THE CAMEO GLASS OF THOMAS AND GEORGE WOODALL

In memory of my grandparents, George Calloway Woodall and his wife, Florence.

Thomas Woodall aged seventy.

George Woodall aged thirty-seven.

FOREWORD

Thomas and George Woodall were two extraordinary brothers who oversaw the production of some of the most wonderful cameo glass ever produced. We are very fortunate at the MSC Forsyth Centre Galleries to have a broad sample of the brothers' works, many of which are illustrated in this book. Texas A&M University together with the Corning Museum of Glass, New York, have two of the best collections of Woodall cameo glass to be found in the United States. This is not surprising when we consider that the glass was initially produced at Thomas Webb & Sons, Amblecote, for sale to a worldwide market. Modern marketing, transportation and communication networks meant the customer in New York or Sydney followed the brothers' careers and acquired the Woodall glass (if one could afford it) with the same keen interest as a buyer in London or Birmingham.

The wellspring of all English cameo glass was the Roman Portland Vase (in the British Museum). First imitated in pottery by Josiah Wedgwood, the Vase was copied in glass after many trials by John Northwood Snr. Northwood was in turn mentor and preacher to the Woodalls, who far surpassed their master in technical proficiency and the number of works they made showing the human figure.

Stop and think for a moment of what it meant to carve the figure or a portrait in glass. In cameo, one removes the upper layers to reveal the underlying colour, usually light on top with dark underneath. One slip of the hand and the work might be ruined. Keep this in mind as you realise that George Woodall's photographs (he was a very good amateur photographer) show substantial alterations in entire figures, even as the work was in progress. What confidence!

These figures are not only capable and correct – they are masterworks of textural illusion. Skin, hair, drapery and water, softened to a matt finish by acid or the engraving wheel, flow one into another. This proficiency in rendering such effects in cameo was unparalleled at the time and has never been equalled by any cameo maker since.

Woodall cameo glass was not restricted to Roman influences. Chinese red and yellow colour were mixed in designs taken from the *Book of Chinese Ornament*. Indian-inspired 'ivory' glass was made into tusks or oriental bottles entwined with serpents and dragons. Colourful cockatoos squawk and brilliant white polar bears lumber across vases. The reach of the British Empire is captured in these translucent and opaque mementoes.

Chris Perry is in an advantageous position to capture the history of Woodall glass. As the great, great-grandson of George Woodall, his widespread family has first-hand knowledge of their illustrious forebears. Situated as Chris is in the Stourbridge (now Dudley) area, he has further access to the records of Webb and other glassmakers. A biography of Thomas and George Woodall bringing together the men and their glass is long overdue. It is a pleasure to greet this book and its accompanying exhibition, *Legends in Glass* at Broadfield House Glass Museum, as it fills this void, informs the reader and celebrates the accomplishments of Thomas and George Woodall.

Timothy Novak
Director MSC Forsyth Centre Galleries, Texas A&M University
March 2000

The Cameo Glass of Thomas and George Woodall

Christopher Woodall Perry

RICHARD DENNIS
2000

ACKNOWLEDGEMENTS

My thanks to the family: Pam Eldred, granddaughter of George Woodall and her husband, Dr Vernon Eldred; Martin and Rita Hambrey; Pamela and Ron Hatch; Robert and Gideon Hatch; John and Lesley Heaselden; David Holds, grandson of George Woodall; Nancy Holds; Graham D. Keightley and his daughter Helen, and sons, David and Andrew; Kathleen Joyce Langford; Bill and Ruth McLaughlin; Norman Pearson, grandson of Thomas Woodall; Ronald Petford, grandson of Thomas Woodall, and his wife Bessie; Doris Scriven; Joan Scriven, granddaughter of Thomas Woodall; Pamela Shannon; Clare Thomas, guardian of Thomas Woodall's archives; Beatrice May Woodall; Rachel, Keith and Christine Woodall; Malcolm Woodall; and Marie Woodall.

Special thanks to other family members including Heather Darby; Enid, Ken and Geoff Holds; John and Gae Holds; Phil Roberts; Mac and Virginia Shannon; and Owen and Margot Williams. My gratitude to my immediate family, Godfrey, Jill and Victoria Perry for their invaluable support.

My appreciation to the following Museums, Universities and Societies: Zelda Baveystock; Christopher Menz, Art Gallery of South Australia; Charles Hajdamach, Roger Dodsworth and John Smith, Broadfield House Glass Museum; Gary Baker, Chrysler Museum of Art; Jennifer Howe, Cincinnati Art Museum; The City Museum, Stoke-on-Trent; Dr David Whitehouse, Elizabeth Hylen, Gail Bardhan, Jill Thomas-Clark and Brandy Harold, The Corning Museum of Glass; Kurt J. Sundstrom, Currier Gallery of Art; Paul Bowen, Dudley Archives Department; The Friends of Broadfield House Glass Museum; The Glass Association; Dr Helmut Ricke, Kunstmuseum Düsseldorf im Ehrenhof; Lois Wolf, Milan Historical Museum, Ohio; Jessie McNab, Metropolitan Museum of Art, New York; Sheila Stamford, Pilkington Glass Museum; Eva Czernis-Ryl and Gara Baldwin, Powerhouse Museum, Sydney; Robyn G. Peterson, Rockwell Museum; Caroline de Guitaut, Royal Collection Trust; Mary Nixon, Sandra Cumming, The Royal Society, London; Timothy Novak, Pamela Schwarz and Cory Ramsey, Texas A&M Memorial Student Centre; Terry Bloxham and Martin Durrant, Victoria & Albert Museum.

My gratitude to: Geoffrey Beard; Bonham's, London; Simon Cottle, Sotheby's, London; Simon Coward; Jon Crisman, Jackson's Auctioneers, Ohio; Martin Davies and the staff of Parkside Junior School, particularly Lorraine (& Digger) Digweed, Pauline Forbes, Pav Malhi and Dave Porter; Richard Down; Annette Dunn; Stanley Eveson, ex-Technical Director of Thomas Webb & Sons; Darren Field; Warren Hamilton; Jonathan and Alison Harris; Dilwyn and Patricia Hier; Robert Hill; Stan Hill, editor of *The Blackcountryman*; Anthony Hoskins, The Edinburgh Crystal Glass Co. Ltd; Graham & Jackie Joel, Leonard Joel Auctioneers, Melbourne; Leo Kaplan; Lo-Co Glass; Helen Millard; Simon Morris, Dunn's Photographic; Adrian E.C. Petford; John and Eileen Sanders; John Sandon and Diana Kay, Phillips, London; A. & J. Speelman Ltd; Paul Tippet, Christie's, London; Tom and Judi Walsh; Jan Walshaw; and Derek Whitcher.

Thanks to Emma Hier and Rick Merrie, photographers.

Edited by Sue Evans

Digital photography, print, design and reproduction by Flaydemouse, Yeovil, Somerset

Published by Richard Dennis, The Old Chapel, Shepton Beauchamp, Somerset TA19 OLE, England

© 2000 Richard Dennis & Christopher Woodall Perry

ISBN 0 903685 77 9

All rights reserved

British Library Cataloguing-in-Publication Data. A catalogue record for this book is available from the British Library

CONTENTS

INTRODUCTION

There are few of us who can remember dusting a piece of cut crystal glass in our childhood, which is now displayed in a museum. Geoffrey Beard wrote his first article on cameo glass before I was born, and my grandfather was a modest man who rarely spoke of his past. As I approached adulthood, I began to realise that my great, great-grandfather was a man of distinction who had helped to revive a form of glassmaking which would have been forgotten without The Portland Vase and the Woodall legacy to remind us. I knew that Stourbridge had connections with the glassmaking industry but only because I drove past the Red House glasscone when I visited Wordsley.

Who was George Woodall, and why was he so passionate about his art? Why was his family so proud and yet also secretive about the man and his private life? And what of Thomas Woodall, George's brother, mentioned and yet strangely absent from records of key events. I read the many books written about cameo glass passed to me by mother. In some accounts, Thomas and George appeared as bitter opponents – split by feuding over forged signatures. Others wrote more diplomatically yet hinted that George had swindled Thomas out of his glory. The 'evidence' in this delicate matter was vague. There were many gaps in information and knowledge and many questions left unanswered.

Then there were the rectangular wooden boxes full of curious glass negatives that cluttered up our garden shed – banished beneath the lawnmower because the boxes might have woodworm. My mother spoke of photographs of Kingswinford, beautiful cameo vases and beautiful women, including her grandmother. And so I embarked on writing this account of the work of two brothers, a task complicated by the insistence of many of their contemporaries that their surname was spelt Wood_h_all. I was fortunate that the Woodall family had kept so much material – sketch books, documents, letters, pieces of glass, tools, and photographs.

This book is an account of a Gladstonian Britain which never died in the hearts of two gifted and skilled men. Each blessed with different talents and one shared skill: the ability to create magic on glass.

George Woodall's collection of glass photographic negatives are gratefully reproduced.

Christopher Woodall Perry
October 1999

PUBLISHER'S NOTE

Family archives, local knowledge, Thomas Webb & Sons' records and contemporary West Midlands newspapers have helped Christopher Perry write an intriguing account of the lives of Thomas and George Woodall. As important has been the unravelling of family legends and the stories and skeletons, handed down from one generation to another. Interwoven with these memoirs are details of cameo glass production at Thomas Webb's. Thus, this book gives an insight into the Victorian artist/craftsman at work and play and provides us with the period setting for the objects we so admire today.

The glass of Thomas and George is a wonder to see and examine, the virtuoso skill of carving in this difficult medium takes one's breath away. The romantic link with the Barberini Vase and Northwood's copy – the brothers' design, so much a part of high-Victorian art (from Lord Leighton to William S. Coleman) – and the 'ivory' pieces inspired by an exotic world of Persian and Oriental art (forerunners of such celebrated cameo glass to be made in Europe), gives the Woodalls' cameo a special place in glass history.

This book is not an in-depth study of the sources, influences or wider historical context of Woodall cameo glass. To quote Chris Perry, '_the focus of this book is a biography of the Woodall brothers and their children with an extensive pictorial record of their work_'. With considerable help from museums, auction houses and collectors, and the miraculous survival of many of George Woodall's glass plates we have been fortunate in locating and reproducing the great majority of the more important Woodall pieces. It has been Christopher's challenge to develop the pioneering work of Geoffrey Beard's _Nineteenth Century Cameo Glass_, and this book is a significant contribution to the study of cameo glass, on which scholars will be able to build.

1827 – 1850

Thomas and George Woodall – Family Background

In the early nineteenth century, Thomas Woodall, a vice maker in a factory producing nails for export throughout the British Empire, married Sara Marsh. Originally from North Yorkshire, the couple lived in Cradley, a small hamlet between Halesowen, Dudley and Stourbridge, in the area now known as the West Midlands and had two sons, Samuel and Thomas. In May 1827, Thomas was baptised at Oldswinford Church, near Stourbridge, one of the three parish churches which bordered Cradley. The Woodalls had received no formal education and nor did their children. However, Thomas was a competent musician from whom his sons inherited their love of music – Samuel learned to play the piano and Thomas Jnr found his forté with the flute.

When Samuel was twenty-one years old, he left Cradley to marry and live in Kingswinford. Seeking employment, the rest of the family followed him to the neighbouring village of Wordsley. As his father before him, Thomas Jnr worked as a nailor. In 1847, aged twenty, he met Emma Bott[1], the youngest daughter of George and Katherine Bott who lived in Kinver. George Bott was a face turner by trade[2] and worked for a manufacturer of spades. Thomas Jnr had become a pillar of the parish church – playing the organ and arranging new hymns – and it was here that he met Emma who worked as a glassmaker at the Heath Glassworks. Their courtship was encouraged by both sets of parents and the couple were married at the Church of St Mary, Kingswinford, on the 1st October 1848. They moved into 100 Barnett Lane and settled unobtrusively into Wordsley's working class. The booming glassworks of W.H., B. & J. Richardson and Co. provided work for Emma, whilst Thomas worked in Robert Dudley's nail factory.[3] They shared the house with Joseph and Mary Phasey and their daughter, Mary Ann, and Emma's younger brother, Thomas Bott, who was an apprentice at William Richardson's glassworks.

On the 25th June 1849, Emma gave birth to a son, named Thomas after his grandfather and father. Determined to provide him with the educational opportunities denied to his parents,

Holy Trinity Church, Wordsley: the site for the family graves of the Webbs, Stuarts, Northwoods, Richardsons and many of the Woodalls. *(Photograph by Emma Hier)*

Emma planned that he should go to school. Her brother, Thomas Bott, encouraged her in this – he had persevered with studies and his ability to read and write was a key factor in his success as a student of porcelain painting.[4] Emma would marvel at his skill in enamelling pictures onto pottery in the Limoges-style.

On the 15th August 1850, Thomas and Emma's second son was born, named George, after his maternal grandfather. On the 6th October, during his christening at Holy Trinity Church, Wordsley, the couple realised that they had failed to have their first son, Thomas Jnr, christened. Anxious to rectify this oversight, they went home and returned to the church with him.

St. Mary's Church, Kingswinford village green. *(Photograph by George Woodall)*

Haymaking on a farm in the Kingswinford area. *(Photograph by George Woodall)*

The towpath at Botterham Lock. (*Photograph by George Woodall*)

This lack of protocol was not appreciated by the Reverend Hickman who, perhaps to show his displeasure, christened Thomas, the first-born, second. The entries were then incorrectly written in the parish register under the surname, Woodhall.[5]

Thomas and George Woodall were destined to achieve far greater fame than their parents could ever have imagined.

[1] Emma Bott was baptised at Oldswinford Church on the 7th October 1826. She had two sisters, Mary Ann, baptised 10th July 1825, Eliza, baptised 6th October 1826, and a brother, Thomas, baptised in 1829 at Kinver. While the Botts lived at the Hyde, the family was extended by twins, Mary and Edward, baptised 2nd December 1832, John, baptised 21st September 1834, Penelope, baptised 20th February 1837, and Janet, baptised 2nd April 1838.

[2] A face turner operates a milling machine, creating the face of steel tools.

[3] Robert Dudley (d 1878) and his family lived at Broadfield House, Kingswinford.

[4] Thomas Bott was educated at Kinver Grammar School. Apprenticed to William Richardson, he worked in the enamelling and gilding departments, subsidising his training by painting portraits in oils. In 1852, after being rejected for a job in London, he spent the night on Worcester railway station. The next morning he went to the Kerr & Binns Porcelain Works, showed them his sketches and was immediately hired. While with the firm, he helped develop the Limoges-style enamelling process. His wife, Eliza, gave birth to three children – Thomas John, Georgina and Thomas Dugmore. After her death, he married his wife's half-sister, Mary Ryder. Thomas Bott died on the 12th December 1870, aged forty-one. His widow tried to prove that his death was caused by arsenic poisoning. However, the factory refused to accept that their paints and the artist's practice of licking the brush, could cause poisoning. His eldest son, Thomas John, had trained under him and began working in 1874 as a contemporary porcelain artist. From 1885-1889, he worked freelance before moving to Brown-Westhead, Moore & Co., at Cauldon Place. He left in 1890, to join Coalport China as an art director and remained there until his death in 1932. He was survived by one daughter, Norah Constance, named after his Woodall cousin.

[5] This slip of the pen was to cause confusion in the future. Many newspapers would refer to a T. Woodall and T. Woodhall in the same article, creating the impression that they were two separate people. Similarly a G. Woodall and G. Woodhall would feature in the same piece.

1851 – 1870

THE WOODALL BROTHERS' EDUCATION

In February 1851, Thomas Bott left Wordsley to seek his fortune in London. He returned often and through a combination of 'instigation and recommendation'[6] persuaded his brother-in-law that Emma should have her way and the two boys be sent to school. Thomas Snr wished them to have a musical education and while Emma agreed, she wanted to expand on this. At the age of five, Thomas Jnr was sent to Wordsley National (Church of England) School.[7] Founded in 1836 with help from the Reverend George Saxby Penfold, past headmasters included Henry Newman and George Yeats. Thomas particularly enjoyed Mr Boultbee's lessons when the curate would play the flute while the children sang, led by Walter Steels. Sunday School reinforced Thomas Jnr's love of music and Jackson's 'Te Deum' became a favourite. After school, Thomas would accompany his father to various musical engagements – the boy became a skilled musician from the age of seven, with a preference for the violin and piano. He chose the latter so that he could play the church organ; John Bournes of Audnam was the organist at Holy Trinity (the main parish church for Wordsley) and Thomas loved to hear the deep notes booming through the windpipes.

The youngsters would often play in the yard with the other children who lived in Barnet Lane. Amongst these was pretty Martha Newman[8] who would sit and listen to Thomas Jnr as he played on a small piccolo. When their father left Dudley's to work in his own nail-making factory, Thomas Jnr and George were taught the skills of iron-manipulation and the extra income earned from this helped to pay for their education.

George followed his brother to school in the autumn of 1855. He had little interest in music and was instead fascinated by his Uncle Thomas' sketchbooks. In 1852 Thomas Bott had given his nephews *The Art of Illuminating* by Digby Wyatt. The book contained decorative borders and patterns from historical sources and George spent a good deal of his spare time tracing the patterns and copying the artwork. Much of the brothers' later commercial 'flower and insect' cameo may have been influenced by the book's text:

> Whenever birds, insects etc are introduced, they should be drawn true to nature; butterflies and moths are truly amongst the most beautiful and appropriate objects.

Indeed, butterflies featured heavily in future Webb designs, though the company did not officially adopt the motif.

At school the children studied reading, writing, arithmetic, Latin and art. Thomas particularly enjoyed drawing honeysuckle while, like his Uncle Thomas, George preferred figure work and quickly became the more proficient at life drawing and copying from the antique. However, Thomas Jnr was very supportive of George and there appeared to be no rivalry. Newman's and Yeats' teaching of drawing and classical mythology (the use of Greek images would be prevalent in the brothers' later cameo work) helped Thomas Jnr when he left school aged eleven, followed by George in 1861.

Thomas Jnr now had to convince a local firm to employ him as an apprentice glass engraver. This task was complicated by high unemployment in the trade as well as in the local area. The recent failure of the Richardson Glassworks had been a disastrous blow to employment prospects. Thomas took his sketches to Messrs Northwood and Guest at Wordsley. John Northwood and Thomas Bott had served their apprenticeship together so Northwood[9] already knew about Thomas Jnr and, after looking at his sketches, took him on. George's reputation preceded him and he too was offered a job in the factory. This was an unusual occurrence in an industry which, while it produced substantial revenue and employed hundreds of people, was so overshadowed by mining, chainmaking and nail manufacturing that the newspapers rarely mentioned glassmaking. Consequently, many people were unaware of the names of firms, or the industry's principal locations.

Thomas Bott gave his nephews a copy of John Flaxman's *Iliad & Odyssey* to use as sketch material. Flaxman was a leading sculptor in the English neo-classical movement and from 1775-1787 had worked for Josiah Wedgwood. Bott also gave the boys some of his source material and a photograph of one of his pieces. Thomas and George were impressed by the skill of the enamelling, but the realistic images provided by the photograph, particularly fascinated George. Bott enjoyed the fact that 'he [Bott] did a lot of fine work and got good prices for it'.[10] However, Thomas' memoirs reveal that he believed his uncle was exhausting himself by working so hard and although he respected his talent and financial security, Thomas was happy to serve his apprenticeship while also enjoying his musical activities. Thomas Bott's artistic and financial success made far more of an impression on George – an early indication of the younger brother's business-minded acumen.

Ecce Homo, used as source material by Thomas Bott, 1866.

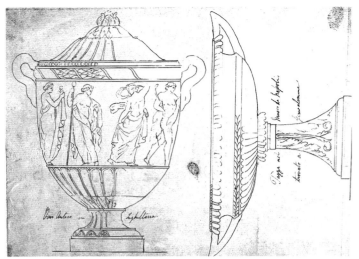

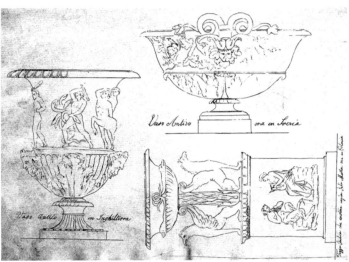

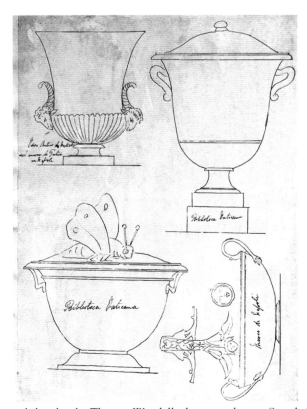

Classical sketches by Thomas Woodall when a student at Stourbridge School of Art. (*Family collection*)

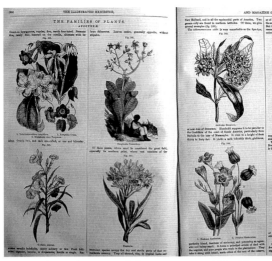

A page from Thomas and George's copy of *The Illustrated Exhibitor and Magazine of Art*, 1852, given to them by their uncle, Thomas Bott. (*C & V Perry collection*)

The boys left the Sunday School at Wordsley and Thomas attended afternoon classes at Mount Pleasant Methodist Chapel where his father played the violin in the choir band. By the age of eleven, Thomas was playing the organ for the Wall Heath Congregational Church on some Sundays and later played the violin for the Methodist chapel. He practised with John Caswell, a fine cellist, and as villagers emigrated in search of employment, also made up numbers by singing in the choir. In contrast, George went to church with his mother, and was content to sit in the pews and return home to play in the lane or practice his drawing. He would draw freehand in a style that was more natural and inspired than Thomas'.

In February 1861, Thomas Jnr started working for J. & J. Northwood[11], alongside John Northwood himself, with Philip Pargeter[12] a frequent visitor. It was hard work: Thomas Jnr worked 66 hours per week (7am-6pm) including Saturdays, and each day walked several miles to and from the factory. New ideas for decorative patterns were encouraged and under Northwood's guidance there were numerous design opportunities. As a pioneer in his field, Northwood's new template technique of glass etching, which was straightforward and easily applied, must have given Thomas and later George, many chances to develop their skill and artistry on relatively inexpensive pieces of tableware. Upon arrival at the small firm, Thomas noticed four pieces of glass, all recently bought from the bankrupt Richardson's.[13] The final piece (no.4), unusual in its etched-out design, was a prototype inspired by Benjamin Richardson Snr who was trying to recreate the Roman glass art of cameo. Thomas had never heard of cameo and found it an intriguing experiment to discuss with George at home. Taught well by John Northwood, Thomas became a highly-skilled artist who eventually outshone his seniors, particularly when using decorative patterns. However, he traced much of his work and, as he wrote in his memoirs, came to regret what he saw as an over-reliance on this. When George arrived at Northwood's in 1862, he was placed in a menial job but quickly learned the trade, his years of practice in freehand drawing proving invaluable. He believed that glasscutting skills alone were insufficient to achieve his desire for social standing and wealth, but was sure that a glassmaker who combined superb workmanship with good business practice would be admired and be able to achieve middle-class status.

In addition to their day jobs, Thomas and George continued their apprenticeship through an education in drawing at Stourbridge Art School.[14] It was a taxing schedule, including work, night-school and church engagements as well as finding time for social activities. Thomas was an imposing figure – he admired his childhood playmate Martha Newman, but she was courting another, and he was too shy to compete for her attention. He helped his father form the Kingswinford Brass Band and the close bond between himself and Thomas Snr left George feeling excluded and deprived of paternal attention. In a bid for praise and recognition at home, George would drive hard for success. At just five foot, he was small, but charming, fashionably dressed and less involved with church activities than his brother. George's flamboyant moustache and short groomed hair made him popular with the opposite sex. He pursued Pamela Parkes[15], a brunette with perfect manners. Of slight build with her hair always in a bun, she was considered pleasant, though her dignified air prevented her from seeming a warm person. However, she was perfect for George and he quickly fell in love. He began to write poetry for Pamela and, attracted by his romantic nature, she returned his feelings.

The register of the Government School of Art shows that on the 22nd July 1866 Thomas passed Practical Geometry and Model Drawing. Because he was colour blind and able to see only two of the primary colours, Thomas realised that he would have difficulties as an artist unless he found a form of glassmaking where colour was not an imperative. On the 5th November, George passed the same exams and despite being younger than Thomas, was regarded as an equally skilled craftsman. In December, Stourbridge School of Art awarded Thomas *The Old Curiosity Shop* by Dickens as a prize for 'satisfactory progress' in Ornamental Drawing from Casts. Recognising the potential of this shy young man, William Bowen, the headteacher, appointed Thomas as a teacher.

By this time the differences between the brothers were becoming more apparent. Thomas was developing a keen love of art and also expressed this through music. A scholar and a temperate man, he showed patience, understanding and found

John Northwood. (*Photograph by George Woodall*)

teaching rewarding. Thomas recorded in his memoirs that his brother drew quickly and with great panache, whereas he was more reliant on tracing and copying other's designs. George also had a firmer self-interest – he wished for the artistic success that would bring royal patronage and financial security. He was more motivated than his brother, and sought publicity by launching *The Kingswinford Monthly Illustrated Journal* which included poetry, historical tales, news and a travelogue. In May 1867, Wordsley village was shocked by the murder of Thomas Porter, a policeman who lived in Cot Lane. Porter was a friend and George wrote a moving poem in tribute. He had already submitted two poems – *A Welcome to Spring* and *The Country Bridge* – to *The Stourbridge Observer* and the three poems were duly printed.[16]

A Brother's Grave
A much lov'd brother now is dead,
Beneath the soil they've laid his head;
His friends now mourn the death of one,
A son and brother, now he's gone.

He in the cold, damp grave is laid
Near to a spot where oft he play'd;
Yes, when a youth, with schoolmates there,
He in their pleasures took his share.

He'd many friends – he'd gained their love,
To please them each he always strove;
Greatly beloved by all he knew,
From earthly ground he'd gone from view.

How solemn was the day they bore
His last remains from his own door,
Unto the deep and narrow grave
O'er which the springing grass will wave.

The bell he heard in youth did toll,
And spoke of some departed soul,
When weeping friends in silence trod
To lay his corpse beneath the sod.

But now he's gone, he's left behind
A mother lov'd, with troubled mind,
And brothers too, and sisters dear,
And many a friend to shed a tear.

Thomas Woodall
aged eighteen.
(*Family collection*)

Cot Lane on the hill overlooking Kingswinford.
(Photograph by George Woodall)

F118, white and light blue on frosted ruby vase with a scene from nature, 10ins (25.5cms) marked Gem Cameo.
(Broadfield House Glass Museum)

They'll never meet on earth again
But when in heaven, free from pain,
They'll join with all the blood-wash'd throng,
To swell the everlasting song.

Bedeck his grave with flowers that bloom,
As though it were a monarch's tomb;
And may green branches hang and wave
O'er our departed brother's grave.

Kingswinford, 13th May, 1867.

Neither Thomas Snr nor Emma had learned to read and they would have been impressed by the publication of their son's poetry, as would the people of Wordsley and Kingswinford. Even George Bott conceded, at a time when state education was in its infancy and few people could write, that the mastery of poetry

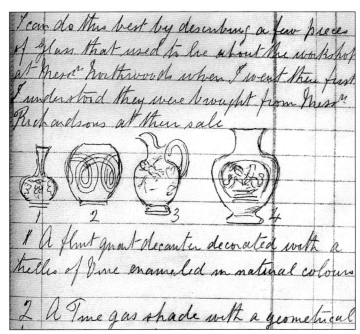

From Thomas Woodall's memoirs: a thumbnail sketch and brief description of four pieces of glass acquired by J. & J. Northwood from Richardson's. *(Family collection)*

was a fine attribute for his grandson. With Thomas Snr and Emma founding a music dealership in Broad Street, Wordsley, it seemed possible that the members of the family could finally pursue their respective ambitions. From 1867-1868, when two Reform Acts gave Thomas Woodall Snr the right to vote for the first time, the brothers' political consciences were stirred. Only two-and-a-half to three million voters were added to the national register, but it was a symbolic gesture by the Liberal government. The passion for social reform and economic prosperity was passed from father to sons, and the Woodall boys were immediate supporters of Prime Minister Gladstone.

Imbued with confidence over the modest success of his poetry, George continued to court Pamela Parkes while Thomas remained attracted to Martha Newman. Her suitor had died in 1868 and Thomas had hopes for the future. As a declaration of his love, he went to Archer Clarke's in Worcester Street, and posed for a portrait photograph which he had mounted and placed inside a romantic wallet containing a birthday poem:

The Birthday
This is the birthday of my love,
Then vanish care and sorrow;
To-day shall mirth and pleasure reign,
Though grief may come tomorrow.

The long hours, heavy workload and missed free time, were rewarded when Thomas Jnr was rated 'Good in Design' at the Local Advanced Art Examination held in 1869 and received a certificate from the Science and Art Department of the Committee of Council Education. Unfortunately, by 1870, the impoverished Woodalls were twelve shillings in arrears at the Stourbridge Art School so, although they attended, they were not allowed to register and enter exams. The brothers were fortunate that Martha's uncle was a senior member of staff at the school and allowed some leeway in their affairs. The passing of the Liberal Government's 1870 Education Act also helped, because legislation decreed that every child attend a primary school, regardless of financial considerations. Education, long accepted as the reserve of the rich, was now becoming a right for a whole new generation.

6 This extract is taken from Thomas Woodall's memoirs which are now in the family collection.

7 The Wordsley National (Church of England) School had several notable scholars at its head.

8 Martha Patience Newman was born on 7th November 1850, baptised 12th January 1851 at Holy Trinity Church, Wordsley.

9 John Northwood, son of Frederick and Maria Northwood, was born in Wordsley and baptised on the 13th November 1836. At the age of twelve, he was apprenticed to W.H., B. & J. Richardson to decorate, gild and enamel glass. He was then hired by Benjamin Richardson when his new factory opened in 1852, and received a medal from the School of Design in 1855. Northwood left Richardson's in 1859 to form a partnership with Joseph Northwood, H.G. Richardson and Thomas Guest. In 1860, this was dissolved and he established J. & J. Northwood. In 1861, Northwood invented the Template Etching Machine and later the Geometrical Etching Machine. He also developed the substance now known as 'white acid' which could be used without the side-effects of hydrofluoric acid. In 1862, he was commissioned by Sir John Benjamin Stone to carve *The Elgin Vase*, completed in 1873. The frieze around the vase depicted two equestrian groups from the Parthenon sculptures, also known as the Elgin Marbles. This fine piece was a forerunner for the invention of rock crystal techniques. George Woodall would have seen its development over the nine-and-a-half years taken to produce it, and heard the praise given to Northwood after the vase was given to the city of Birmingham. Its reception was warm but the trade papers did mislabel the piece as a 'beautiful cameo vase entirely the labour of his own hands.' The vase was actually made of pure flint glass. Like cameo carving that was to follow: 'the breaking off accidentally of a small piece scarcely larger than the head of a pin, would have totally spoiled the work. It is almost amusing to contemplate now the various dangers the vase has passed through since its earlier days. M. Northwood relates that he, upon one occasion, let the tool he was working with fall upon the foot, and it was some minutes before he dare examine it, to find the vase uninjured. Another time, the steel point of his tool broke between the handle and the body, and many days passed before he could extract the piece, which was eventually done by consuming it with acid.' (*The County Express*, 2nd Nov 1878.) His son, John Northwood II, continued to carve cameo work and was a Director and Technical Manager at Stevens & Williams.

10 From Thomas Woodall's memoirs.

11 After dissolving his partnership with Northwood et al, Tom Guest went on to found Guest Brothers, flint glass decorators with his brother, Edward. In 1886, Edward Guest died and Tom Guest worked alone until his death on 24th May 1892. Based in Brettell Lane, Amblecote, the firm, Guest Brothers, continued to prosper after its founder's departure. It was responsible for decorating a large number of ivory cameo pieces in the 1890s and continued to engrave for Thomas Webb & Sons until the 1950s.

12 Philip Pargeter (1826-1906) was initially apprenticed to Benjamin Richardson; when W.H., B. & J. Richardson failed, Pargeter created his own glass decorating business at Audnam. After eleven years, he joined William James Hodgetts and his uncle Benjamin Richardson to form Hodgetts, Richardson & Pargeter. In 1871 the partnership was dissolved and Pargeter took over the lease on the Red House Glassworks. His work involved cameo, crystal and coloured glass production. In 1882, frustrated by restrictive trade practices, he sold the business to Frederick Stuart. He then pursued property deals and developed Mount Pleasant at Wordsley, the Platts at Amblecote and land in Walsall. On his death his estate included the Pargeter-Northwood copy of The Portland Vase and three cameo tazzas of *Newton*, *Shakespeare* and *Flaxman*.

13 Richardson's suffered from the slow growth in the glass trade and the fierce competition for sales.

14 The school, founded in 1851, was a breeding ground for ambitious, skilled craftsmen. Its reputation had been earned by years of successful teaching. The first master at the school, Henry Alexander Bowler, became a Professor of Perspective at the Royal Academy and was succeeded by many other scholars including William P. Bowen in 1863. When Bowen left in December 1881, he had improved results, increased student numbers, and achieved a healthy pay rise under the government's system of payment by results.

15 Pamela Parkes was baptised in 1852 at West Bromwich. Her father was Joseph Parkes, a miner. They moved to Kingswinford in 1853 and were a respected family in the neighbourhood.

16 *The Stourbridge Observer*, 11th, 18th, 25th May 1867.

1871 – 1880

JOHN NORTHWOOD AND THE PORTLAND VASE

Pamela Parkes aged twenty-one, shortly after her marriage to George Woodall. (*Author's collection*)

1871 proved to be a turbulent year for Thomas Jnr – his apprenticeship at Northwood's had ended and he was now unemployed. He became a freelance artist, sketching pieces that were engraved by others, did some drawings for local gentry and taught piano and violin. It was a difficult time but he was consoled by having won Martha's love and support. They wanted to marry but without any regular income, he felt unable to ask her father's permission. Fortunately, John Northwood came to his aid.

Philip Pargeter had challenged John Northwood to produce a copy of The Portland Vase[17] for his personal collection and for exhibition, and Northwood decided to assemble a team of engravers to work on the vase. It would appear that this was done in some secrecy as there were no references to the project in the trade or country press until the work was unveiled. Though recognised as a talented engraver, presumably George was considered too young for the task but he reminded his mentor that Thomas was looking for work. Thomas was rehired to work on the vase in a team and feeling confident that his future was assured at Northwood's and beyond, he and Martha

decided to marry on the 25th December at Oldswinford, the parish from which her family originally came.

Just three weeks later, George announced that he was to marry Pamela Parkes. With so much family spread throughout the Black Country, All Saints Church in Moxley, near Bilston, was chosen – George's cousin, Samuel Thompson was churchwarden there.

Thomas and Martha's simple wedding took place on Christmas Day 1871. At the reception, Thomas presented his bride with a white on brown cameo brooch depicting a lovers' scene, that he had made for her at Northwood's – a very good attempt at the primitive new technology that John Northwood was trying to perfect. The couple moved into The Park, Kingswinford, and over the years, Martha became a well-known figure in the village.

On the 11th February 1872, George married Pamela and they settled in Townsend, Kingswinford. Their wedding was something of a double celebration as Thomas had announced that Martha was expecting a child; by early March, Pamela was also pregnant.

The Woodalls attended Liberal Party meetings and supported Gladstone's government as it passed the 1872 Secret Ballot Act. This ensured that people's votes were private,

Thomas and Martha Woodall with Noel aged one, and Eva aged two. (*Author's collection*)

thereby strengthening the Liberal position as employers were no longer able to pressurise their employees to vote for the Conservative party.

Northwood and Thomas examined a copy of Wedgwood's Jasperware version of The Portland Vase and determined to make their own. To produce a glass copy the white outer layer would have to be marvered onto the blown blue glass inner casing. The problems were many for this technique: matching the coloured batches of glass to prevent 'flying'; forming shapes without bubbles or defects; and the art of annealing (cooling) the different layers of glass simultaneously. Correct temperatures were required to prevent cracking and, consequently, the cup method was developed.[19]

Once a suitable two-layered blank was created, Thomas sketched out the drawings for the vase on the outer layer of glass and painted a bitumen resist for acidizing away the unwanted parts of the top layer. When dipped in acid several times, the outer layer of white glass would be eroded except for the parts protected by the acid-resist. This was time-consuming and required great concentration. Northwood took over the rough relief and hand-carved the remainder of the vase, a process which took two years. Meanwhile, George was also busy at Northwood's. For his wife's twenty-first birthday, he engraved a crystal jug with a scene of stags in a landscape (see opposite).

On the 3rd November 1872, Martha gave birth to a boy: Thomas thought of the child as a gift from God and so named him Handel Newnam Woodall, after the composer of 'The Messiah'. The following month, Pamela gave birth to Florence Amy Woodall (hereafter known as Amy, her preferred name). On the 5th January 1873 Noel Handel Newnam Woodall was christened at Holy Trinity Church, Wordsley. Later that year, Thomas became the organist at the Wesleyan Chapel, Kingswinford, and on the 19th September his daughter, Eve Adelina Woodall, was born (hereafter known as Cis, because she was the eldest sister). She was baptised on the 9th November at Holy Trinity, once again incorrectly surnamed, Woodhall.

Pamela was pregnant for the second time by February 1874 and she and George moved into a larger, rented house at 27 Market Street, Kingswinford. Also known as Luton House, the couple turned part of it into a milliner's shop – with Pamela working in the shop, they could afford a live-in domestic nanny and other maids came in to clean.

Crystal jug, copper wheel-engraved with stags in a wooded landscape, and a castle ruin in woodland on the reverse, 12³⁄₄ins (32.5cms), by George Woodall. (*C & V Perry collection*)

On the 18th April 1874, the Stourbridge Choral Society was formed and Thomas conducted performances of 'The Messiah', 'Elijah', and Costa's 'Eli' which were well received at the Market Hall. On the 14th November of that year, George and Pamela had another daughter, Beatrice Maud Alice (hereafter known as Alice). As Thomas came to the end of his work on The Portland Vase, his third child Ida Mabel was born on the 1st April 1875 (again mistakenly christened as Woodhall!). Needing more living space, Thomas and Martha moved to lodgings in Broad

George and Pamela Woodall's marriage certificate.

George Woodall standing in front of St. Mary's Church. During exposure the dog moved and therefore appears twice in the photograph. *(Photograph by George Woodall)*

From left, George and Thomas Woodall with their children, Amy, Alice and Cis, c1875. *(Author's collection)*

Street and later to Summer Street, Kingswinford. Despite the demands made by rapidly growing families and full diaries, Thomas and George continued to actively support Gladstone as he sought wider electoral reform and addressed social welfare issues. Even the Conservative party, now in government headed by Benjamin Disraeli, was promising social legislation. Joseph Chamberlain, as Mayor of Birmingham 1873-75, ran gas and water supplies as municipal undertakings, started slum clearance, built public parks and laid recreation grounds.

During the last week of August, Noel Woodall contracted German Measles and died from pneumonia on the 31st October 1875. He was buried at Holy Trinity on the 4th November. At the Sunday service the following day, Thomas played the opening Voluntary, 'I Know that my Redeemer Liveth' as a tribute. On the 6th August 1876, Martha gave birth to a fourth child, George Harry Newnam (named, as was customary, after his paternal uncle, and hereafter known as Harry). Thomas began searching for employment as his work with Northwood

Pamela and George in front of Luton House, Market Street, where the couple would live until George's death. *(Photograph by George Woodall)*

The original sketch of Dennis Hall, Amblecote, by Arthur Arrowsmith of *The Express and Star*. The site was expanded to include houses, more factory space and an iron foundry. The conservatory housed many pieces of fine glass. (*Author's collection*)

A *Country Bridge* by Thomas Woodall, a contribution to George's publishing venture. (*Family collection*)

was finished and George was keen to follow his brother. They applied to Messrs Thomas Webb & Sons, Dennis Hall Works[20], who were looking for draughtsmen to sketch patterns for engraving onto glass exclusively copyrighted to Webb's. Wilkes Webb was aware that stiff competition from British glassworks and the many foreign companies was eroding Webb's market share and it was necessary to find new sources of revenue. Thomas was assigned to continue with the work of John Northwood[21], the results to be displayed in the British section at the forthcoming Paris Exhibition in 1878.

After his foray into poetry, George's work on *The Kingswinford Monthly Illustrated Journal* became more news-based. On the 11th November 1876, the *Brierley Hill Advertiser* reviewed the journal's earlier issues, stating:

> It is a new experiment in the neighbourhood... set forth as a local magazine of information and instruction... and having looked through the number sent us, we are bound to say that this is a fair and true description of the periodical.

But publishing was only a sideline. George was employed full-time by Webb's to draft sketches and engrave existing forms of glass. He was an innovative craftsman and constantly tried to improve the quality of the product. Together with Wilkes Webb and William Fritsche (glass engraver and part-time publican of The Red Lion, Brettell Lane), they discovered the

manufacturing process for rock crystal glass[22] during the summer of 1878[23]. (A vase made at this time, *Aphrodite Rising from the Waves*, was later to become a design for a cameo plaque.) Many pieces were made and sold and George was widely applauded for his engraving skills. A designer foremost, he nevertheless signed what little glass he actually made, a practice he would continue throughout his career. He used the signature 'G Woodall' and added the year afterwards. However, as he carved more and more pieces in the same period, he frequently omitted the year. At this stage George had no real interest in cameo carving, his work on rock crystal was commercially successful and he saw a great future for it.

In 1876, Wilkes Webb[24] had also commissioned John Northwood to produce a piece of cameo glass. He was determined that the popularity of The Portland Vase which would be on its debut display at Paris on Danielli's stand (on Philip Pargeter's behalf) would not detract from Webb's three-dimensional cameos. Wilkes Webb had not underestimated the competition for the top prizes at the Paris Exhibition. As well as The Portland Vase, Pargeter intended to display Northwood's unfinished *Milton Vase* and four tazzas.[25] Additional competition

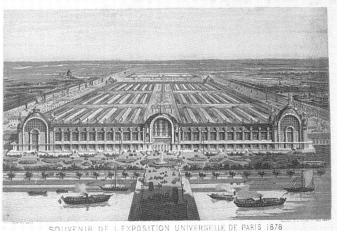

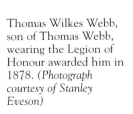

SOUVENIR DE L'EXPOSITION UNIVERSELLE DE PARIS 1878
VUE GÉNÉRALE DU PALAIS DE L'EXPOSITION

Thomas Wilkes Webb, son of Thomas Webb, wearing the Legion of Honour awarded him in 1878. (*Photograph courtesy of Stanley Eveson*)

The wrythen glass jardiniere and stand dominates the conservatory of Dennis Hall. (*Photograph by George Woodall*)

From Thomas Woodall's memoirs: sketch of *The Aurora Vase* showing how it was designed in three pieces. (*Family collection*)

came from glassmaking companies Hodgetts & Richardson, Walker, and Stevens & Williams.

Hodgetts & Richardson displayed their copy of The Portland Vase as well as three other cameo vases by Locke: *Cupid Sailing on a Cockleshell*, *Unhappy Childhood* and its companion vase, *Happy Childhood*.[26] The latter two were carved by Joseph Locke in 1877. Alphonse Lechevrel also exhibited *Birth of Venus*, *Hercules Restoring Alcestis to her Husband Admetus*, *Raising an Altar to Bacchus* and *Venus Rising from the Sea*.[27] These early pieces of cameo impressed public and trade alike but in press reports, they were not as widely applauded as the Webb exhibits.

The Webb stand was planned around two centrepiece vases: one to be carved by Thomas Woodall and the other, John Northwood's *Dennis Vase*. By March 1878, Thomas was behind schedule as he struggled with the decorative borders – even so, he steadfastly refused to work overtime on Sundays, believing it to be a day of rest. His vase was so intricate that even the often indifferent local press was eager to see it. (In forty years there were scarcely any articles about the glass trade in *The County Express* and what few there were mainly consisted of quotes taken from *The Pottery Gazette*.)

Completion of Thomas' vase was further delayed when a small flaw was discovered in the lip, but there was no time to restart the piece. (Early cameo carvers were frustrated by flaws and air bubbles between the layers of glass that were unseen until work was underway. Sometimes the piercing of an air bubble could cause a piece to crack, thereby destroying several months' work. Many cameo blanks were discarded before a perfect one was found.)

The forty-foot stand in Paris, designed by James O'Fallon, Art Director at Webb's, featured a dazzling array of glass. Every style was represented: Egyptian, Persian, Assyrian, Gothic, Greek, Japanese, Grotesque, Byzantine. Wilkes Webb had patented a new form of iridescent (also known as Russian) glass, which refracted light to imbue the glass with the colours of the rainbow. O'Fallon worked closely with Thomas Woodall on many brilliant designs that followed.

As well as cameo, Wilkes Webb had revived making glass as imitation bronze. Two elaborately ornamented and deep-cut 'Queen Anne' chandeliers added to the spectacle. The Paris International Exhibition (*Paris Exposition Universelle*) opened on the 1st May 1878 with exhibits from many countries – the 'unusual scale of magnificence'[28] of the event was reported in the press. Despite the excellence of so many exhibits, Northwood's latest piece and Thomas Woodall's *Aurora* vase were singled out for special praise. The latter was white, carved against a blue background with a representation of Guido Reni's painting *Aurora* on it (see page 43).[29] Thomas Webb & Sons was awarded the only Grand Prix for glass and Wilkes Webb was awarded a Legion of Honour. (Initially, he refused it insisting that it should go to Charles Webb, but he declined.)

The Grand Prix was awarded for 'all styles and periods... in the ornamental glass'. The judges praised Webb's for being the first company (or so they thought) to produce cameo glass in the style of the Roman Portland Vase:

> These exquisite vases were... purposely excluded by the jury... for the display has been judged on its true decorative and technical merits, quite apart from the unique characteristics of the cameo-sculptured vases.[30]

Hitherto, the term 'cameo' had become virtually redundant in the glassmakers' vocabulary.

Door furniture, a cameo glass fingerplate attributed to George Woodall. (*Photograph by George Woodall*)

Charles Webb, brother of Thomas Wilkes Webb and Walter Wilkes Webb and joint managing director of Thomas Webb & Sons, in the grounds of Dennis Hall. (*Photograph courtesy of Stanley Eveson*)

While Thomas was enjoying Webb's success in Paris, Martha had moved the household into George Street, Audnam, in readiness for the birth of their fifth child, Cecil John Newnam (hereafter known as Jack), born on the 3rd November 1878. The following year, Gladstone embarked on his 'Midlothian Campaign' touring the country and appealing directly to the voters he had enfranchised to concentrate on social reform rather than imperial ambitions. By going directly to the people in this way, Gladstone won the case for reform and the Liberals were returned with a 137-seat majority.

As 1879 gave way to a new decade, the rock crystal market declined. The Webb's pattern books show that far fewer pieces were made throughout the 1880s, and in an interview with *The County Express* many years later, George recalled his concern about the impact of cheap glass imports undercutting prices. Thomas wrote in his memoirs that engraved crystal glass versions of the cameo pieces were difficult to sell. By the time that George and Pamela Woodall's third child was born on the 11th February 1880 (hereafter known as George Parkes), George had realised that he would have to find a new niche for his talents and the popularity of cameo in Paris convinced him that the finest work would fetch high prices and make its carver a wealthy man. He had attempted a family piece in 1878 – a plaque of *Diana and Nymph Bathing*, which he had based on *Le Bain du Diane*, a painting by François Boucher. The figure carving was a straightforward copy from the painting but the background was far simpler. George admired Thomas' cameo pieces with their ornate designs, but felt that if cameo glass was to become a commercial venture its costs needed to be reduced and it required an edge to set it apart from its competitors. Wilkes Webb agreed that George should go to London to visit the South Kensington Museum in order to study the classical exhibits. He duly went in June 1880 for three months, leaving the management of the household in Pamela's hands. Whilst there, he greatly impressed Sir Philip Cunliffe-Owen, the Artistic Director of the South Kensington Museum, and returned to Staffordshire with a book which proved to be inspirational, *The Industrial Arts: Historical Sketches; The South Kensington Museum Art Handbook*.

Meanwhile, Webb's antipodean exploits were booming. The Sydney Exhibition of 1879 had been a success and for the Melbourne International Exhibition, Webb's shipped over the first cameo glass to touch Australia's shores and its impact was tremendous. The company invested heavily in this venture: £8000 worth of stock, Thomas Wilkes Webb and three assistants, including an engraver, were dispatched to the continent to sell the products, with B.W. Gribbon already their appointed representative. *The Argus* made special mention of *The Aurora Vase* when it reviewed the exhibition in October 1880:

> The body of the vessel consists of under and upper shells or layers of glass – the one being blue and the other white opal. The drawing is represented in white, whilst the surrounding blue serves as a background. The opposite side of the vessel is filled in with scrollwork... and the leaf decorations on the lid and base are executed in the same way. The first step in the process was to form the outer shell by blowing into a cap or mould, and the next to blow in the blue, which in turn lined

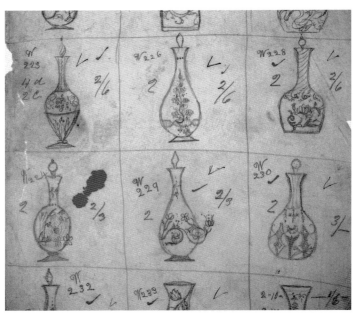

Early sketches of engraved designs for decanters with Woodall pattern numbers, attributed to George Woodall. (*Family collection*)

the white shell. The two shells become firmly united before cooling. They were then reheated to enable the glassblower to bring them to the shape of a perfectly oval vase, completed by the addition of base and cover, fashioned separately. The vase had to be kept fourteen days in the furnace, in order that the glass might be thoroughly annealed, the opal being a very fractious material to deal with compared with the blue. After the annealing had been effected, the vase was taken in hand by Woodall, who with pen and ink sketched a reproduction of Guido's picture upon the opal surface and next gradually scraped away portions of the outer shell in order to expose the blue ground. Where considerable blanks had been left, acid was used to hasten the operation; but along the outlines of the figure, only the graver's tools could be employed.

On the domestic front, George missed the birth of his brother's sixth child, Ethel Janet Woodall on the 31st May (hereafter known as Janet, her preferred name). Thomas and Martha moved house to Rose Cottage, where they remained until Thomas' death many years later.

17 The Portland Vase was a Roman vase, originally made in Alexandria about the first century A.D. There is speculation as to its ownership but most of the evidence points to the Emperor Augustus, the earliest Caesar. It was discovered in the late-sixteenth century in the sepulchral chamber of the Emperor Alexander Deverus on the Frascati Road, near Rome. It was owned by the Barberini family for two hundred years and known as the Barberini Vase before being acquired by Sir William Hamilton and then by Margaret, Duchess of Portland. On her death, her son the Duke purchased the vase from her estate for 1000 guineas. In 1810, the Duke, then Prime Minister, left the vase in the British Museum where it became known as The Portland Vase. On the 7th February 1845, William Lloyd entered the Hamilton Gallery and smashed the vase and its case. Unable to pay the fine imposed by the courts, Lloyd was sent to prison but released when an anonymous benefactor (believed to be the Duke of Portland) paid the fine. The vase (in 187 pieces) was repaired in 1845, 1947 and 1989. The Romans used the cameo technique to create other decorative pieces, but The Portland Vase is the only known piece in the UK. Benjamin Richardson brought a Wedgwood copy of the vase into his works and promised £1000 to the first engraver who could reproduce it. Pargeter renewed Richardson's challenge, Northwood accepted using a blank made by the 'chair' at Pargeter's works: Daniel Hancox, Joseph Worall, Charles Hancox and Benjamin Downing. It was completed three years later in 1876, but when it was taken to London to compare with the original, the sudden temperature change caused it to crack. The Pargeter-Northwood copy was a 10ins, white on blue, two-handled vase with a carving of the myth of *Peleus and Thetis*. However, Joseph Locke and Alphonse Lechevrel also undertook a copy for Hodgetts & Richardson & Co., which was never finished. Richardson was in fierce competition with Pargeter to achieve the best vase and he pushed his team too hard. The $9^7/_8$ins vase featured carving in white opaque on a dark blue background. A pioneer in many ways, Northwood began the practice of using local girls as models to demonstrate classical poses and it is reputed that he used Ellen Rowley to pose for the first vase. Northwood made two later versions, *The Milton Vase* and *The Dennis Vase* (also known as *The Pegasus Vase*). In the style of The Portland Vase, these featured original engravings taken from classical sources. *The Pegasus Vase* was awarded a Gold Medal at the 1878 Paris Exhibition and was finished in 1890. Northwood said in an interview: 'My first cameo work was a copy of the Elgin Frieze, on a vase for Stevens & Williams, which got smashed on its way to London. My next was a treatment of the Parthenon Frieze on a vase which is now in the Birmingham Museum. [*The Elgin Vase* is not cameo as defined today.] My third, a copy of The Portland Vase was bought by Philip Pargeter, who also had *The Milton Vase*. The Portland Vase was found near Rome. [It was placed in auction and bought by the Duke of Portland who lent it to Josiah Wedgwood to copy.] The early meaning of the word cameo was simply an onyx (having different layers of stone) but it is now taken to imply an anaglyph. The engraving of stones and gems is a very ancient art... in *Exodus XXVIII, Chapter* 9 Moses (in 1491BC) was commanded to take onyx stones and engrave on them the names of the children of Israel. Tryphon engraved the celebrated cameo in the

collection of the late Duke of Marlborough, representing the marriage of Cupid and Psyche, in about 300BC... When a youth, I worked for Benjamin Richardson, who often said a thousand pounds for the one who could execute a good copy of it in glass. Afterwards I saw The Portland Vase and from that time began experimenting with the aim in view of reviving the glass cameo. My first successful essay in cameo work was a claret jug for this firm, in January 1865. This, on account of the long process of execution, was a failure commercially, but I believe it was the first cameo produced since the ancients. Wedgwood made copies of The Portland Vase which were in jasperware. My first work was done with a steel point, but a lot of cameo work is done now with the engraving wheel, though the fine parts must still be touched up by steel tool.' (*The County Express*, 28th January 1893.) A white marble replica of the vase can be seen on Northwood's grave in Holy Trinity Church, Wordsley.

18 The white opal outer layer covered only the sides of the vase where Northwood intended to carve.

19 The glass technology used to create the blanks is a highly complex process. Through discussion with the Pilgrim Glass Company, Okra Glass and other individual artists, it has been possible to conduct a series of experiments. Lo-Co Glass, Louise Edwards and Colin Hawkins, have examined the probable methods of cameo blank production used by Victorian glassblowers. A blank plaque took them approximately forty minutes to complete, a small vase took an hour. The first method involved taking the blowing iron and gathering about three-quarters of the amount of glass required to make the article from a pot containing the base or underlying colour. After slightly blowing and truing the gather, the glass required for the outer layer was gathered from another pot. This was then manipulated so as to coat or thoroughly encase the first gather. The second method which was probably a secondary development, was referred to as the cupping method. This involved producing an open cup from the glass required for the outer layer and whilst this was still at a working temperature placing a preformed bubble of glass on a blowing iron into it. This was then blown and expanded in such a way that it expelled all the air from between the two items of glass and the cup could be picked up and manipulated. This process had the advantage of being able to more easily control the thickness of the layer and be repeated where multicoloured layers were required. Original blanks had very thick layers of white. Within five years, that opal layer had become only 2mm thick, because the thicker layers took longer to carve and placed more stress on the piece. A trick was to put more chalk in the white to make it softer to cut. It is highly probable that the glassblowers used other tricks of the trade. A typical blank contains little coloured glass, the main body of glass is colourless crystal. The base colour is generally a very thin layer on the inside of the crystal and the outer layer(s). The gathering process would be used to cover a small amount of coloured glass with the main body of the crystal and the outer layers applied using the cupping method. The colourless crystal provides the mechanical strength of the article. Also, since crystal takes on the colour of any glass in contact with it, less coloured glass needed to be used and more subtle colours could be achieved. These extra layers of glass provide the artist with a greater tolerance of error in the depth of etching, cutting and carving needed when producing the design. One hundred years ago, the stress on the blank during these processes was enormous. The annealing process took several days and results were erratic. The expansion and contraction of each layer of hot glass has to match or the layers shear away from each other. Much wastage must have occurred in the process. Hence, many later pieces were actually cut from larger blanks that had been faulty in some way, with the flawed area being discarded. Some of these sections were in the possession of the Woodall family.

20 Situated at the rear of Dennis Hall in Dennis Park, Amblecote, the Dennis Glass Works covered an area that is now largely modern housing estates. In 1829, Thomas Webb Snr (1804-1869), Benjamin Richardson and William Haden Richardson formed Webb & Richardson at the Wordsley Glass Works. In 1836, Webb left and founded Thomas Webb & Sons at the White House Works. By 1840 he was at The Platts. In 1860 the words '& Son' began to appear on letterheads. The Richardson business was expanded to include Jonathan Richardson, hence the name W.H., B. & J. Richardson. By 1856, Webb's had moved, and owned and occupied slightly over four acres. Dennis Hall included a 'House, Manufactory, Lands and Gardens'. The young Woodall brothers arrived at the firm where

Charles Wilkes, Thomas Wilkes and Walter Wilkes Webb in tripartite partnership managed Thomas Webb's after Webb Snr retired in 1863. After a dispute involving a pay cut for all Webb's employees Thomas Ernest Webb formed a breakaway company in 1897 with John Corbett – Webb & Corbett.

21 It seems probable that the Woodalls left Northwood's because John Northwood was sub-contracted to the post of artistic director at Stevens & Williams. (His etching and engraving shop was subsequently employed to carve cameo pieces for Stevens & Williams.) This created several problems for Thomas and George: their work would have been constantly overshadowed by Northwood's work, promotion to Head of Department would have been impossible unless Northwood left freely, and the prospect of working for a Brierley Hill firm on a freelance basis may have seemed too risky financially and too embarrassing socially as Brierley Hill was perceived as an urban slum.

22 George Woodall said in a later interview: 'Mr Webb brought... a specimen of real rock crystal and we found out a method of polishing the glass by acid in such a way as to resemble exactly the natural product. This system was afterwards adopted by the manufacturers of the district, and a new era commenced, the rock crystal glass quite superseding the old dull-coloured engraving.' (*The County Express*, 20th January 1912)

23 The term rock crystal first appears in the Webb factory pattern books next to pattern numbers 10991, 10992 and 10993, dated 6th July 1878.

24 George Woodall later described Thomas Wilkes Webb as 'The leading spirit of the trade... he was not only an artist but he knew the trade... in other ways. He... encouraged his men in every possible way in the right direction.' (*The County Express*, 20th January 1912)

25 *The Milton Vase* was 13³/₈ins, two-handled, white on blue. Its subjects were from *Paradise Lost* and depicted the angel Raphael sent by God to instruct Adam and Eve who were carved on the reverse. Also, at the Paris Exhibition, 'There are four tazzas, or flower dishes, each of which will be furnished with a carved head, the four being Shakespeare, Newton, Flaxman and Watts, as the representatives of the arts in which they have their peculiar excellences.' (*The County Express*, 23rd March 1878) Another tazza of Shakespeare was also produced without public knowledge, possibly a prototype or private commission.

26 The display also featured a Renaissance-style dessert service on several stands, having ruby studs and a set of plates to match. There was also a liqueur service of blue tints and an Egyptian-inspired table service. Engraved water sets, two Moorish-style vases and a Dutch Scheedam bottle were used to show deep cutting skills. A stand, using patented threaded glass, became the centre piece for a display of other threaded pieces. A richly cut toilet service and a set of glasses combining threading and moulding completed the display.

27 *Birth of Venus*: an 11¹/₈ins, two-handled vase; *Hercules Restoring...*: a 14¹/₄ins white on blue vase; *Venus Rising...*: an 11¹/₄ins white on blue two-handled vase. A.E. Lechevrel (b Paris c1850), whom Thomas Woodall described as a 'French seal engraver', was invited to Wordsley in 1877 by Hodgetts, Richardson & Co. to teach students how to engrave and carve.

28 *The County Express*, 30 March 1878.

29 The vase was blown in three pieces – the lid, the body and the foot – the body and foot joined by a nut and bolt. The opal is very thick and Thomas turned this into an asset, creating beautiful 3-D perspectives, particularly with horses, three-deep, pulling a chariot. The decoration is flawed where small air bubbles have burst but this does not detract from the magnificence of this unsigned and unmarked piece. The cobalt blue inner layer is identical to the colour used by Richardson's which suggests that the blank may have been made by the same team that created Richardson's blanks. This raises the hypothesis that the Red House may have scored blanks for all manufacturers in the earliest days of production. A hairline crack on the base bears witness to its turbulent history. After the Paris Exhibition, *The Aurora Vase* was returned to Webb's where it was finished by Thomas. He believed that the piece was lost in a shipwreck on its way to the 1880 Melbourne Exhibition, his memoirs report that the wreck was salvaged and the vase sold for £800 to an art gallery where it was destroyed by fire. In reality the Art Gallery of New South Wales bought the piece at the Exhibition for £250 and eventually loaned it to The Powerhouse Museum, Sydney, in 1987, where it was kept in storage until briefly displayed in the mid-1990s. It is due to be exhibited in 2001.

30 *The County Express*, 2 November 1878.

Thomas Webb & Sons' paper label with details of the *Crane* jar, see page 60.

1881 – 1890

WEBB & SONS, COMMERCIAL CAMEO PRODUCTION

W376 (centre) and two other pieces of early cameo. *(Family collection)*

Between 1881-1882, Thomas and George experimented with the production and carving of cameo glass. George was determined to refine the process used by John Northwood and Thomas and make it more cost effective and less prone to breakage. Their knowledge of 'cutting, engraving, shaping and the use of acids was sorely tested'[31] as the brothers attempted to make commercial cameo production viable. Much of their experimentation involved using acids to etch pieces, usually in preparation for carving. Gradually it became clear that only the very skilled engravers carved the best cameo. The glass industry was in recession from 1882-1886 and this enabled the brothers to assemble a team of engravers at low cost. Many of these artists, like Kretschman, continued to work in rock crystal as well.

Craftsmen and apprentices were employed to produce commercial cameo pieces – small vases, bowls and scent bottles that used simple line borders and mainly floral designs. Branches, leaves and vines were combined to make overall designs. Fruit designs also became fashionable and the layers of colour helped create the desired effect.

In later years, in an interview with *The County Express* (1912), George boasted that 70 people had worked for the Gem Cameo team, but this was an exaggeration. There were 72 engravers of commercial cameo working for Webb's (30% of the total workforce), but the Woodall's chose only the finest craftsmen for the Gem Cameo team. As department head, Thomas would decide which specimens were suitable after examining blanks from Webb's and these pieces would be taken to the Woodall's 'secret' workshop. (In an interview Stan

Eveson, Works Manager of Thomas Webb & Sons from 1961-1978, recalled that when he began at Webbs in 1929 he was unable to find any trace of the Woodall workshop. Josef Palmé told him it was in a secret location in order to stop theft – Eveson discovered that the team used to work in a converted storeroom at the rear of Dennis Hall in an L-shaped building.) Thomas would sketch onto the vases and the junior engravers would then apply an acid-resist paint onto the outer opaque glass layer for the sections they wished to retain. Once dipped in acid, the unwanted parts of the outer layer would be eroded and the engravers could carve the finer detail. This application of Northwood's process saved considerable time. The inner layer would normally be a dark colour in order to create a contrast.

The engraving team, as signified by five sets of works numbers in the factory price book, initially consisted of five sections: the numbers being preceded by an **F, K, L, W,** and **I**. Fridolin Kretschman[32], Jacob Facer, Jules Barbe[33] and Charles Nash worked on pieces identified by an **F** (for Fritsche), **L** (possibly for Lionel Pearce) or **K** (for Kretschman). Kretschman and George Woodall chiefly designed **I** (for 'ivory') pieces. Thomas and George Woodall carved little of the final output and rarely signed pieces of commercial cameo. **W** signified the work of the Woodalls (originally **TW** until George joined the department). As Facer and Kretschman left, George Woodall took over their numbers and unfinished projects. Thomas and George worked mainly with Barbe and Nash, the latter being the linkman between both sections – Nash as a finisher and acid-resist painter, Barbe as enameller, painter and gilder. By 1884, the Woodalls were being assisted by Harry Davies[34], Tom

Farmer, William Hill, Hanke Keller, William Mullett, G. Round, Frances Smith, Tom Guest, Joseph Muckley, Mr Shuker, Mr Burke and J.T. Fereday.[35] The team, under the Woodalls' direction, produced vases, scent bottles, candlesticks, fingerplates, menu boards, tazzas and cups. Thomas specialised in oriental designs using dragon and floral motifs and symmetrical patterns of scrolling foliage

In early 1882, George decided that he would also begin sketching designs for other engravers. He was reasonably satisfied that the cost of the process had been reduced and the quality improved sufficiently, to make cameo a commercial success. Wilkes Webb was delighted with the progress that had already been achieved; examples of the new vases were taken to the 1882 Worcestershire Exhibition and proved very popular. The official report stated:

> A tiny bit of this cameo glass stands before us as we write – a little vase with a white convolvulus sculptured on a rose background – every vein in the leaf, every fold and dimple in the flower being exquisitely cut and so delicately whithal.

George was a perfectionist and was unhappy with the finished work of the other engravers in his team. Increasingly he worked alone, sketching his own designs and carving his own vases. In the spring, he tried a different approach. He rejected the conventional shapes that were being carved in favour of a plaque. This offered Thomas new opportunities for designing and carving borders and the two brothers collaborated on their first piece of joint carving. *The Favourite* was a 13-inch white on light brown plaque, which George signed, 'T and G Woodall 1882'.

The plaque was not intended for sale; Thomas took it home for his wife but, inadvertently, it proved to be a harbinger of things to come. It was the first instance of the Woodalls co-signing their work, and Wilkes Webb encouraged this, realising that their signature increased the value. It was also an unusual piece because it was solely the brothers' work. Until then, and for some time to come, Thomas had insisted that the Woodall team pieces should be stamped 'Gem Cameo' (to signify the tradition of gem carving) since he did not wish to take credit for other people's work. His refusal to sign meant that his work seemed poorly represented at exhibitions. He also carved

Thomas Woodall's designs for engraved glass vases illustrated in *The Art Journal*, 1882. *(Family collection)*

proportionally less and designed more and was busy with managerial duties. (In 1878, George had signed his plaque, *Diana and Nymph Bathing*, which was not intended for sale; he continued to design but only signed the pieces he carved.) On some occasions the team would duplicate a piece, using George's original drawing. *Before the Race* and *The Race* are examples of this.

As the two brothers finished this experimental period, they enjoyed increased leisure time with their families. More children were born: 11th February 1883, Kathleen (known as Kate) was born to Thomas and Martha and fifteen months later on the 14th May, they completed their family with Nora May (known as May). With his large family requiring attention, and a baptism and organ recital at Bethel Chapel[36] to prepare for, Thomas chose to stay at home rather than attend the International Health Exhibition held in London in June 1884.

A glassblower shapes and finishes a cameo blank to form a vase. *(Photograph by George Woodall)*

George Woodall at his desk in Dennis Hall. *(Family collection)*

A Thomas Webb & Sons Sales Catalogue

The following illustrations are of pieces made between 1884-1886. As well as Woodall (W-) and Thomas Woodall (TW-) pieces, there are entries with the prefix L (see page 22). (*Photographs reproduced courtesy of the Broadfield House Glass Museum*)

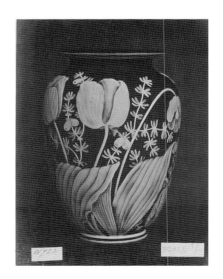

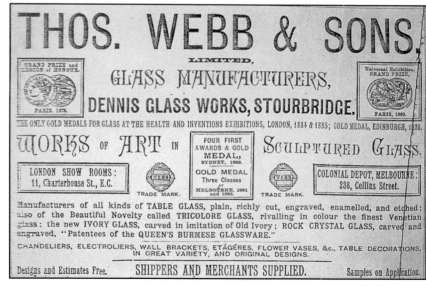

INTERNATIONAL HEALTH EXHIBITION, LONDON, 1884

Health: Food, Dress, the Dwelling, the School and the Workshop.

Education: Apparatus used in primary, technical and art schools.

Objects of the Exhibition:

The object of the exhibition will be to illustrate as vividly and in as practical a manner as possible, Food, Dress, the Dwelling, the School, and the Workshop, as affecting the conditions of healthful life, and also to bring into public notice the most recent Appliances for Elementary School – Teaching and Instruction in Applied Science, Art and Handicrafts. The influence of Modern Sanitary Knowledge and Intellectual Progress upon the welfare of the people of all classes and all nations thus be practically demonstrated, and an attempt will be made to display the most valuable and recent advances which have been attained in these important subjects.

The sixth group will comprise all that relates to Primary, Technical and Art Education, and will include Designs and Models for School Buildings; Apparatus and Appliances for Teaching; Diagrams, Text-Books etc. Special attention will be directed to Technical and Art education, to the results of industrial teaching, to the introduction of manual and handicraft work into schools, and also to specimens illustrating the results of Art and technical teaching.

General Committee members:

W. Woodall Esq., M.P.
Sub-Committees (Selected from Members of the General Committee)
The Workshop: W. Woodall Esq., M.P.
School and Education: W. Woodall, Esq., M.P.

6th December 1884 Science and Art Department Students Exhibition International Health Exhibition. Section III Glass

Objects selected for consideration for purchase:

Catalogue No.:451
Object: glass vase, cameo cut, designed and executed by T Woodall, manufactured by Messrs Webb
Remarks: Already sold

Catalogue No.:473
Object Glass Bowl, carved designed by T Woodall, manufactured by Messrs Webb
Price: £31.10.0

Catalogue No.:480
Object: Two Glass Panels, cameo cut, designed by G Woodall, manufactured by Messrs Webb
Price: £30.0.0 (Pair)

Catalogue No.:486
Object: Glass Vase, cameo cut, designed by T Woodall, manufactured by Messrs Webb
Price: £21.0.0

Catalogue No.:487
Object: Glass Vase, cameo cut, designed by T Woodall, manufactured by Messrs Webb
Price: £10.0.0

Catalogue No.:494
Object: Glass Vase, cameo cut, designed by T Woodall, manufactured by Messrs Webb
Price: £38.0.0

No. 473 carved by Francis Smith
No. 480 is unsigned
No. 486 carved by Benjamin Hollis (not recorded at Webb's)
No. 487 carved by J.T. Fereday
No. 494 carved by William Hill

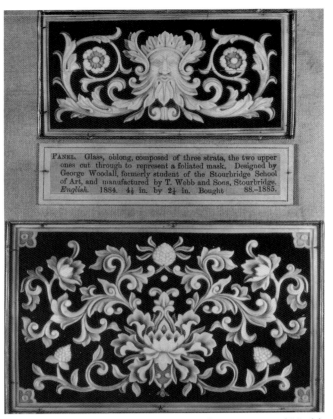

Exhibition panels. Catalogue No.480 from the International Health Exhibition, 1884. *(Victoria & Albert Museum)*

His work was given a seal of approval when the new Victoria & Albert Museum purchased pieces (see opposite and page 54) and the above panels.[37]

112 past and present glass designers from the Stourbridge area were represented on various stands. Thomas was acclaimed in the press for the team's work and his own decorative carving, gaining a Bronze Medal for Glass Vases and Bowls. George attended the exhibition but at this stage was a minor figure. Over the ensuing years Thomas frequently chose to stay at home, leaving George to act as showman for their work. A review of the exhibition read:

> The cameo glass of Messrs T Webb and Sons… far surpasses anything else in the whole of the exhibition. Webb and Sons have succeeded in resuscitating a lost art, and are without equals, if not without rivals. We… call attention to the plaques (nos. 478 and 481) by Thomas and George Woodall, in which the figures are wonderfully executed in white on black grounds, and the two exquisite vases by Fereday (nos. 451 and 494).
> *(Introduction to the Report on the 1882 Worcestershire Exhibition)*

Less than four weeks after his return from London (which was excited by the news that Gladstone had passed a further Franchise Act extending the electorate to about five million people – one sixth of the population), George and Pamela's fourth child, Pamela, was born on the 17th July. Thomas and George worked together and their families enjoyed regular musical evenings: Alice played piano, Amy the piano and concertina, George Parkes the violin – all taught by Thomas.

George pursued an interest in photography, bought a new and expensive light-oak box camera and gradually became a talented photographer. He captured many scenes of ordinary Kingswinford life as well as photographing many of the large houses, providing an insight into a cross section of Kingswinford 'society' from 1885-1910.

W1538, white on blue vase, 8¹/₂ins (21.5cms), signed G Woodall and Gem Cameo. A later, similar vase was given the title *Cloches*. (*The Metropolitan Museum of Art, gift of Ethel Lyman Mackey and Ruth Hellum, 1960*)

Mrs J.J. Winans, white on brown portrait plaque, 11ins x 8¹/₂ins (28 x 21.5cms), signed G Woodall 1885. (*Photograph courtesy of Stanley Eveson*)

Photography finally met cameo in January 1885 when George realised that photographs of his pieces could add to their commercial success and Webb's sent copies to potential dealers. His earliest attempt was of the unusual piece, *Minerva*. In the future, he would photograph much of his work and keep a copy for himself to display at Luton House, and give others to members of his family.

George's daughter, Alice, with her straight nose, rounded chin and upright bearing, was to be the inspiration for many of

A rustic summer house under construction at Luton House. From left, a servant, Amy, another servant and Alice. (*Photograph by George Woodall*)

his cameo maidens. From an early age, it was clear that Alice was very close to her father. Their personalities were similar – like him, Alice was stubborn, took violent dislikes to people, and could be vindictive. George used the nickname 'Flip' to characterise his particular closeness to his daughter – like her, his temper would flip into a rage and just as quickly evaporate. George collected over 200 photographs of actresses (dressed in a variety of styles), but his principal inspiration remained his daughters who provided the detail for many ancillary maidens. Amy and Alice were the source for the female figure studies before 1900 but draped figures were assumed by other craftsmen to be based upon a generalised female. Occasionally, however, Amy and Alice did pose nude. *The Works of Antonio Canova*[38] was a source for George's nudes and he also possessed a lay-figure that he could turn to any angle to shape a pose. George's personal effects included many books of classical inspiration including *L'amour Allare* and the painting *Knight Errant*.[39]

Minerva was the last Woodall piece to use a white opaque layer over a cobalt blue. Due to differences in the expansion and contraction of the glass layers, a lack of stability in the white layer on top of the blue piece caused frequent cracking. The process had been unavoidable until George discovered that a similar colour effect could be achieved by using a flashed (or ultra-thin) layer of blue between the outer layer and the innermost layer, creating three layers of glass. As the white layer was thinned down, the blue underneath became more transparent. This middle layer would enable George to create blue backgrounds of great delicacy.

The brothers continued to collaborate on special pieces, whilst the team worked on smaller cameos. A stand was taken at the 1885 International Health Exhibition and George began to carve portraits as special commissions, starting with two companion pieces, *Judge J. Winans* (who sat in the USA Supreme Court after 1864) and his wife. By now the Woodall team had established a working pattern: Thomas was the

Sketches from Thomas Woodall's pocket notebook showing the influence of Japanese, Chinese and Persian styles. Furniture also provided inspiration for decorative borders. *(Family collection)*

The Woodall team working on *The Great Tazza*. From left: back row, Tom Farmer, Harry Davies and Thomas Woodall; front row, William Hill, J.T. Fereday and George Woodall (seen working on a separate vase, illustrated on page 101, perhaps to establish that he often decorated his own pieces). (*Photograph by George Woodall*)

department head, chief designer and principal carver of decorative borders on plaques; George was the technical innovator and principal carver of figures. At the beginning of 1886, the brothers agreed that George would be free to work uninterrupted on solo pieces; W733 *Dancers* was the first of many to be signed by George alone. Significantly, this piece was one of the first plaques entered in Webb's Price Book. The book

was introduced quite late and over 1000 pieces had been sold before records were kept. The Woodalls, like other engravers, were paid bonuses for piece work and the glass was sold so quickly that pieces were often not being entered into the Price Book. Consequently, Thomas felt that workmen were being either under- or over-paid, leading to financial disparities.

Albeit unofficially, George now had equal managerial status with Thomas. While this did not cause difficulties between the brothers, the other engravers had to tread carefully. Thomas was a mild-mannered man who forgave mistakes and disliked fuss – George, though kind, was passionate about his work, expected the highest standards, and did not easily forgive errors. For production of *The Great Tazza* in 1886, the Woodalls assembled a close team of their finest engravers. The design was inspired by Owen Jones' *Examples of Chinese Ornament*, published in 1867, and the work would not be finished until 1889.

George's fifth child Norah Constance (hereafter known as Connie), was born on the 14th November 1886, the same day as Alice's birthday, who described it as 'the rottenest birthday present', a joke shared by the two sisters for many years. Much of 1887 was dominated by work on *The Great Tazza* with its seven layers of glass, but George also found time to create one notable, independent piece: *Origin of the Painting,* a $9^{1}/_{2}$-inch vase based upon Eduard Daege's *Invention of Painting*, 1832. The vase sold immediately and wealthy clients ordered copies; George recreated the principal picture of the vase on five additional pieces in future years. Other designs would also be repeated in this way, with slight alterations or different borders on plaques and vases.

In the garden of Luton House. From left: back row, Thomas, Thomas Snr and George; front row, Martha, Emma and Pamela. (*Photograph by George Woodall*)

The Factory Price Book shows that although imitation jade cameo had previously been carved, Wilkes Webb did not actually patent his 'imitation of old carved ivory' (no.16487) until the 30th November 1887. This variation on the cameo process gave the glass an 'ivory' effect. It involved staining the glass to produce a dark tint in the recesses of the carving while the top layer retained some colour. 'Ivory' production was technically complex. Up to fourteen processes, including gilding, jewelling, painting, padding and polishing, were employed to create a single piece. The Factory Price Book indicates that 'ivory' production became a mainstay of Webb's work as a result of falling demand for commercial cameo work in 1888. Supply exceeded demand: Stevens & Williams had assembled its own team, Stuart Crystal was making medallion cameo pieces, and Walsh Walsh was advertising Vesta Ware, a lattice-patterned product which created a cameo-like effect.

Webb's were luckier than most – helped by the exclusivity of their 'ivory' patent and the brothers being under sole contract, the impact of the recession was not so severe. The Woodall team increased production of 'ivory' glass. However, because of the popularity of George Woodall commissions, the larger pieces of exhibition work, special projects and figure work remained largely unaffected. The importation of 'a German imitation came into vogue'[40], and the Government, lobbied by many interested parties, was keen to prevent imports being bought under false pretences. The Merchandise Marks Act 1887, reinforced the Customs Consolidation Act 1876, to prevent foreign goods being imported unless they were marked as being non-British. It was a particularly sensitive issue in the glass and pottery trades which suffered huge import levies on any goods shipped to other countries. *The Pottery Gazette* led a campaign for a Merchandise Marks Amendment Act to specify the foreign origin of goods in greater detail and this bill entered Parliament for its first reading in October 1887. Although cameo production continued for another ten years, the imports signalled the beginning of the end.

With no more children planned, and business flourishing, Thomas joined the first of many committees on which he would serve. Already engaged with Wordsley Choral Society (as Honorary Secretary) alongside his work as church organist, Thomas became a member of Kingswinford Parish Church

Vase with dancing girls, white and pink on yellow, 12ins (30.5cms). *(Photograph courtesy of Geoffrey Beard)*

Council. On the 18th April 1888, he was elected as a sidesman under the chairmanship of the Reverend J.J. Slade, MA.

By mid-1888 the Government Protectionism Bill was nearing completion. George and Pamela's last child, Thomas Bott Woodall (hereafter known as Thomas Bott Jnr), was born on the 31st July, the day after the tenth Glassmakers Picnic in the Heath Park.[41] The event began with a procession from Wordsley with £1000 worth of exhibition glass being carried to the park. The 'I' Company First Worcestershire Rifle Volunteers joined the Willenhall Templar Prize Band, the Brierley Hill Operatic Band, and the Wordsley Brass Band. There was a funfair, and the £124.0.0 raised from admission to the glass tent covered the day's costs. Stevens & Williams exhibited a jug, with the handle cut above and underneath; Richardson's included cut goblets, but Thomas Webb's exhibits were particularly elaborate with enamel and Burmese work, a 'Queen Anne' jug from the 1878 Paris Exhibition, and a Woodall cameo vase.

From left, W1797 *Origin of the Painting*, white on brown vase, 9½ins (24cms), signed G Woodall 1887; W1753 *Dancing Girls*, white on pink on yellow vase, 12ins (30.5cms), signed G Woodall. *(Photograph by George Woodall.)*

From left, Tom, Connie and Pamela Woodall. George doted on his children. *(Photograph by George Woodall)*

Members of the Woodall family in the garden at Luton House. From left: back row, Amy, Thomas Snr, Harry, Alice, George and Jack; middle row, Emma and Pamela; front row, Connie, Tom and Pam. (*Photograph by George Woodall*)

Amy and Alice Woodall pose in an aesthetic interior. George's daughters were the principal inspiration for much of his female figure work. (*Photograph by George Woodall*)

Shortly after the Picnic, the Woodall brothers learned that they had each received a Gold Medal for cameo work at the 1888 Melbourne Exhibition in Australia. As *The Great Tazza* neared completion, George finished further pieces of magnificent work: W2403 *The Fruit Seller*, W2501 *Pandora*, W2609 *Cupid and Psyche*, W2476 with lovers on a swing, and a two-handled vase. By using an engraving wheel to speed up the carving process, he had significantly reduced the time taken to finish a piece of work. This discovery helped to maintain Webb's profits in the slowing market.

By January 1889, *The Great Tazza* was finished and was dispatched to the continent, destined for the Paris Exhibition in May. *The Pottery Gazette* reported that due to a shortage of space, the British section was split into three areas, leading to furious arguments with the hosts. Webb's fared better than most, though all complained that the problem was caused by the large metallic structure, which the French had erected and was now covering too much space. *The Pottery Gazette* dismissed the Eiffel

Tower as a 'gimmick that will not last the test of time'! Upon its unveiling, *The Daily Telegraph* described the Webb stand as:

> the most remarkable [cameo glass]... the world has ever seen... a large vase and plateau in low-toned red, lilac and white – is cast in no fewer than seven layers, all its designs being in strong, sharp relief, and its lower surfaces first bitten out with acid and then finished with the cold steel graver. There are vases, coupes and plaques by the score ranged round these masterpieces. Each a gem in its own way. I observed that those most closely following the antique models in form, and enriched by figures in relievo, drawn with a charming freedom and vivacity... all bore the name of Woodhall (*sic*).

The many individual pieces produced by George were now signed only by him. Whilst much of Thomas' output with the Woodall team had been marked with the usual 'Gem Cameo' (with 'Tiffany & Co., Paris Exhibition 1889')[42] stamped as well, George ensured that his pieces received extra prominence. Other pieces of his own work on display included *Cupid and Psyche* and the *Pandora* vase. As he had little interest in playing the showman, Thomas was happy for his brother to take the limelight. A busy family life and many other interests engaged his time and remarkably, though perhaps predictably, rather than travel to Paris he chose to stay at home and attend the Fourth Grand Evening Concert of Wordsley Choral Society on the 13th May. George took Pamela to France, leaving their children in the care of the nanny. The Paris Exhibition opened on the 11th May, to mark the centenary of the French revolution. As Thomas and Martha listened to Rossini's 'Stabat Mater' in a half-empty drill hall in Wordsley, the Prince of Wales stopped at Webb's stand and spoke to George of 'the intricacies of the work'.[43] While in Paris, George and Pamela went shopping: at that time Oriental influences were prevalent on the continent and they bought a selection of Japanese woodcuts that were to inspire George in new directions for later pieces.

The Pottery Gazette reviewed the exhibition, praising the Webb's stand:

> The chief attraction... is the large bowl and plate as a centrepiece with vases as side pieces. This bowl is composed of

Front and reverse of W2685 *Pompeiian Maidens*, jar and cover. (*Photograph by George Woodall*)

Right, George Woodall photographed many prints by R. Caton Woodville. These romanticised scenes of Egypt would inspire many of the designs on later cameo works. *(Photograph by George Woodall)*

Far right, vase, 12ins (30.5cms), signed G Woodall, marked Gem Cameo and Theodore B. Starr, New York. A drawing of this figure features in Daniel Pearce's sketch book. *(Private collection)*

seven strata of glass, each of a different colour and tint. When a bowl with these seven layers of coloured glass had been produced, properly and safely annealed and cooled, the beautiful Oriental design it now bears was cut out of these layers by skilful artists. I was told that nearly one thousand pounds was paid for salaries and wages alone in the production of this one set. They have been specially made to the order of Mr Goode.[44]

Over the next eighteen months, many pieces of cameo were produced, including more solo work by George: W2567 *Night*, and in October 1890, W2576 *Chinese Dogs*.

The brothers' eldest children were now teenagers. After a good schooling, Amy and Alice, went into millinery, their mother's trade, and Amy, approaching eighteen, was courting George Calloway, a builder. George Parkes Woodall intended to follow in his father's footsteps and become a glass engraver. Thomas encouraged his children to enter professions. His eldest son, Harry, was a gifted musician, while Jack had inherited his father's social conscience and was a Liberal supporter, and the daughters were eventually to become teachers.

The 1890s saw great changes in society: local authorities were democratised by creating elected county and borough councils, and administrative duties which had been carried out by unelected Justices of the Peace and local boards, were now transferred to these new bodies. Thomas and members of his family were to serve on many of these councils.

[31] *The County Express*, 20th January 1912.

[32] Fridolin Kretschman specialised in engraving and hand-tool finishing of pieces. After 1886, his name no longer appears in the Webb's Price Book as a member of the Woodall team, and the prefix K- for his own work appears in 1887 mainly with his own 'ivory' cameo designs, suggesting that he left the Woodalls in 1886 to produce independent work, including a 7$^{1}/_{2}$ins white on red plaque of the German Chancellor, Bismarck.

[33] Jules Barbe was a specialist in gilding and enamelling, working with Kretschman and George Woodall on many pieces.

[34] Harry Davies (1862-1937). Dates are sourced from *English Cameo Glass* by Ray and Lee Grover.

[35] John Thomas Fereday (1854-1922) was an engraver for Thomas Webb & Sons throughout his forty-year career. When cameo work

The Webb's Pattern Book drawing for GW5 *Morning*. George Woodall carved several version of the subjects *Night* and *Morning*, compare with GW24, illustrated on page 101. *(Edinburgh Crystal Glass Co)*

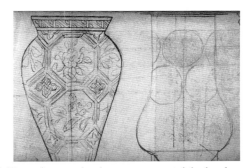

Sketches from Thomas Woodall's pocket notebook, source material for border and vase designs. *(Family collection)*

finished, he worked on crystal tableware and designed the Egyptian-style set 'Dynasty' which was given to The Princess Royal as a wedding gift in 1922. He retired in the same year, and died in Llandudno, Wales. He was an executor of George Woodall's estate.

36 Bethel Chapel, Kate's Hill, Dudley. Thomas Woodall Snr raised £160 to pay for a harmonium organ while Thomas Jnr sang.

37 The Victoria and Albert Museum began as the South Kensington Museum but was renamed after the death of Prince Albert.

38 Antonio Canova (1757-1822), an Italian sculptor specialising in neo-classical works. The Emperor used Canova as a cultural ambassador to retrieve stolen artwork from Paris after the fall of Napoleon. George Woodall owned a copy of *The Works of Antonio Canova*, featuring outline engravings by Henry Moses.

39 This picture now hangs in the Tate Gallery, London.

40 George Woodall described it as 'a sort of enamel painting so like the

glass that... those could not tell the difference. The imitation goods were sold at one-tenth the price.' *The County Express*, 20th January 1912.

41 This so-called annual tradition had been forgotten for fourteen years until H. Turney offered his Park to revive it. However, this was the last picnic.

42 In a recent conversation with the author, Charles Hajdamach and Timothy Novak questioned the legitimacy of this stamp. *The Pottery Gazette* reports that Tiffany's bought many pieces in 1893, many of which were featured at the Chicago World Fair and in Paris four years earlier. It seems probable that the stamp may have been added as provenance for the pieces.

43 *The County Express*, 20th January 1912.

44 *The Pottery Gazette*, 1st July 1889.

1891 – 1900

GEORGE WOODALL WORKS ALONE

Sadly, 1891 began badly with Thomas Wilkes Webb's death from diabetes on the 21st January – a personal blow to Thomas and George who greatly admired him.

However, production was hectic and there was little time for grieving. George produced solo pieces including W2720 *The Minuet* and a two-handled vase that was bought by the Melbourne Tennis Club and presented to W.D. Coldham on 25th May 1892[45], a purchase indicative of Webb's successful overseas market.

In addition to George's independent work, the Woodall team continued on 'Gem Cameo' collaborations and worked on a third strand of the enterprise – the joint pieces. In figure work, Thomas had never developed sufficient confidence when drawing or carving hands and feet, whilst George had less patience with the ornate borders at which Thomas excelled. According to Thomas' memoirs, George would concentrate on the figure work and Thomas the patterns. This cooperation finished such pieces as *The Favourite* in 1891, a reworking of an earlier cameo design. In late 1891, the brothers began working on exhibits for the Chicago Exhibition which was to be staged two years later: George on two solo pieces, W2732 *Aphrodite* and W2734 *Cupid in Disgrace*, and collaborating with Thomas on W2759 *Feathered Favourites*, W2786 *Diana and Endymion* and W2794 *Intruders*.

Fruit and Flower Girls, opal on deep claret vase, 12¹/₂ins (32cms), signed Fruit and Flower Girls, attributed to the Woodall team. (*Photograph courtesy of Stanley Eveson*)

W2765 *Penelope*, white on brown on flint jar, signed T & G Woodall and inscribed: 'Presented to Mrs Parker by the Liberals of Wordsley and the district in recognition of the gallant attempt made by her husband, Thomas Parker Esq. to win for the popular cause the Kingswinford Division of Staffordshire, at the parliamentary election of 1892.' (*Photograph by George Woodall*)

The brothers' continued their support for the Liberal Party though when a general election was called in 1892, Thomas declined to be actively involved with campaigning for Thomas Parker, the Liberal candidate for the Kingswinford division of Staffordshire. He felt that his quiet work on various councils might be jeopardised if he was associated with the election manifesto, which was labelled as 'extreme' by opponents. Instead, George agreed to publicly support Parker and printed leaflets on his behalf. At several political meetings his text, 'An honest man's the noblest work of God. Be true to yourself and vote for honest Tom Parker', impressed the electorate. It also did his career no harm to share the platform with Philip Pargeter the president of the local Liberal Party and the Richardson family. Parker rallied greater support in Kingswinford than in Wordsley but it was no surprise when he was defeated on polling day by a Tory candidate supported by the powerful Earl of Dudley and Stuart family. Thomas and George presented Mrs Parker with a piece of cameo, W2765 *Penelope*, as a gesture of appreciation for her husband's hard work.

In late 1892, at Charles Webb's request, the curator of the South Kensington Museum inspected *Aphrodite* and *Cupid in Disgrace* and 'pronounced them to be perfect in execution'.[46] An analysis of the Thomas Webb accounts ledger 1887-1892 reveals that the price of Woodall work had rapidly increased. One of the reasons for this growth in income was that, ever the showman, George and his photography had marketed the glass so well.

W2732 *Aphrodite*, white on blue on claret plaque, 13ins (33cms), signed G Woodall 1892 and Gem Cameo. (*Photograph by George Woodall*)

Adam and Eve plaque, 18ins (46.5cms), signed Geo Woodall, the only known Woodall cameo with a biblical subject. (*Photograph by George Woodall*)

W2786 *Diana and Endymion*, white on brown plaque, 17½ins (45cms), signed T & G Woodall. (*Photograph by George Woodall*)

W2734 *Cupid in Disgrace*, white on blue on claret plaque, 13¼ins (33.5cms), signed G Woodall 1892. (*Photograph by George Woodall*)

From left, W3111 *Iris*, opal on brown two-handled vase, signed Geo Woodall; W2848 *Cleopatra, The Egyptian Princess*, white on raisin brown, 11ins (28cms), signed Geo Woodall and Gem Cameo; W2726 front and reverse of *A Quiet Nook*, white on brown covered jar, 7ins (18cms), signed Geo Woodall. (*Photographs by George Woodall*)

W2718 *Diana and Nymph*, white on brown covered jar, 10ins (25.5cms), designed by George in 1878 after a painting in the Louvre by François Boucher. *(Photograph by George Woodall)*

W2802 *Wandering Star* panel. *(Photograph by George Woodall)*

By early 1893, the Woodall exhibits for the The World's Fair in Chicago were ready to be sent to the USA. The long distance, and the high cost of transportation resulted in no glass companies leasing stands. Instead, London agents such as Phillips were paid to organise sales displays. The local newspapers were invited to look at Webb's pieces in January 1893, and their praise was overwhelming:

> We were fortunate enough to see some five plaques which are to follow... the bulk of the exhibits, many of them having been sent away.[47] Foremost among these is one of some thirteen inches in diameter, on which the decoration is Aphrodite rising from the sea. Beautiful and entirely new effects in this material are obtained... The waves seem churned into foam, and from this the lithe and graceful figure of the goddess is emerging, her long hair rippling into the water, and her limbs perfectly exposed in the foamy brine, while sea birds hover near or wing their way over the waste of waters in the far distance. In three panels of the outer circle are Zephyrs who wafted the goddess to the shores of Oythera and the ornamentation on the edge between the panels appropriately consists of scallop shells.[48]

The County Express concentrated on *Cupid in Disgrace, Feathered Favourites* and *Diana and Endymion*:

> *Cupid Disgraced* (sic) illustrates a story of classic love. Cupid was sent by Venus, whose envy had been excited by the superlative beauty of Psyche to punish her, by inflaming her with hopeless love. But Cupid, instead of afflicting the heart... himself fell victim to her charms. The artist has chosen the moment of Cupid's return to his mother's palace... and Venus is chiding him for his disloyalty to her cause. Symmetry and proportion are carefully observed.

> *Favourites* is the *pièce de résistance*, and it is one that is bound to be admired... In this plaque the customary circular form has been departed from, and the outline has been divided into a

series of six graceful curves. Upon a terrace which overlooks the waters of a lake, are two female figures. The features are modelled to a high type of classic beauty, we may remark Mr G. Woodall's forte seems to be his ability to create beautiful women – and through the folds of their flowing diaphanous draperies, the outlines of their vigorous and shapely limbs are plainly traced. One figure is leaning – in an attitude which combines stateliness and grace – against an ornamental balustrade; the other is seated upon one of the steps. In the foreground are a couple of jars, from which the flight of doves, which circle overhead, and alight on the floor and finger and shoulder, are evidently expecting to be fed. The architectural

Alice Woodall, aged eighteen. *(Photograph by George Woodall)*

Webb's engraving and etching team became known through the mark 'Gem Cameo', unfortunately only some of them can be identified. Back row, second from left, Thomas Woodall, fifth from left, William Hill, Harry Davies and Tom Farmer, far right, J.T. Fereday; front row, far right, George Woodall. *(Family collection)*

W2384 *On the Terrace*, white on brown panel, 12¼ins x 8½ins (31cms x 21.5cms), signed T & G Woodall. *(Photograph by George Woodall)*

parts in this piece and others are very striking, tiled floor and marble pillars with elaborate carvings and mouldings being represented with astonishing effectiveness. The landscape effects, also – water, cloud, foliage, and distant hill – are not less noticeable and natural. When finished... this will form a very striking centre piece.

Another peerless piece of work will be *Endymion and Diana*.[49] Endymion (a shepherd) asked Jupiter to grant him eternal youth and the capacity of sleeping as much as he wished. Diana, represented as a huntress, discovers him as he lies in a state of somnolency, and, struck with his beauty, falls in love with him. The artist has selected for his subject the moment when Diana discovers him as she is returning from the chase, bearing her bow and quiver and accompanied by her dogs. Endymion is reclining on the mount, and Diana is gazing upon him, the scene being a happy conception. Only a true artist could venture to undertake any of this delicate and exquisite work.[50]

The papers were quick to notice that George had become the principal figure carver and the tiled floor, which became a feature in many of their plaques, was making its first appearance.[51] The praise for the cloud formations must have particularly pleased George, because he had photographed them in order to study their perspective in more detail.

An example of one month's travelling expenses at Thomas Webb's confirms that George was the driving force behind the cameo revival, whereas Thomas was foremost a skilled craftsman and administrator. In February 1893, George claimed a total of £5.11.0. In a similar period Thomas travelled just once (with George), claiming only £2.11.6.

The rush to finish the Chicago display pieces prevented Thomas attending the Parish Church Council from the 7th December 1892 onwards. In particular he missed a key meeting on the 19th April 1893 when the Council unanimously supported the motion: 'To defend the Church against

Amy Woodall aged twenty-one. (*Photograph by George Woodall*)

W2797 *Greek Girl*, white on brown oval plaque, 7¹/₂ins x 5ins (19x15.5cms), dated March 1894 in Pattern Book. (*Photograph by George Woodall*)

disestablishment and disendowment.' This was a clear conflict between the Council and the Liberal party. For many years Gladstone had advocated equal rights for secular and other non-Anglican churches. Thomas agreed with him, and did not return to the Council until October 1894 when the issue had been resolved by parliament. A man of principle, he did not wish to compromise his beliefs, but neither did he wish to antagonise his friends.

As predicted, the Webb's exhibits were a success in Chicago and orders came flooding in. Following the exhibition, the Woodall team continued to produce pieces such as *Floralia* and throughout 1894, exceptional pieces such as W2797 *Greek Girl* and W2685 *Pompeiian Maidens* were finished. The two brothers had much to celebrate at the annual Church Garden Party that summer. As in former years, George had been asked to print the programme of games – he had developed a business selling his publishing and photographic skills from his millinery shop in Luton House. The brothers had given their elder daughters

cameo brooches as small gifts and George also carved Alice a special cameo vase for her birthday (see page 51). It was a symbol of the close bond between father and daughter which grew stronger as Amy pursued her private life with George Calloway, and posed less.

By mid-1895 the brothers had completed two more joint pieces, W2834 *On the Terrace* and W2830 *Vestal*, but problems were emerging. Many of the Woodall team who had worked on *The Great Tazza* were now engravers in their own right. Thomas was happy to teach the apprentices and lead the other engravers, but George was restless about having to work, and be known, as part of a wider team. A mixture of imported glass from America, the Continent and UK businesses had begun to flood the market and as sales of the genuine article suffered so surplus stock began to mount. The United Kingdom firms named their product 'Cameo Glass' – a vase was painted with acid resist in the required design and then dipped to remove parts of the unwanted outer casing. The result was pleasing, and technically

A 'society' celebration in Kingswinford. An intriguing posed photograph by George Woodall.

W2733 *Floralia*, white on plum plaque, 13ins (33cms), signed
G Woodall 1892 and Gem Cameo. (*Photograph by George Woodall*)

W2677 *Dancing Girls*, white on dark brown covered jar, 11¹/₂ins
(29cms), signed T & G Woodall. (*Photograph by H.C. Ash*)

it was cameo, but the designs were inferior to those of the Woodall's. The 'Florentine Art Cameo' and 'Lace-De-Boheme-Cameo' from the Bohemian factories also gained sales: the designs, normally floral or figural, were painted on a satin glass body with heavy white enamel. More common was the 'Mary Gregory' style of glass from Bohemia and America, decorated with figures which were principally white enamel on transparent coloured glass. These three processes were quicker and cheaper and therefore popular with a public who wanted to buy something decorative. Charles Webb may well have been tempted to radically reduce production at this stage, but two events threw the cameo team a lifeline. Firstly, the Honourable George Brookman, a keen visitor to the earlier Australian exhibitions, commissioned a large plaque, *The Moorish Bathers*, for which he paid 800 guineas. As a result 'Gem Cameo' was gradually phased out and, instead, pieces were made to order.

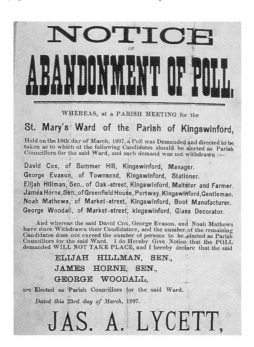

George enjoyed a higher profile in the art world and society as he was receiving commissions for solo pieces. Consequently, from 1895 new works numbers appeared in the Webb's price book: GW1 *Poetry* was the first to be marked as solely George's work. Increasingly, Thomas was left overseeing the smaller Woodall team, signalling the end of an era. Secondly, the discovery by Wilhelm Konrad Röntgen of a form of light radiation that could pass through various substances resistant to ordinary light. The successful completion of a project at Birmingham University to recreate the world's first experiments with X-rays, meant that flaws in cameo blanks could now be seen *before* work began. This was a breakthrough for the Woodall brothers – discovering a fault in the glass when a major work was nearly completed, must have been devastating.

In November, Luton House celebrated Alice's twenty-first birthday and George presented her with two cameo perfume bottles. Unfortunately, she became ill and, following an operation for acute appendicitis, developed a rash which left the side of her face scarred – whenever photographed, she would turn her face away from the camera. George's favourite model was disfigured for life and Alice's hopes of courtship and marriage were devastated. To compensate, George used her features on many pieces but in such a way that the scar was not visible. On a 6¹/₄-inch white on brown plaque, *Song of the Sea* (also known as *Siren*), he signed the piece and wrote on the case, 'Alice Woodall, A Song of the Sea.' The younger daughter, Pamela was now expected to become a model, but she refused to pose naked as a classical figure, so George used her instead for figures dressed in diaphanous drapery and clothing. She appears on only a few plaques because of an estrangement from her father.

Thomas and George completed their penultimate joint work, *The Attack*, in March 1896; much of the year was taken up with George's preliminary sketching and carving of the W3139 plaque which George christened *Moorish Bathers*. Other works included W2840 *Aurora* Version II, W2832 *Euterpe*, W2848 *Cleopatra*, *The Egyptian Princess*, and W3111 *Iris*.

The Pargeter-Northwood version of The Portland Vase, white on cobalt blue, 9³/₄ins (24.5cms), completed 1876. (*The Corning Museum of Glass, bequest of Mrs Leonard Rakow*)

GW10 *Flora*, white on brown on flint vase, 7ins (18cms), signed Geo Woodall. (*Leo Kaplan Ltd*)

The Pearl Necklace, red slab, 4ins (10cms). Given to Pamela Woodall as a parting gift on her emigration to Australia. (*Family collection*)

Cupid and Psyche, white on cobalt blue covered vase, 13ins (33cms), marked Tiffany and Co Paris Exhibition 1889 and Gem Cameo. (*Runyon Art Collection, Texas A&M Foundation, MSC Forsyth Centre Galleries, Texas A&M University, College Station*)

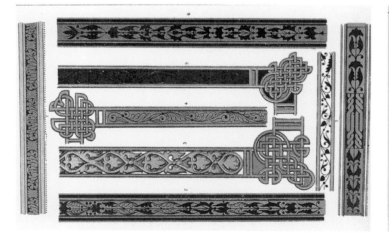

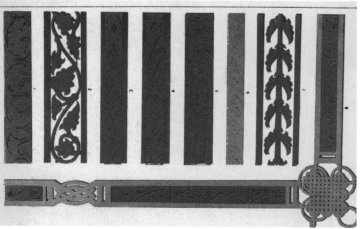

Design motifs from the Woodall brothers' copy of *The Art of Illuminating* by Digby Wyatt, used as source material for decorative borders on cameo pieces. (*Author's collection*)

The Aurora Vase after Guido Reni's painting *Aurora*, white on cobalt blue, 17ins (43cms), by Thomas Woodall, completed 1879. (*The Art Gallery of New South Wales and The Powerhouse Museum, Sydney*) See page 18

Water Nymph, white on claret plaque, 13ins (33cms), signed G Woodall 1884. (*The Corning Museum of Glass, gift of Mrs Rakow in memory of Dr Rakow*)

W2581 *Dancing Girl*, white on red on blue tapering vase, 8¹/₂ins (21.5cms), signed G Woodall. Pattern Book shows different borders. (*Cincinnati Museum of Art*)

Untitled, white on blue two-handled vase, 12ins (30.5cms), signed G Woodall and marked Theodore B Starr, New York, and Gem Cameo. (*Texas A&M Foundation, MSC Forsyth Centre Galleries, Texas A&M University, College Station*)

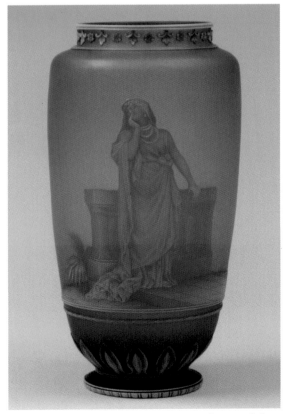

Angling, white on blue vase, the young woman holds a fishing rod in her left hand and, in her right, her catch, 9¹/₄ins (23.5cms), attributed to the Woodall team, c1880. (*Sotheby's*)

Untitled white on red on light blue vase, a maiden stands by a wall, 8¹/₄ins (21cms), signed G Woodall and marked Gem Cameo. (*Texas A&M Foundation, MSC Forsyth Centre Galleries, Texas A&M University, College Station*)

W2358 *Industry,* white on flashed blue on brown two-handled vase, 15³/₄ins (40cms), signed G Woodall and marked Gem Cameo, c1889. (*Texas A&M Foundation, MSC Forsyth Centre Galleries, Texas A&M University, College Station*)

Right, W1400,
plaque with five
cherubs, white on
flashed blue on
cinnamon brown,
10¼ins (26cms),
signed G Woodall.
(*Texas A&M
Foundation, MSC
Forsyth Centre
Galleries, Texas
A&M University,
College Station*))

Far right, *Idle
Moments,* white on
light brown vase,
8½ins (21.5cms),
signed G Woodall.
(*Leo Kaplan Ltd*)

Right, *Minerva,*
white on cobalt
blue ewer, 12¾ins
(32.5cms), signed
G Woodall 1885.
The stand was
silver-plated in-
house under the
direction of Lionel
Pearce. (*Texas
A&M Foundation,
MSC Forsyth Centre
Galleries, Texas
A&M University,
College Station*)

Far right, W2741
The Wader, opal on
deep blue on light
blue vase, a boy
helps a girl across a
stream, 12ins
(30.5cms), signed
G Woodall and
marked Gem
Cameo. (*Sotheby's*)

W2725, white on blue two-handled vase with an angel and cherub, 15½ins (39.5cms), signed G Woodall and marked Gem Cameo, c1891. *(Texas A&M Foundation, MSC Forsyth Centre Galleries, Texas A&M University, College Station)*

Vase with magpie design, white on aquamarine on raisin brown with mica flakes between the coloured layers, 5ins (12.5cms), attributed to the Woodall team. *(Texas A&M Foundation, MSC Forsyth Centre Galleries, Texas A&M University, College Station)*

White on blue vase with flowers, given to Connie Woodall as a wedding present by Thomas Webb & Sons, 4¹/₂ins (11.5cms)1916. *(Family collection)*

W1444, white on ruby vase with honeysuckle, 9¹/₂ins (24cms), marked Gem Cameo. *(Private collection, Melbourne)*

Vase with flowering vine on a shaded red and white ground, 9ins (23cms), attributed to the Woodall team, impressed mark Thos Webb & Sons patented. *(Author's collection)*

Woodall team pieces all marked Gem Cameo, the vase on the right with Oriental flower design, 19ins (49cms), and marked Tiffany & Co Paris Exhibition 1889. *(Leo Kaplan Ltd)*

Plate decorated in the Oriental style, 9¹/₄ins (23.5cms), marked Gem Cameo. *(Leo Kaplan Ltd)*

Plate decorated in the Oriental style with Birds of Paradise, 9¹/₄ins (23.5cms), marked Gem Cameo. *(Leo Kaplan Ltd)*

Nov 14 1894, white on red vase, 6ins (15cms), marked Gem Cameo. Made for Alice Woodall. (*Broadfield House Glass Museum*) See page 39

Vase, red on white on citron on flashed white on flashed ivory, 12ins (30.5cms), marked Gem Cameo. (*Texas A&M Foundation, MSC Forsyth Centre Galleries, Texas A&M University, College Station*)

Above, vase with honeysuckle, amethyst overlaid with white, 6ins (15cms), attributed to the Woodall team. (*Cincinnati Art Museum*)

Right, white on flint on lime green vase with marine design, 14³/₄ins (37.5cms), marked Tiffany & Co Paris Exhibition 1889 and Gem Cameo. (*Texas A&M Foundation, MSC Forsyth Centre Galleries, Texas A&M University, College Station*)

Vase with apples, flowers, insects and butterfly, white on claret, 5ins (12.5cms), by George Woodall. *(Family collection)*

Bowl with Oriental scene, white on blue, 7ins (18cms), marked Gem Cameo. *(Jackson's Ohio)*

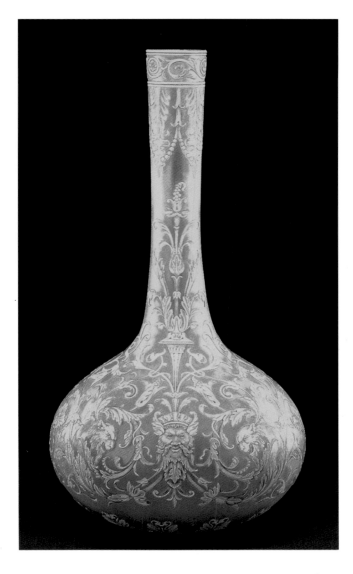

Left, white on brown vase with a cherub, 8¹/₂ins (21.5cms), marked Gem Cameo with 18431 scratched on base. *(Private collection)*

Far left, two-colour bottle vase with renaissance-inspired scrollwork and masks, 16ins (40.5cms), signed G Woodall and marked Gem Cameo and Tiffany & Co Paris Exhibition 1889. *(Sotheby's)*

The Great Tazza, translucent red over opal on translucent yellow-green on white on dark green, 15¼ins x 19¼ins (39cms x 49.5cms), 1889. *(The Corning Museum of Glass, bequest of Mrs Leonard Rakow)* See page 30

Vase, white on translucent yellow, 7¹/₂ins (19cms), designed by
Thomas Woodall, carved by J.T. Fereday. (*Victoria & Albert Museum
Picture Library, Museum No.91-1885*)

Vase with peonies, white on brown, 5¹/₄ins (13cms), designed by
Thomas Woodall, carved by William Hill.
(*Victoria & Albert Museum Picture Library, Museum No.89-1885*)

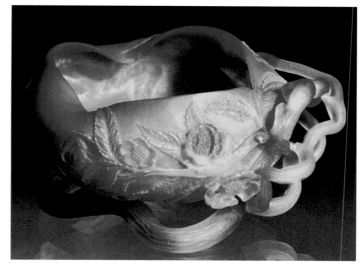

Above, vase carved as an open flower with blossom and tendrils in
the manner of a Chinese hardstone carving, 3¹/₄ins (8cms), designed
by Thomas Woodall, carved by Francis Smith. (*Victoria & Albert
Museum Picture Library, Museum No.86-1885*)

Left, pink on flashed green vase, 6¹/₂ins (16.5cms), designed by
Thomas Woodall, carved by Benjamin Hollis.
(*Victoria & Albert Museum Picture Library, Museum No.90-1885*)

See page 27

Bronze medal awarded to George Woodall at the 1884 International Health Exhibition. (*Family collection*)

The Siren by Thomas John Bott, son of Thomas Bott, signed and dated TJB 1883. This Limoges-style enamelled plate illustrates the similarity in style of the two cousins, Thomas John and George. (*The Potteries Museum and Art Gallery, Stoke-on-Trent*)

George Woodall's gold cravat ring. (*Family collection*)

Scent bottle with cupid and lily of the valley, white on citron, 9³/₄ins (24.5cms), by the Woodall team. (*Leo Kaplan Ltd*)

William E. Gladstone, white on blue medallion, 2¹/₂ins (6.5cms), signed G Woodall and marked Gem Cameo. (*Private collection, USA*)

Cameo blank with two unfinished pieces which were abandoned when Thomas Woodall detected flaws in the glass. (*Family collection*)

Three-layered vase with dragon inspired by Chinese cameo glass, the reverse with an octopus and snake design, ruby on 'snow'-filled crystal, 8¹/₄ins (21cms), marked Tiffany & Co Paris Exhibition 1889 and Gem Cameo, c1889. *(Private collection, London)*

W2588, ginger jar with cover, Oriental design, 11³/₄ins (30cms), marked Gem Cameo. (*Sotheby's*)

Vase with cameo-carved tulips and intaglio-engraved roses, red on flint with gilt design on neck, 7³/₄ins (19.5cms), marked Gem Cameo. (*Texas A&M Foundation, MSC Forsyth Centre Galleries, Texas A&M University, College Station*)

Above, bowl with rose design, 'rainbow' glass on red, 3¹/₂ins (9cms), marked Gem Cameo. (*Texas A&M Foundation, MSC Forsyth Centre Galleries, Texas A&M University, College Station*)

Left, W1444, white on ruby vase, 9¹/₂ins (24cms), marked Gem Cameo. (*Private collection, Melbourne*)

W2542, front and reverse of vase with leopard and snake, black on ivory, 3½ins (9cms). (*Texas A&M Foundation, MSC Forsyth Centre Galleries, Texas A&M University, College Station*)

Above, W1356, vase decorated with flowers, white on amethyst, 4ins (10cms). (*Private collection*)

Right, W2055 *Before the Race*, white on brown vase, 13¾ins (35cms), marked Gem Cameo. This is the second version, the earlier W2043 was the first piece of glass made for sale that is signed by both the Woodall brothers and can be dated 1887-88. (*Leo Kaplan Ltd*)

The Race, white on brown vase, 12³/₄ins (32.5cms), marked Gem Cameo, c1888. There is another version of this vase signed by T & G Woodall. *(Phillips)*

W1624 *The Water Iris*, white on blue vase, 16ins (40.5cms), marked Gem Cameo. (*The Art Gallery of South Australia, Morgan Thomas Bequest Fund 1904*)

W2815, white on blue on light green fire-polished bowl, 4ins (10cms), marked Gem Cameo. (*Leo Kaplan Ltd*)

W2712 *The Crane*, white on dark blue jar (cover missing), 6ins (15cms). The panels depict a crane preening under its wing, standing on one leg, and eating fish. (*Private collection*)

W2719 *The Storm*, white carving of fish and marine life on a translucent green vase, 15³/₄ins (40cms), designed by George Woodall, marked Gem Cameo, c1890. (*The Art Gallery of South Australia, Morgan Thomas Bequest Fund 1904*)

W2791 *The Attack*, white on brown plaque, 17¼ins (44.5cms), signed T & G Woodall, 1891. Formerly in the collection of H.C. Ash, and shown in the Phillips' Exhibition of 1899, a companion to the plaque *Intruders*, illustrated on the page opposite. *(Private collection)*

The Favourite, white on light brown plaque, 13ins (33cms), signed T & G Woodall, 1891. *(Phillips)*

W2794 *Intruders*, white on brown plaque, 16³/₄ins (42.5cms), signed T & G Woodall, 1891. *(The Chrysler Museum of Art, Norfolk, Virginia, gift of Rebecca Hill in memory of Billy Hill and Museum purchase with the assistance of Mr and Mrs J.S. Shannon)* See caption to the companion plaque on the page opposite.

W2510 *Ceres Receiving from Bacchus a Restorative Cup*, white on topaz two-handled vase, 8³/₄ins (22cms), marked Gem Cameo. *(Texas A&M Foundation, MSC Forsyth Centre Galleries, Texas A&M University, College Station)*

TW569 *Giraffes*, white on amber vase, 7ins (18cms), signed G Woodall and marked Gem Cameo. *(Leo Kaplan Ltd)*

Vase with two cherubs, white on raisin brown, 8ins (20.5cms), signed Geo Woodall and marked Gem Cameo. *(Bonham's)*

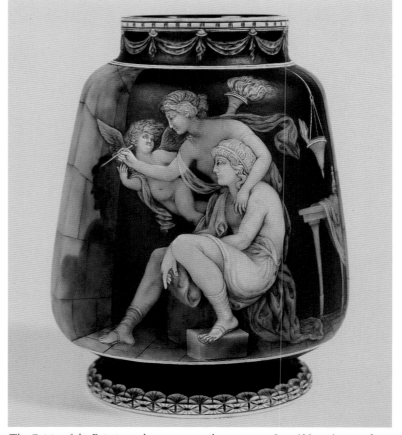

The Origin of the Painting, white on raisin brown vase, 9ins (23cms), signed Geo Woodall. The reverse is decorated with an artist's palette. *(C & V Perry collection, on loan to Broadfield House Glass Museum)*

Vase with insect decoration, white on flint on yellow, 6ins (15cms), attributed to the Woodall team. *(Texas A&M Foundation, MSC Forsyth Centre Galleries, Texas A&M University, College Station)*

W2811, white on sea green on flint vase with a mermaid, 8¹/₄ins (21cms). *(Texas A&M Foundation, MSC Forsyth Centre Galleries, Texas A&M University, College Station)*

Mars, the God of War, white on topaz vase, 7³/₄ins (19.5cms), marked Gem Cameo. *(Texas A&M Foundation, MSC Forsyth Centre Galleries, Texas A&M University, College Station)*

W2532, white on citron lampbase with Athena holding an owl, 10³/₄ins (27.5cms), marked Gem Cameo. *(Texas A&M Foundation, MSC Forsyth Centre Galleries, Texas A&M University, College Station)*

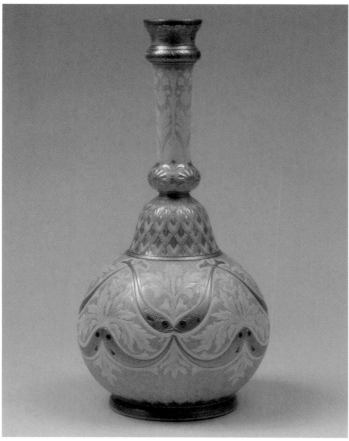

'Ivory' vase with fish, gold and platinum-enamelled, 11¼ins (28.5cms), marked Gem Cameo. A similar vase is illustrated in *British Glass* p230 by Hajdamach. *(Texas A&M Foundation, MSC Forsyth Centre Galleries, Texas A&M University, College Station)*

Islamic-style vase, enamelled, gilded and silvered on opaque 'ivory' glass, 8 ins (20.5cms), decorated by Jules Barbe from a cased blank, W2195, marked Tiffany & Co Paris Exhibition 1889 and 88 on the base. *(Private collection, London)*

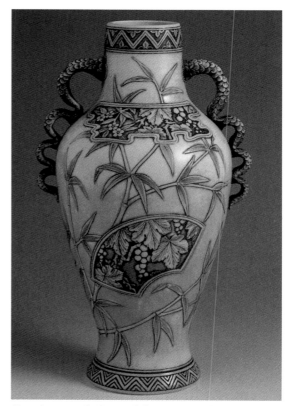

W2312, 'ivory' double gourd vases with Persian designs in shaped panels, 9ins (23cms), designed by George Woodall. *(Leo Kaplan Ltd)*

'Ivory' vase with Oriental design, 10ins (25.5cms). Illustrated in a George Woodall glass plate negative (reproduced in *British Glass* p230 by Hajdamach). Numerous 'ivory' vases of similar design are in the Webb Pattern Book. *(Private collection)*

Vase, opaque white on clear, with enamelled sunflowers, 9ins (23cms) by Lionel Pearce. The branches, leaves and buds have been carved intaglio on the base layer. (*Private collection, London*)

F100, vase with tadpoles, opal on dark green with blue and gilt enamelled neck and handle, 6½ins (16.5cms). The reverse of the vase also shows tadpoles. (*Private collection, London*)

'Ivory' vase with padded-on cherries in ruby glass, the vase enriched with gilding, 9ins (23cms). 195 is scratched on the base, possibly the Webb pattern number. (*Private collection, London*)

W3218 *Seaweed, Sea Nymph and Fishes*, olive green, brown and Burmese on flint vase, 8¼ins (21cms). (*Texas A&M Foundation, MSC Forsyth Centre Galleries, Texas A&M University, College Station*) See page 124

Vase with grapes and a spider's web on the reverse, white and blue on amber, 9ins (23cms), marked Gem Cameo. Similar in design to F164, this form of cased glass blank was used to produce many such pieces. (*Private collection, Melbourne*)

W3139 *Moorish Bathers*, white on flashed blue on raisin brown plaque, 18ins (46.5cms), signed Geo Woodall, completed 1898. The Webb's Price Book describes this plaque and others as brown but, with transmitted light, it appears red. Nominated by George Woodall as his finest piece of work. (*The Corning Museum of Glass, bequest of Mrs Leonard Rakow*) See page 97

Feathered Favourites, white on flashed blue on brown panel, 5³/₄ins (14.5cms), signed Geo Woodall, 1892. *(Texas A&M Foundation, MSC Forsyth Centre Galleries, Texas A&M University, College Station)*

W2716 *The Flower Gatherer,* white on topaz flatsided vase, 7¹/₂ins (19cms), signed G Woodall and marked Gem Cameo. *(Texas A&M Foundation, MSC Forsyth Centre Galleries, Texas A&M University, College Station)*

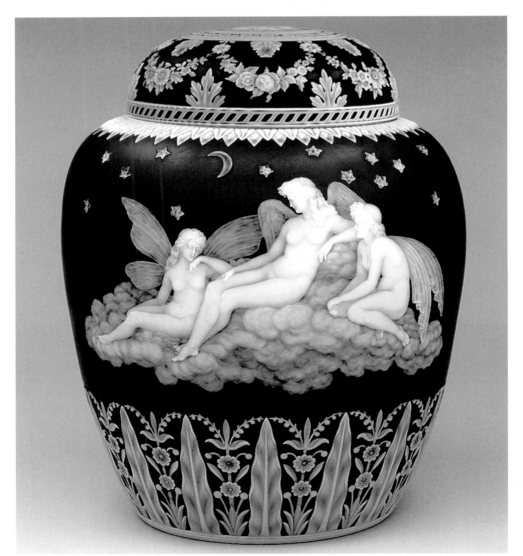

W2567 *Night,* white on flashed blue on raisin brown jar with cover, 10¹/₂ins (26.5cms), signed G Woodall 1890. *(Texas A&M Foundation, MSC Forsyth Centre Galleries, Texas A&M University, College Station)*

W2660 *Love's Awakening*, white on flashed blue on raisin brown covered jar, 11½ins (29cms), signed G Woodall and marked Gem Cameo, c1887. This piece was given the working title *Cupid* in the factory pattern book. (*Texas A&M Foundation, MSC Forsyth Centre Galleries, Texas A&M University, College Station*)

W3185 *Toilet of Venus*, white on blue on plum plaque, 17¹/₄ins (44.5cms), signed Geo Woodall, completed 1898. 'When the artist had reached the last stage but one in the original specimen, a flaw was discovered in the glass, and the whole of the work, which had occupied him for many months, had to be recommenced on a fresh piece of glass.' (*The Lady Magazine*, June 1899) (*Texas A&M Foundation, MSC Forsyth Centre Galleries, Texas A&M University, College Station*)

W2723 A *Maid of Athens*, white on blue on black vase, 10¼ins (26cms), signed T & G Woodall and marked Gem Cameo, c1891. Amy Woodall was the model. (*The Corning Museum of Glass, gift of Mrs Rakow in memory of Dr Rakow*)

W2807 *Muses*, white on brown vase, 8ins (20.5cms), signed T & G Woodall, c1891. This depicts five of the nine classical Greek muses: Euterpe, Erato, Terpischore, Clio and Thalia. (*The Corning Museum of Glass, gift of Mrs Rakow in memory of Dr Rakow*)

At Cupid's Shrine, white on thin blue on claret plaque, 18ins (46.5cms), signed Geo Woodall, 1908. Experiencing difficulty in finding a drawing of an upright Cupid, George arranged for Beryl Holds to pose. (*The Corning Museum of Glass*)

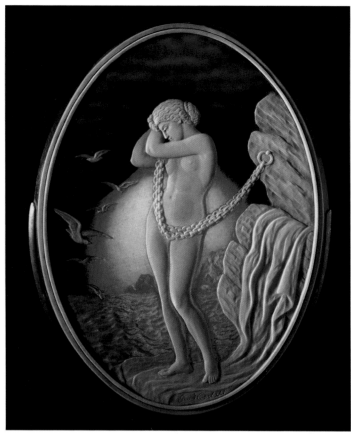

Perseus and Andromeda Version I, white on amethyst oval panel, 6¼ins (16cms), signed Geo Woodall. The model is Amy Woodall in one of her last poses. The piece was later mounted onto a marble base with a silver mount, London 1902. (*Private collection, Melbourne*)

Perseus and Andromeda Version II, white on brown plaque, 6½ins (16.5cms), signed Geo Woodall. On loan to the Birmingham Museum and Art Gallery for twenty years but returned to its owner in 1996. It was then sold to a private collector. (*Phillips*)

Perseus and Andromeda Version III, white on claret oval brooch, 4ins (10cms), signed GW. (*Family collection*)

Dr and Mrs Samuel Parkes Cadman, white on claret portrait medallions, 6¼ins (16cms), signed Geo Woodall. Parkes Cadman was Pamela Woodall's nephew. (*The Corning Museum of Glass, gift of Mrs Rakow in memory of Dr Rakow*)

Aphrodite Rising from the Waves, white on blue on red plaque, 8¹/₄ins (21cms), signed Geo Woodall, completed 1920. *(Family collection on loan to Broadfield House Glass Museum)*

Dancing Girls, pair of blue on brown vases, 12³/₄ins (32.5cms), signed T & G Woodall and marked Gem Cameo. On the reverse of both are the Arms of Cure of London quartered with Cheyney of Berkshire and Upavon, Wiltshire. The drawings for the two figures are in Daniel Pearce's sketch book, now at the the Broadfield House Glass Museum. *(Toledo Museum of Art)*

Left, W1776 *The Milkmaid*, blue-white on blue two-handled vase, 12ins (30.5cms), signed G Woodall. *(Christie's)*

Far left, W2730 *Pandora*, white on brown vase, 13¹/₂ins (34.5cms), signed T & G Woodall. *(V&A Picture Library. On loan to the Victoria & Albert Museum)*

W2840 *Aurora*, white on flashed blue on raisin brown vase, 13ins (33cms), signed T & G Woodall, c1895. *(Texas A&M Foundation, MSC Forsyth Centre Galleries, Texas A&M University, College Station)*

Vase with lovers on a swing, white on red on blue, 10ins (25.5cms), by George Woodall, marked Tiffany & Co Paris Exhibition 1889. (*Texas A&M Foundation, MSC Forsyth Centre Galleries, Texas A&M University, College Station*)

Vase with shaped panels displaying geisha girls in exotic robes, ruby on green on opal enriched with gilding around the figures, 5³/₄ins (14.5cms), by the Woodall team. Pattern number 3366 is scratched on the base. (*Private collection, London*)

Vase with cyclamen, white on amber, 5ins (12.5cms), by the Woodall team. The price code, CXXX is scratched on the base rim. (*Private collection, London*)

W2356, perforated 'ivory' on ruby-lined bowl, with a chinese bat and fruit and foliage decorating the sides, 4¹/₂ins (11.5cms), by the Woodall team. (*Private collection, London*)

Light brown on opal on clear glass vase with cameo flowers and intaglio-carved leaves on the crystal base layer, 3³/₄ins (9.5cms), designed by Lionel Pearce. A larger version of this vase, W2693, is in the Art Gallery of South Australia. (*Private collection, London*)

Right, cameo vase, 13³/₄ins (35cms), designed by Lionel Pearce. The brown base colour has two layers of crystal glass, with padded-on ruby, white and lemon flowers enriching the design. *(Private collection, London)*

Far right, gourd-shaped vase with padded-on birds and flowers in an Oriental style, 10³/₄ins (27.5cms), designed by Lionel Pearce. *(Private collection, London)*

W3260 and W3261, companion vases, olive green on a shaded ground, 7¹/₂ins (19cms), stamped with an unusual long hexagon-shaped mark, Thomas Webb & Sons. The vase on the left with a landscape and the other with figs. *(Private collection, London)*
See page 124

Above, W1148, vase decorated with an Oriental pattern, ruby on clear citron on opal, 3ins (7.5cms). *(Private collection)*

Left, vase decorated with a Persian pattern, white on yellow on brown, 10^1/$_2$ins (26.5cms), marked Gem Cameo. *(Sotheby's)*

Right, vase in a Persian design, ruby then white then ruby on citron 17ins (43cms), c1884. The base is also decorated and has a Thomas Webb & Sons mark around the rim. *(Private collection, London)*

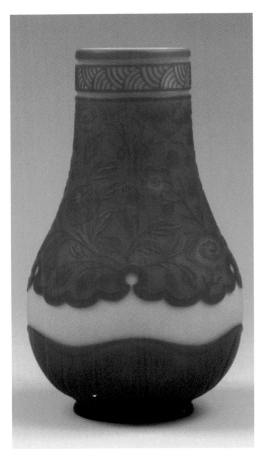

Above, W2448, imitation jade bowl, with flowers and a bat carved in the Chinese style, 3^1/$_2$ins (9cms). *(Private collection)*

Left, five-layered vase, red on white on citron on flashed white on flashed ivory, 8^3/$_4$ins (22cms), marked Gem Cameo. *(Texas A&M Foundation, MSC Forsyth Centre Galleries, Texas A&M University, College Station)*

Right, vase, dark blue on crystal base with red birds, a white dove and a stork in padded-on colours, intaglio-carved clouds embellish the scene, 5^1/$_2$ins (14cms), marked Gem Cameo. *(Private collection, London)*

Vase with 'Dogs of Fo' chasing each other between the waves, white on translucent green, 15¹/₂ins (39.5cms), c1892. The cased blank for these pieces was designed by George Woodall and also used to carve *The Storm* and *The Polar Vase*. (*Private collection, London*)

Companion to vase opposite, 15¹/₂ins (39.5cms), c1892. The scene depicts imperial sea dragons between the waves. (*Private collection, London*)

Thomas Woodall's last, unfinished vase, white on amber, 4ins (10cms). The Oriental-style piece has been dipped three times in acid to remove unwanted white glass, but hand carving has not begun. *(Family collection)*

Above, George Woodall's hand tools, toolbox and unfinished tazza.

Fine steel tools used by George Woodall between 1914-1923. *(C & V Perry collection on loan to Broadfield House Glass Museum)*

W2824 *Music*, white on flashed blue on brown plaque, 12ins x 9¹/₂ins (30.5cms x 24cms), signed WOODALL. *(Leo Kaplan Ltd)*

GW1 *Poetry*, white on flashed blue on brown plaque, 12ins (30.5cms), signed Geo Woodall. *(Leo Kaplan Ltd)*

GW26 *Diana*, white on flashed blue on raisin brown vase, 7¹/₂ins (19cms), signed Geo Woodall. (*Texas A&M Foundation, MSC Forsyth Centre Galleries, Texas A&M University, College Station*)

GW13 *Psyche*, white on brown vase, 6³/₄ins (17cms), signed Geo Woodall. It is likely that the figure is Pandora opening her box, but the Price Book states otherwise. (*Broadfield House Glass Museum*)

GW21 *Ceramia*, white on brown flatsided vase, 6¹/₄ins (16cms), signed Geo Woodall. (*Phillips*)

GW153 *Sea Gulls (sic)*, white on flashed blue on raisin brown vase, 7¹/₂ins (19cms), signed Geo Woodall. (*Texas A&M Foundation, MSC Forsyth Centre Galleries, Texas A&M University, College Station*)

Above, *John the Baptist*, cut crystal brooch. A family piece by George Woodall given to Dr S. Cadman in 1899. Other than *Adam and Eve* this is the only example of the Bible being used as source material. *(Hulbert of Dudley collection, on loan to Broadfield House Glass Museum)*

Right, W2759 *Favourites*, white on flashed blue on brown, 12ins (30.5cms), signed T & G Woodall 1892, commonly known as *Feathered Favourites*. *(Victoria & Albert Museum Picture Library)* See page 37

'Ivory' candelabra listed in the Webb Pattern Book as I 499. There were originally four candelabra with the Woodall number W2151. Designed by George Woodall and painted by Jules Barbe. *(Private collection, Melbourne)*

GW31 *An Undine*, white on flashed blue on brown panel, 6½ins (16.5cms), signed Geo Woodall and *A Choice Bit*. (*Texas A&M Foundation, MSC Forsyth Centre Galleries, Texas A&M University, College Station*)

GW155 *The Pearl Necklace*, white on claret oval panel in gilt frame, 6¼ins (16cms), signed Geo Woodall. (*Broadfield House Glass Museum*)

Antony and Cleopatra, white on brown plaque, 18ins (46.5cms), signed Geo Woodall, 1897. (*Family collection*)

Lord Kelvin, white on flashed blue on brown plaque, 18ins (46.5cms), signed Geo Woodall, 1904-5. (*The Royal Society of London*)
See page 104

GW154 *Sappho*, white on claret on blue oval panel, 6¼ins x 5ins (16cms x 12.5cms), signed Geo Woodall. *(Family collection)*

Syrene, white on blue plaque, 4¼ins x 6¼ins (11cms x 16cms), signed Geo Woodall. Unlike other versions of this subject, a boat has been added to the background. *(Leo Kaplan Ltd)*

Venus, white on brown vase with the goddess and cupid rising from the waves, within a decorative shell border, 8ins (20.5cms), signed Geo Woodall. *(Leo Kaplan Ltd)*

Morning, white on brown vase, signed Geo Woodall. *(Leo Kaplan Ltd)*

Right, *Wild Waves*, white on cobalt blue two-handled vase, 12ins (30.5cms), signed Geo Woodall. *(Texas A&M Foundation, MSC Forsyth Centre Galleries, Texas A&M University, College Station)*

Far right, GW7 *Pharaoh's Daughter*, white on brown vase, 11ins (28cms), signed G Woodall. *(Family collection)* See page 124

Right, *Mischief*, white on red vase, 8½ins (21.5cms), signed Geo Woodall. Made in 1916, the Lord Mayor of Birmingham, Wiggins Davies (1944-45), owned this together with *Perseus and Andromeda* version II and three other pieces. *(Photograph courtesy of Broadfield House Glass Museum)*

Far right, *Phyllis at the Fountain*, opal on dark blue on aquamarine blue vase, 10ins (25.5cms), signed Geo Woodall. Sold by Alice Woodall in May 1938. *(Sotheby's)*

GW33 *Andromache*, white on blue on red panel, 12¹/₂ins (32cms), signed Geo Woodall, 1902. (*The Corning Museum of Glass, gift of Mrs Rakow in memory of Dr Rakow*)

Above left, *The Polar Vase*, 15³/₄ins (40cms), signed Geo Woodall, 1908. Albert Revi suggested that the Shackleton Expedition had inspired the design of three Polar vases. Others have suggested that the real inspiration was the British National Antarctic Expedition of 1901-1904. (*Texas A&M Foundation, MSC Forsyth Centre Galleries, Texas A&M University, College Station*)

Above right, GW157 *Syrena*, white on purple vase, 8¹/₄ins (21cms), signed Geo Woodall. (*Sotheby's*)

Right, *Crane and Palm*, white on cobalt blue two-handled vase, 12ins (30.5cms), signed Geo Woodall. The blank is reminiscent of early Richardson pieces and may have been carved by George Woodall for Richardson's. (*Broadfield House Glass Museum*)

Left, *Love's Areo*, white on cobalt blue vase, 7ins (18cms), signed Geo Woodall and marked Tiffany & Co Paris Exhibition 1889 and Gem Cameo. Carved by Alphonse Lechevrel and remodelled by George Woodall to aid its sale. (*(Texas A&M Foundation, MSC Forsyth Centre Galleries, Texas A&M University, College Station)*

Far left, *The Armenian Girl*, oval portrait plaque, 5ins (12.5cms), signed Geo Woodall. This private piece, not intended for sale, was possibly based on a painting, *Armenian Girl*, which hung in Luton House. (*Broadfield House Glass Museum, gift of E.P. Lucas*)

Left, *Venus Rising from the Sea*, white on blue vase, 12ins (30.5cms), signed 'AL 1887' (Alphonse Lechevrel) originally, George Woodall's signature was added later. (*Broadfield House Glass Museum*)

Far left, *Birth of Venus*, white on blue vase, 12ins (30.5cms). Carved by Alphonse Lechevrel with additional cutting by George Woodall, the handles were later removed. Now signed, AL and Geo Woodall. (*The Corning Museum of Glass*)

Front and rear view of W2795 *Pomona*, white on brown vase, 10ins (25.5cms), signed T & G Woodall. *(Private collection)*

Front and rear view of W2731 *Feathered Favourites*, white on brown vase, 12³/₄ins (32.5cms), signed T & G Woodall. *(Private collection)*

W2830 *Vestal*, white on brown vase, 9ins (23cms), signed T & G Woodall. (*V&A Picture Library. On loan to the Victoria & Albert Museum*)

W2806 *A Pompeiian Girl*, white on brown vase, 9ins (23cms), signed T & G Woodall. (*V&A Picture Library. On loan to the Victoria & Albert Museum*)

W3930 *Cleopatra*, white on flashed blue on brown plaque, 17½ins (45cms), signed T & G Woodall, completed 1898. (*V&A Picture Library. On loan to the Victoria & Albert Museum*)

W2790 *Sappho*, white on brown panel, 12¹/₂ins x 7¹/₂ins (32cms x 19cms), signed T & G Woodall, completed 1894. Amy Woodall was the model. *(Broadfield House Glass Museum)*

Although a supporter of the Liberal election campaign of 1892, George had since avoided activities outside his family and work. However, Thomas persuaded him to join the campaign to raise funds for a new Wordsley Art School. The Wordsley Science and Art classes held their prize-giving ceremony on the 26th February 1897. Sitting with the management committee were several influential people including William Northwood[52], Frederick Carder[53] and J. Silvers Williams.[54] Williams used the occasion to condemn the flood of cheap German imitation cameo:

> Cameo... has been horribly mutilated in a cheap way by the Germans, and this has done much to destroy... a most progressive art in the district. The time would come when art education would spread to such an extent that the British public would be able to distinguish and appreciate the difference between a work of sculptured glass and a horrible piece of daubed paint glass of German production.[55]

The applause was resounding, and Thomas rose to second the motion to borrow money for a new Art School. Plans were already underway to celebrate Queen Victoria's diamond jubilee by constructing the 'Victoria' Technical School in Stourbridge. The following day the brothers discussed the meeting and George began to consider how his business interests could be positively affected by street lighting, drainage, road widening, tramlines and the other improvements now being considered for Kingswinford. He had many influential friends but was unfamiliar with committee politics. Deciding that a stint on a local body would help to establish more contacts George attended the annual meeting for the election of parish councillors for the St Mary's ward of the parish of Kingswinford. The meeting discussed the need for a new Reading Room in the parish and three of the councillors standing for re-election (James Horne Snr, Elijah Hillman and George Evason) maintained that the present room was satisfactory. George voiced a strong objection, 'The reading room is sectarian and political. It is called Conservative and I am not Conservative!' Despite the councillors' attempts to prevaricate, George pursued this theme and stood against them for election. His two Liberal colleagues, David Cox and Noah Mathews, joined him and the meeting voted the three on to the parish council. James Horne demanded an election be arranged and a poll was called for the 23rd March. After five days of intense local lobbying, Cox, Mathews and Evason withdrew their names and Woodall,

Horne and Hillman were elected, unopposed. Thus began George's entry into political life.

The Woodall team was redeployed to work on crystal and intaglio carved work and Thomas mainly worked alone on smaller pieces. He devoted his extra time to playing the organ for the Primitive Methodist Church in Wordsley, as well as community work. He also made extra money by tuning pianos, selling sheet music and giving piano lessons; among his pupils was Connie Woodall – George would pay Thomas £1.10s per quarter for her lessons.

In the midst of George's political manoeuvres, work continued and he was still carving his most impressive piece so far, the eighteen-inch plaque, *Moorish Bathers*. Charles Webb showed a *Pottery Gazette* reporter around the works in early May and commented that, 'when completed the plaque would be the finest piece of work Mr Woodall has ever executed.'

Webb's press notice. (*Author's collection*)

"Moorish Bathers,"

BY GEO. WOODALL.

Reprint from Press Notice.

It was part of John Ruskin's indictment of our modern manufacturing system that it reduced the workers to the level of mere "cogs and compasses"; and truly from the results of "process work" and mechanical multiplications of various kinds the æsthetic mind—forgetting the utilitarian aspect of the question—is apt to turn with fond regret to the "good old times" when artist-craftsmen living in times less hurried than ours, were able to linger long and lovingly over their work, putting into it mind and feeling, creating "things of beauty" worthy to endure and be "a joy for ever," works which to this day are the pride of their possessors and the admiration of all beholders. But the race of artist-craftsmen is not yet extinct, and here and there in our manufacturing districts men may still be found labouring, like their forerunners, with unwearying patience day after day and month after month at a single piece of work, lavishing upon it skill and taste, and giving form and embodiment to their ideals of beauty in some unique specimen of industrial art worthy to rank with the productions of the old masters.

We have been led to these reflections by a visit we paid a few days ago to the glass works of Messrs. Thomas Webb and Sons, Limited, Dennis Park, where, among other beautiful productions of this famous firm, we had the pleasure of inspecting a remarkably fine cameo plaque designed and carved by Mr. George Woodall, and now receiving its finishing touches at the hands of this gifted artist, whose work of a similar kind we have had occasion from time to time to notice in our columns.

The plaque is some eighteen inches in diameter, and is made of a layer of white or opal glass superimposed on a thicker layer of chocolate hue. The decoration is sculptured out of the upper layer. A rich and effective bordering of Arabesque ornament, which runs round the circumference of the plaque, is marked by that lavish and careful elaboration of detail which reminds one of an Alhambraic frieze. It fittingly frames the general design, which has been named "Moorish Bathers," and represents a scene in a Moorish palace, where a bevy of fair damsels are seeking relief from the summer heat—or, may be, the ennui of a too luxurious existence—in the pleasures of the bath. The buildings which enclose the court are of the Mohammedan style of architecture. Rows of slender columns and toothed arches support structures whose facades are fretted and carved with a profusion of embellishment as great as if we had here represented to us a wing of the world-famed Palace of Granada itself. Striking effects of perspective are obtained in the architectural parts of the design. This is especially noticeable in a colonnade which, starting from the front of a building, runs away towards a door of exit distant and dim. A step or two lead down from the pavement of the court to a bath which occupies a large part of the open space. A splashing fountain, flowering plants, graceful palms, and other forms of foliage lend their aid to the general artistic effect. But these things are only the setting in which are held and displayed the jewels of the piece. It is upon the rendering of his conception of various styles of womanly loveliness that the artist has expended his best skill and achieved his greatest triumphs. The bevy of beauties grouped around this bath and sporting in its waters exhibit enough of grace of pose, beauty of line, and loveliness of feature to satiate the appetite of the most ardent admirer of the "female form divine." The eye is at once arrested by the symmetrical figure of a girl, who stands in bold relief in the foreground of the picture. Her outline presents a series of captivating curves, and her pose is charmingly graceful. She is in the act of disengaging from her shoulders an embroidered scarf, and has caught up the hem of her only remaining garment in her left hand, thus leaving the lower limbs bare to the knee. At her waist a jewelled girdle confines her draperies, and to these, by some mysterious application of technical skill, the artist has imparted a semi-transparent texture through which the undulations of her Venus-like form bewitchingly suggest themselves. Her feet rest upon a patterned rug, and here again the artist's mastery of technique is manifested. The rug has been made to look soft and woolley in contrast to the smooth and solid pavement around. The head of this figure is strikingly handsome, and the features lovely. The abundant hair is elegantly bound with strings of pearls. A fan, a hand mirror, a pair of bracelets, and other knick-nacks diversify the foreground, and a perfora-

ted jar or brazier emits a cloud of vapourous perfume. To the left of these objects is a carved settee, the arm of which affords a resting place for a figure of fine proportions. Her back is turned to the spectator, and she is stooping to doff her slipper. As one knee is thrown over the other to facilitate the removal of her footgear a splendid shoulder—which her style of dress leaves uncovered—is thrown into view, and the head and face are seen in profile. The pose is a difficult one, but admirably managed. Just beyond, lazily stretched out on the floor, one hand propping her chin, the other hanging over the side of the bath, a youthful beauty is watching a companion who has just taken a plunge into the water. The loosened tresses of the nymph in the water are floating on the wavelets which her impact has thrown up around her and sent splashing over the steps of the bath. A few subordinate figures which complete the design are drawn and modelled with the same masterly skill.

When one considers that all the varied effects present in this remarkable piece of sculpture—the softness of flesh, the smoothness of marble, the sheen and ripple of water, the diaphanous texture of drapery, distant perspective and bold relief—are all obtained by the manipulation of a comparatively thin layer of a material so brittle and intractable as glass, one is forced to the conclusion that only the highest technical and manipulative skill allied to true artistic taste and perception could hope to achieve such astonishing and beautiful results, and that in Mr. Woodall we have

"an artist skill'd.
With sense of beauty and proportion fill'd."

The works which have issued from Mr. Woodall's studio have won for him fame among connoisseurs of art, and we venture to say that this, his latest production, will still further enhance the high reputation which he already enjoys.

These productions, of course, are not of every day sale, and not every plaque as it comes from the hands of the glassmaker is fit for the hands of the sculptor. There is, on the contrary, very considerable waste before one can be found sufficiently perfect to justify the placing of cameo work upon it. Then such work is a long time under hand. Mr. Woodall has been engaged on this one some years. Three being the circumstances in which these works are undertaken Messrs. Thomas Webb and Sons, and the credit they reflect upon the firm redounds to the credit of the district, which they place in the very forefront of the districts in which art industries flourish.

An early version of *The Toilet of Venus*, discarded after an air bubble burst damaging the surface layer. *(Photograph by George Woodall)*

Wordsley School of Art. *(The Corning Museum of Glass)*

Thomas Snr died on the 27th May 1898 and to Pamela's dismay, it was decided that the widowed and impoverished Emma should move into Luton House as it was larger than Thomas and Martha's cottage. Pamela's resentment towards her in-laws over this intrusion into her domestic life increased the tension between the brothers and Thomas and Martha were no longer welcome at Luton House.

Details of the new sewerage system for Kingswinford and Brierley Hill, polarised the Rural Council (on which Thomas served) and the Parish Council (on which George sat), who had each proposed their own scheme. George's business acumen came to the fore during these negotiations. He bought parcels of land that would eventually be needed for the sewage scheme in the belief that he could sell these on to the council at a profit.

Relations between Thomas and George continued to deteriorate. Since the cameo market was accessible only to the rich and Thomas objected on principle to elitism, the brothers worked together less and less. In July they finished their final joint plaque W3930 *Cleopatra*, destined for the Paris Exhibition in 1899. Thomas worked on more decorative pieces while George finished GW26 *Diana*, GW17 *Terpischore* and the

Nude bathers used as source material by George Woodall. *(Photograph by George Woodall)*

masterpiece, W3185 *Toilet of Venus*. Gladstone died on the 19th May, and both brothers felt a sense of loss; George carved a portrait medallion in tribute to the inspirational Liberal leader.

Thomas and George were very preoccupied with their families. Harry, now a Professor of Music, had just returned from London to work in the provinces and enlisted his father in his new band. Consequently, Thomas was kept very busy by his musical activities as well as his council work. He saw his daughter, Janet, receive her Advanced Stage certificate for Drawing in Light and Shade at the Wordsley Science and Art classes; she and her sisters, Kate and May, were planning to enter the teaching profession. George also had a large and time-consuming family as well as an ailing mother to care for. Pamela's resentment towards Thomas and Martha continued, and it was inevitable that the brothers and their families, met less. The only close contact was via Harry and his Uncle George who, from 1898, typeset and published Harry's musical works.

In October 1898, *Moorish Bathers* was finished. The plaque was sent to Charterhouse Street, London, for exhibition at Webb's showrooms and the press notice issued by Thomas Webb demonstrated their admiration for George Woodall's work. *The Pottery Gazette* also commented:

> Only those who have witnessed the exceedingly delicate process of sculpturing these successive layers of brittle glass can form any idea of the patience, as well as the marvellous skill required. Only an artist – one who loved his work for the sake of the pleasure he found in it – could expend so much time, so much anxious care, on one subject. Mr Woodall's 'capacity for taking pains' (which was Thomas Carlyle's definition of genius) can only be fully appreciated by those who have seen how very slowly this delicate cameo... must be done.[56]

George received international fame as a glass artist – Thomas and his family were more respected in the local community. Harry Woodall's first concert which took place in the same month was well received and bolstered his teaching work. He began to court Bernice Pearson, the daughter of the Woodalls' family doctor. May Woodall made her stage debut on the 21st January when she sang with Messrs Kempson's String Band.

Moorish Bathers, work in progress. *(Photograph by George Woodall)*

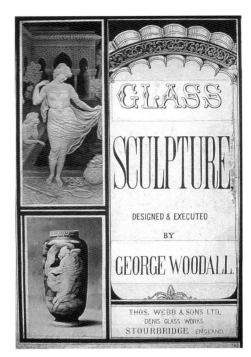

The cover of Webb's booklet Glass Sculpture *with a detail from* Moorish Bathers. *(Broadfield House Glass Museum)*

Thomas' younger children also went on to achieve success, while George's children avoided the limelight.

On the 6th February, amid falling snow, hundreds of people lined the street for the opening of the Wordsley Art School. Members of Staffordshire society assembled and, as the church bells rang, Lord Dartmouth opened the building, accompanied by the leading organisers of the campaign for the art school, including Thomas Woodall, who was Chairman of the Concert Committee. After the opening ceremony there was a public luncheon in the National School. George sat alone as Pamela refused to attend those functions where she would meet her sister-in-law. Toast after toast applauded Wordsley's reputation as a centre for excellence in glassmaking. To illustrate this, the Drill Hall had an extensive display of fine glassware on show[57], including *Toilet of Venus* and Locke's copy of The Portland Vase. The display was still standing four days later when the Woodall brothers went to the final prize distribution for the old Wordsley School of Art. Many of the students, including George Carder, A.J.H. Bohm and Enoch W. Horne received prizes and were later to achieve fame. Surprisingly, despite his intention that his sons would become glass engravers, George had not sent either of them to art school.

As the year passed, George increasingly worked alone. In April, Pamela and he went to Paris, in advance of the Exhibition to be held in May, in which *Cleopatra* was a prominent exhibit. Thomas, as usual, remained at home. On his return, George immediately left for London to attend a selling exhibition of his work. Over the following six weeks, many people would visit the Phillips' Exhibition in Mount Street to marvel at the range of cameo work exhibited and to watch George carving a fresh plaque. To accompany the display, George had asked Charles Webb to produce a souvenir brochure for which George had provided photographic plates of his work.

The promotional booklet, *Glass Sculpture* was based in part upon an earlier press notice about *Moorish Bathers* and several articles from *The Pottery Gazette*. It was a beautifully written testimonial to George's work and was still for sale long after his retirement. A photograph of a George Woodall piece illustrated each page and a collaborative work, *Sappho*, was included. The joint signature was noted on the photograph, but Thomas was not mentioned in the brochure. This was intentional as the exhibition was of George's solo work – also, because of Thomas' low profile, the trade papers who wrote the text, had not featured him since 1893. George highlighted his own signature in pencil so that, while the 'T' of Thomas would still be noticeable, it would be less prominent.[58] This infuriated Janet Woodall, who felt her father was being deliberately undermined by his younger brother.

The national and local press excitedly reported the success of George's London work. *The Times* wrote, 'He is at once the artist and the executant workman... vases and plaques become something that is half picture and half sculpture.' *The Daily News* reported, 'The work, as we have said, can be seen in progress, but the progress is slow, for the plaque will represent the labour of nearly half-a-year.' *The Morning Post* commented:

> Mr Woodall differs somewhat from the methods employed by The Portland Vase decorators, inasmuch as he relies less on relief and more on gradations of light and shade, which he

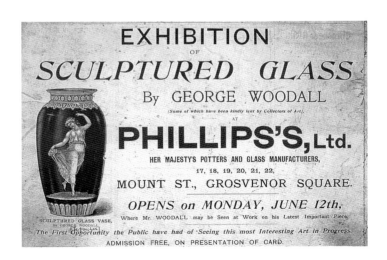

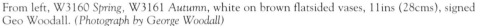

From left, W3160 *Spring,* W3161 *Autumn,* white on brown flatsided vases, 11ins (28cms), signed Geo Woodall. *(Photograph by George Woodall)*

Seaweed vase, 7³/₄ins (19.5cms), signed Geo Woodall. *(Photograph by George Woodall)*

Cupid seated on rocks, white on blue vase, 10¹/₄ins (26cms), signed G Woodall and Gem Cameo. *(Photograph courtesy of Geoffrey Beard)*

obtains by cutting into the thin layer of white glass superimposed on the dark metal underneath, thus securing a range of grey tones that increase in depth as he gets nearer to the dark under surface.

The Gentlewoman reviewed some of the specific pieces on show:

Look at the beautiful picture of the *Toilette of Venus* (sic) and note the dainty diaphanous drapery floating round the lovely form of the goddess. In the companion picture[59], where the cupids playfully try to rob her of her garment, how fine and beautiful is the workmanship. A veritable *chef d'oeuvre* is the *Antony and Cleopatra* in which the flimsiness of the drapery falling from Cleopatra's couch is perfectly suggested. How finely, too, the vigour of the soldier is contrasted with the sinuous grace of the 'Serpent of Old Nile'. So slow is the process that you may watch it for an hour without seeing any perceptible progress made.

The *Queen* magazine summed up opinion:

everyone who visits... will agree that Mr. Woodall's name fully deserves to rank with those of Cellini, Palissy, Quentin Matsys and all the other artist-craftsmen of olden days.[60]

George returned from his triumphant trip to London to normal working conditions and a family wedding. Thomas' daughter, Ida, married Ernest Petford, and the couple moved to Beeston, Nottingham, where Ernest opened a branch of Boots The Chemist. Harry's musical career successfully continued: two cantatas, *The Pride of the Village* and *Harvest Home* met with considerable critical acclaim. The Woodall girls were to meet their future suitors at Harry's musical engagements under the watchful eye of their father.

1900 began as a difficult year for Webb's and the future of the cameo market. Charles Webb[61] retired and was replaced by Congreve William Jackson who was well known to George as he

From left: top row: W2724 *Inspiration*, white on brown vase, 12ins (30.5cms), signed Geo Woodall; W2730 *Pandora*, side and reverse views of vase on page 76; W2831 *Psyche*, white on brown vase, 7¹/₂ins (19cms), signed T & G Woodall; W2721 *Psyche*, white on brown vase, 10ins (25.5cms), signed G Woodall and Gem Cameo.

Middle row: GW24 *Morning*, white on brown vase, 8¹/₂ins (21.5cms), signed Geo Woodall; GW23 *Night*, white on brown vase 8¹/₂ins (21.5cms), signed Geo Woodall; W2403 *The Fruit Seller*, white on raisin brown two-handled vase, 15³/₄ins (40cms), signed G Woodall 1889 and Gem Cameo; W2609 *Cupid and Psyche*, white on brown two-handled vase, 15³/₄ins (40cms), signed G Woodall and Tiffany & Co Paris Exhibition 1889 and Gem Cameo; two-handled vase, 16ins (40.5cms), marked Gem Cameo (see page 30).

Bottom row: W2792 *Pandora*, white on claret brown panel, signed Geo Woodall; *Polar Vase* Version II, white on flint green, 16ins (40.5cms). (Photographs by George Woodall)

101

Nora May Woodall as 'Pride of the Village'. (*Author's collection*)

W2805 *Nymph of the Sea,* white on brown oval panel, 8ins x 5³/₄ins (20.5x14.5cms), signed Geo Woodall. (*Photograph by George Woodall*)

had organised the Phillips' display while London agent in 1899. He realised that Webb's profits were falling because decorative glassware such as Burmese glass or cameo was too expensive to make and sell. Pressure was brought to bear and the Woodall team was disbanded. Thomas remained to work on small pieces but in truth, Jackson was uninterested in continuing to employ him. George's name was recognised, so there was still a market for his work. Thomas was not greatly concerned over this:

W2728 *Nature's Mirror,* white on raisin brown vase, 11ins (28cms), signed T & G Woodall. (*Photograph courtesy of Geoffrey Beard*)

although retired from the Wordsley Parish Council he was still a busy man with work on the Poor Law Committees, and semi-retirement suited him, though the drop in his income had to be supplemented by musical enterprises. In January he helped to relaunch the Wordsley Choral Society which Harry Woodall had agreed to conduct. On the 15th January, *The Fairy Queen, the Goblin and the Mortal Child,* the last of Harry's three cantatas written with the Reverend Graham, were performed at the Drill Hall, with May Woodall playing the Fairy Queen. Another musical extravaganza followed on the 5th February when Harry Woodall and a colleague staged a grand concert. The following Monday, he staged another concert at the Drill Hall. Preoccupied with his involvement in such a busy round of musical engagements, and his daughter, Eva Adelina's, marriage to Charles Roberts due to take place on the 14th April, Thomas Woodall was unperturbed by his diminishing role at Webb's.

Examination results and prizes for the Wordsley Art School were announced on the 9th March. Standards had improved with all students passing Advanced Freehand and Geometry. The school was now open thanks to charitable donations, mainly from the Richardson family who gave the final £40. The names from the prize list included a number of future glass artists: A.J.H. Bohm received first prize and a County Council prize for a vase design, decanter and wineglass, Norman Wilkes received second and C. Hambrey, third; Percy Scriven, Percy Horne, D. Shuker and James Hill all received second class design awards. T. Turner, the director of Technical Education in Staffordshire, spoke of the high standards in the school and congratulated the principal, Frederick Carder, and the teachers, who included Thomas Woodall and J.T. Hambrey. A motion was carried that funds should be raised to build an extension.

The new century had started well for George – in late 1900, he was approached by the American Society of the Chemical Industry who commissioned him to produce a cameo portrait of the eminent scientist, Lord Kelvin.[62] After visiting and photographing the British physicist, production of the fourteen-inch portrait, *Lord Kelvin,* would take four years to complete. Readers of *The Pottery Gazette* were already aware of the talented George and Thomas Woodall but, because of the publicity of his work in the national press, George's fame was growing.

Concert programmes. (*Author's collection*)

Opalescent glass created by adding an excess of arsenic to form a vaseline colour from the uranium compounds. These photographs were taken by George Woodall to create a portfolio to be used by travelling salesmen.

[45] *Studio Pottery*: Art Nouveau and Art Deco and Cameo Glass. Sold by auction at Christie, Manson & Woods Ltd., on 3rd June 1975. No.153: *The Milkmaid*, a fine and rare documentary 12ins, cameo two-handled vase, by George Woodall, of cylindrical shape with short, flared neck. The solid blue ground is overlaid in translucent blue and opaque white with bluish tinge and finely carved with a young girl, a milk-churn over one arm, running in a landscape vignette with a spray of foxgloves and blackberry on one side; the reverse with a vase of roses and trailing fern; the short angular handles with flowerheads and petal terminals; the neck with a blackberry spray and with stiff leaves to the rim, the lower part with a border of arum-lily leaves and with foliate foot rim. The wood stand bears a silver plaque inscribed 'Melbourne Tennis Club Trophy, Presented by M. O'Shanassy, Won by D. Coldham, May 25th 1892'. Sold to Alan Tilman for £8925. Source: Christie's Auctioneers.

[46] *The Brierley Hill Advertiser*, 21st January 1893.

[47] Since only Woodall work was sent to this Exhibition, the other work must have been 'Gem Cameo' produced by the team.

[48] *The Brierley Hill Advertiser*, 21st January 1893.

[49] I am unsure why *The County Express* used different titles for some of the Woodall pieces. These names may have been the preferred titles of Charles Webb or one of the brothers who was present at the display.

[50] *The County Express*, 28th January 1893.

[51] The workmanship mentioned in these pieces was later commented on by George Woodall: 'I found a different metal, a white with a blue tinge which when carved down upon the brown background became semi-transparent and... a most delicate, beautiful blue, thus increasing enormously the range of the artist's possibility of scene-painting. The light and shade, and the 'distance' which I can depict in my reproductions of architecture is wonderful. By pressing into my service the cutting-wheel... an infinity of time and labour is saved and the cost of production... lessened.' Transcript for 'Picture Sculpture' *The County Express*, 20th January 1912.

[52] William Northwood (1857-1937), a schoolfriend of Thomas and nephew of John Northwood, carved the cameo plaque *Venus and Dancing Cupid* and *Venus Interesting Cupid*, in 1895. Having a paralysed left arm, his work was particularly remarkable.

[53] Frederick Carder (1863-1963) began as a potter but, inspired by The Portland Vase, moved to glassmaking. He left J. & J. Northwood in 1880/81 to join Stevens & Williams as a designer under Northwood's instruction. In 1888 he won a silver medal for vase design, *Cupid and Psyche*; in 1889 he won a gold medal for *The Muses* and in 1890 he carved *Immortality of the Arts*. For many years he was an art master and eventually Principal at the Wordsley Art School. He emigrated to the USA in 1903 and managed the Steuben Glass Works, becoming a director until 1933, then becoming Art Director at Corning Glass Works and its associate Museum of Glass.

[54] Richard Honeybourne founded Stevens & Williams in 1776. The company acquired its name when William Stevens and Samuel Williams took over in 1846. The partnership continued until 1879 when S. Cox Williams and his son became directors. When the former died, Joseph Silvers Williams inherited the site. The business was eventually incorporated into Royal Brierley Crystal.

[55] *The County Express*, 27th February 1897.

[56] Reprinted in *The County Express*, 15th October 1898.

[57] Among the non-Woodall exhibits were some pieces from Tiffany; majolica tiles and *Loved of the Ladies*, a collection of Royal Worcester and Coalport porcelain. Other cabinets featured armour, coal shoes, Chinese ivory toys, an enamelled cup by Jules Barbe and an array of paintings.

[58] I have examined over 150 of George Woodall's photographs of cameo pieces. *Sappho* is the only photographic plate that bears this pencil overwriting of 'G' for George. Whilst this does highlight the 'G' it does not hide the 'T' for Thomas. In *Nineteenth Century Cameo Glass* Geoffrey W. Beard suggested that George may have recarved cameos to remove his brother's name. While it is a fact that the brothers became estranged, family interviews make it quite clear that this was because of domestic circumstances rather than professional differences.

[59] The piece mentioned is *Intruders*.

[60] As reproduced in *The Brierley Hill Advertiser*, 22nd July 1899.

[61] Charles Webb worked for Alderman Copeland in his Bond Street china dealership before entering Webb's as a director. In 1886 the business became a limited company: Wilkes retired because of ill health and Charles Webb became managing director. When he retired he left Dennis Hall and moved into Claremont, Kingswinford. He died on the 12th May 1908.

[62] Baron Kelvin of Largs (1824-1907), mathematician and physicist, President of the Royal Society from 1890-1894 and received the Order of Merit in 1902.

Left, *Night*, right *Morning*, white on brown companion vases, 10ins (25.5cms) signed Geo Woodall. (*Photograph by George Woodall*)

On the 22nd January 1901, Queen Victoria died. While the country went into a long period of mourning, George worked prolifically, completing many pieces he had been carving since 1899. GW3 *Night* and GW5 *Morning*, a companion set of vases, was complemented by GW7 *Pharoah's Daughter* in September 1900. There was also GW10 *Flora*, GW13 *Psyche*, GW25 *Sirene*, GW12 *Penelope* and on the 13th June 1901, GW22 *Painting* and another set of companion vases GW23 *Night* and GW24 *Morning* were sold at auction (as annotated in the Price Book).

Emma Woodall died in April 1902, aged seventy-four, with Thomas and George at her bedside. Dr Pearson certified the death and only three months later his daughter, Bernice, would marry Harry Woodall. The couple had courted for several years and for some time had intended to marry. However, at the time of their marriage, Bernice was four months pregnant – a scandal in Victorian times. To avoid the inevitable comment and gossip, Harry and Bernice left the district and married at St Chad's Church in Lichfield. Although Thomas and Martha attended the wedding, Thomas, a devout Christian, was devastated and

Left, Pamela Woodall aged eighteen. (*Photograph by George Woodall*)

Far left, Bernice Woodall in costume. (*Author's collection*)

refused to act as witness. George and Pamela were not invited. Thomas was deeply embarrassed by the affair and, in the interests of 'respectability', George did not wish to be seen as too closely involved with his brother and sister-in-law. With the loss of their mother and this damaging social blow, the relationship between the brothers became yet more distant. After their wedding, Harry and Bernice moved to Wollaston, Stourbridge, where, because Harry was a minor celebrity, their arrival was welcomed. No-one in the village was aware that the couple were newlyweds – in the era before telephones and television, Wordsley and Wollaston seemed poles apart – and on the 12th December, Bernice gave birth to a daughter, Beryl Rogers Woodall.[63]

To increase prices, Webb's placed more of George Woodall's pieces in auctions. In October, a selection of his recent work was auctioned: GW32 *Calypso* and GW33 *Andromache*, failed to sell. Three more vases followed: GW114 *Sirene*, GW115 *Sirene* and GW116 *Flora*, then a succession of oval brooches with smaller versions of George's earlier work, *Nature's Mirror* and a *Greek Slave*. He had sketched plans for more impressive vases and plaques, however these were put on hold when, in February 1903, George learned that his unmarried daughter Pamela, was pregnant by Herbert Holds, a house furnisher. The couple

Photograph of Lord Kelvin by George Woodall, used as source material.

married at the Register Office in Stourbridge on the 6th March but, fearful of the prospect of public scandal, neither set of parents went to the wedding. Only Amy, Pamela's eldest sister, attended as witness and bridesmaid. The newly weds were outcasts: Herbert was disinherited and Pamela was ignored by her parents and other members of her family. However, she miscarried at three months, and as there was now no evidence of any misdeed, some degree of rapprochement took place between the young couple and their families. George softened towards his daughter and, eventually, she reappeared in cameo wearing a pearl necklace – a smaller red slab of *The Pearl Necklace* was later given to her.

During those difficult months George had chosen three more oval blanks for carving brooches. By the 30th March he had carved *The Dove*, *Sea Nymph*, *The Dance*, *Gathering Pearls*, *Venus Rising from the Sea*, *Sappho*, *Penelope* and *A Syrene* in

GW30 *The Dance* plaque, 20ins (51cms), signed Geo Woodall. *(Photograph by George Woodall)*

W733 *Dancers*, white on brown plaque, 13¹/₄ins (33.5cms), signed G Woodall 1886. *(Sotheby's)*

miniature. However, his work had suffered with the news of his child's civil rather than church wedding (a register office was considered suitable only for divorcees who were not allowed to remarry in church). The social repercussions could not be avoided and George was 'unburdened of many social duties'. Apart from the continuing work on *Lord Kelvin*, on the 2nd May, George completed seven more brooches which were carved on the engraver's wheel without the need for prolonged concentration: *Diana, Pandora, Nature's Mirror, Girl in the Clouds, Venus Rising from the Sea* (twice) and *Bacchanate*.

1904 began as a quiet year for Thomas Woodall. A heart scare shortly after Christmas resulted in his retirement from many public duties. Webb's business was sluggish and the company continued with aggressive marketing in order to sell its cameo stock. A letter to George Brookman in Adelaide, South Australia (a collector and influential figure in the fledgling Public Library and Museum of South Australia), illustrates Webb's keenness to sell cameo through a network of secret deals:

17th May 1904
Dear Sir,
We trust by the time this reaches you, you will have reached home safely...
We are sending you by this post a copy of the newspaper *Madame* which we think may interest you as it contains an article on Woodall's Cameo work accompanied by illustrations. We also send you (inside the paper *Madame*) an unmounted photo of his latest placque *(sic) Dancers* which you so admired when visiting the works. As you will remember this is the largest piece of glass which Woodall has ever undertaken measuring no less than 20ins in diameter. It is therefore unique as a specimen of sculptured glass, besides representing some of the very finest work of its kind that Woodall has ever done. We think it possible that the Museum may be desirous of securing this splendid piece of work and we therefore beg to say that after careful consideration we are prepared to dispose of it for £425 which is £50 below the wholesale cash price.
If the Museum secures this specimen they will have one of the very finest pieces of sculptured glass in existence and a larger piece than we are ever again likely to successfully produce.
We have added a few specimens to the collection which we made when you were at the works for the Museum and trust that all will arrive safely and help to make a unique and interesting display.

We are also enclosing bottles containing samples of various ingredients which go to make glass, each bottle being labelled with the name of the ingredient.
If the Museum should decide to secure the *Dancers* placque (sic) on the terms we propose we should esteem it a great favour if you would arrange for a cable to be sent us containing the code word 'Adelaide'.
We suggest this because this is a season of the year when our leading American customers visit this country and they always purchase one or more of Woodalls finest pieces and it would prevent any possible disappointment if we knew in good time your decision on the matter.
We are, dear sir, etc.

On the 19th September 1904, George signed an agreement with W. Davidson, his close friend and Master of the Aston Union, to borrow £350 (interest 4% per annum) in order to buy Luton House.[64] A great deal of George's glass remained unsold and was being auctioned by Webb's at regular intervals. To compensate, George had reduced his output of major pieces, and his smaller brooches sold well. In a new business enterprise from Luton House, George was to sell insurance for the Royal Lancashire Insurance Company, and also act as agent for *Exchange & Mart* and George Morris of Dudley, who kept stables and hired out carriages for weddings and funerals. With the added profits from his land deals, George was able to pay £50 off his mortgage by the spring of 1905, a sizeable sum in so short a time. Alice Woodall later described Luton House as being full of the finest porcelain, with many cameo pieces adorning the shelves and a beautiful grandfather clock ticking away in the sitting room.

The *Kelvin* plaque was handed to The American Society in early 1905 and George's workmanship was greatly applauded. W.H. Nichols, President of the Society of Chemical Industry, presented it to the Royal Society in November 1905. It earned George 100 guineas and many influential friends. In January 1906, he borrowed a further £250 from Davidson, possibly to pay for extensions to Luton House, in particular to enlarge his photographic studio into a cameo workshop. George was now approaching retirement age from Webb's and would soon need his own premises.[65]

On the 25th December 1905, a second child, Alfred Cecil Woodall (hereafter known as Frank), was born to Harry and

Sketch for a cameo bowl the factory pattern book (No.26752), possibly indicating a background of mica flakes. *(Edinburgh Crystal Glass Co.)*

Bernice. A third child, Geoffrey Hargreaves Woodall followed on the 3rd December 1906, by which time, the family lived at Holmcroft in Clifton Street. Thomas' daughter, Janet, met Percy Joe Scriven while both were students at Wordsley Art School. During their courtship the opportunity had arisen to emigrate to America. Three years earlier, Frederick Carder had pleaded with Percy to accompany him to the United States but Janet had strongly opposed the idea. The couple married on the 28th July 1906 and settled in Wood Street, Wollaston, then South Avenue, Stourbridge, before going to Whitehall Road, Pedmore. George and Pamela did not attend the wedding, another indication that the brothers now led separate lives. Percy was works manager for Stevens & Williams and later became a director of the company.[66] The couple had three children: Marjorie on the 22nd July 1907; Charles Roger on the 19th May 1915, and Kathleen Joan on the 6th March 1918.

A lifetime's ambition came to fruition in the following October when Thomas and George appeared together to celebrate the completion of Wordsley School of Art. Wordsley now had its own school, with a national reputation. It was a proud moment for Thomas who had been treasurer and now, along with the Reverend Slade and Benjamin Richardson, became a trustee of the building. It had taken fifteen years to finish the project.

GW139 *Morning* and GW140 *Night*, companion vases, 7ins (18cms), both signed Geo Woodall. *(Photograph by George Woodall)*

Meanwhile, Herbert Holds had become a cabinet master maker and he and Pamela had largely regained their social position. The arrival of Georgina May Beryl Holds (the first grandchild), was a happy event. (Sadly, she fell from her pram, aged two, damaged her spine and died in Australia while a teenager.) However, George was conscious that a stigma remained. He advised the pair that emigration to Australia would offer them the chance of a respectable life and in 1907, George subsidised their assisted passage on the SS *Dorset*. Herbert made a will leaving George Woodall and James Hartill as executors of his estate. It was agreed that the rents from his houses in Dudley Road were to be sent to Australia to provide additional income for the Holds. However, for reasons never given, once the couple left England, George never again spoke to his daughter. The couple had seven children and life in Australia was extremely hard.[67] Pamela wrote many times asking for the rents on their properties, but to no avail. George maintained the houses and paid water rates and other taxes promptly, but he kept the rents for himself.

Rose Cottage, Wordsley, home of Thomas and Martha Woodall.

A further auction in July 1907 sold GW15 *Chase* and GW16 *Caught*, and *Narcissus* was sold a month later on the 3rd August. In an attempt to enhance business and increase prestige in December 1907 the Wahliss Galleries at 88 Oxford Street, London, staged another of their magnificent exhibitions of glass and pottery. Crown Derby, Dresden and Wedgwood were augmented by a selection of George Woodall's pieces. One review stated:

> When one bears in mind that any morning the artist may come to his studio to find the work of months... shattered by some flaw in the glass, it is obvious that Woodall's work must always be rare, and that the glass sculptors worthy of mention in the same breath with him can be counted on one hand. [68]

On display were *The Dancing Hours, Diana and Endymion, Phyllis, Calypso, Siren, Aphrodite, Diana, Hebe, Sea Foam, The Chase, Iris* and *Caught*. A claret decanter featuring the Elgin Marbles as a design was also exhibited.

Thomas remained at Rose Cottage, living modestly as a glass engraver. He continued to teach at Wordsley Art School at night; in June 1906, a County Council Grant together with several donations had finally led to the School's completion of the first glass laboratory in the UK. However, he suffered from angina and his son's father-in-law, Dr Pearson, bluntly told him,

From far right: GW15 *The Chase*, white on brown vase, 6¹/₂ins (16.5cms), signed Geo Woodall.

GW16 *Caught* (also known as *The Captive*), white on brown companion vase to *Chase*, signed Geo Woodall.

Phyllis, white on blue vase, 8ins (20.5cms), signed Geo Woodall.

GW27 *Hebe*, white on brown vase, 7¹/₂ins (19cms), signed Geo Woodall. (*Photographs by George Woodall*)

'If you want to live Tom, retire!' Thomas left the glass industry in 1908 and became a music teacher and instrument dealer, happy to give concerts as a violinist. In contrast to his early apprenticeship days when he could find little work as a music teacher, the Woodall name now opened doors to many wealthy local families seeking music instruction. He had few worries: Harry was a well-established musician, Jack worked hard as a Relieving Officer, helping to keep people out of the workhouse, and Kate was musical director of the Woodall entertainments. In one final flourish in April, Thomas left local politics. He disagreed with his old Liberal colleagues, and voted to abolish the class-biased system of allocating pews, which forced the poorer members of the congregation to sit at the back of the church.

After Herbert and Pamela's emigration to Australia, George was once again able to concentrate on his work and had returned to carving major pieces of cameo. Webb's had asked him to carve several pieces for a forthcoming exhibition and Lionel Pearce[69] had designed *The Polar Vase* for George to carve. In June, Congreve Jackson planned a magnificent display for Franco-British Exhibition 1908 being staged at the White City. Instead of the large stands used in previous exhibitions, Webb's built a small glasshouse, allowing the public access to a three-tiered platform (entry sixpence) in order to watch the stages of glassmaking. The papers reviewed Stand No.73, at the Decorative Arts Palace, with enthusiasm:

> The Cut Glass forms a larger proportion of the whole collection than has been given to this branch in any previous exhibition – designed by Mr James R. Service and Mr L. Pearce, and the work executed under the supervision of Mr E. Parrish, the foreman. One of the finest specimens of glass cutting is a large eighteen-inch dish, designed by J.R. Service. The engraved or intaglio glass has been designed by William Fritsche, and many of the finest examples have been executed by him and bear his signatures. Among the many examples... are vases in combined rock crystal and intaglio effects typifying the seasons: one large pair of vases representing summer having beautifully engraved peacocks, one with tail feathers grandly arched, the other gracefully dropped, and each sheltered in a wonderful bower of rambling roses, which may be counted by a hundred on each vase. The scheme of ornamentation being completed by conventional arrangements of peacocks' feathers modelled appropriately to suit the beautiful outline of the vase form. Autumn is typified on another form of vase, cut by a similar method of decoration, in which a flight of swallows, exquisitely engraved, may be seen passing over a broad expanse of foaming sea, a very realistic effect of rolling waves and glittering spray being worked into the picture by methods peculiar to Mr Fritsche.

The cameo glass is all the work of Mr George Woodall, who is also responsible for the designs of the examples included in the exhibit. An eighteen-inch plaque representing *Cupid's Shrine* is Mr Woodall's latest work. A very carefully executed border, three-inches deep, encircles the subject which completely fills the centre space and represents a Greek waiting maid (Phyllis) who has been sent to the fountain for water, and finds Cupid guarding his shrine and obstructing her path. Forgetful of her purpose she lays her pitcher aside and seats herself in front of the chubby little cherub and becomes lost in thought, and presumably speculates as to the possibility of one of the remaining arrows from the quiver of the 'god of love' being directed towards her.

A smaller plaque shown is *The Wild Waves*, in which a nymph of the sea disports herself on the surface of the falling ocean waves, with two solitary seabirds hovering near her, as though prepared to give a warning if assistance should be needed in battling with the elements, a friendly but needless precaution, for the nymph is quite at her ease. A conventional border of shells and seaweed, with dolphins placed between the groups, completes this thirteen-inch plaque which makes a companion to an earlier work of similar character and size, in *Aphrodite*.

GW6 *Sea Foam*, white on brown vase, 10ins (25.5cms), signed Geo Woodall. (*Photograph by George Woodall*)

The Webb stand, 1908 Franco-British Exhibition. Among the glassblowers at the furnace is Albert Saunders forming a swan. (*Photograph by George Woodall*)

Shown in a good light and position between these two examples, is the twenty-inch plaque, *The Dance*, perhaps Mr Woodall's most ambitious effort, and the largest object he has worked upon in this class of production. The easy, graceful pose of the dancing figures give evidence of Mr Woodall's mastery over his work, and the airiness of their flowing robes demonstrate almost unlimited possibilities in manipulation in this presumably intractable material. A range of vases with single figure subjects, most of a classical nature and a few

medallions and miniatures in cases are included in a most interesting contribution.

The richly gilt and enamelled pieces shown have been designed by Mr J. Barbe... The metal work used in the mounting of many of the pieces shown has all been executed at the Dennis Works from designs by Mr L. Pearce, who has also designed the remarkable *Polar Vase*. This novel example of sculptured glass gives a very interesting picture of Arctic life and scenery. In the foreground Ursus Polaris, in all his solitary grandeur, is seen 'at home', the home also of the seal and walrus, the penguin and the albatross, surrounded by mighty fields of floating ice, with jagged peaks and towering ridges that look like the teeth of a gigantic saw, possibly the very fringe of that mysterious and uncertain region beyond the ice line, still unknown to man.[70]

On one day during the month-long exhibition, the Woodall brothers were seen together – Thomas' first appearance for many years. George appreciated this gesture and Thomas returned to Wordsley in good spirits, perhaps regretting not having visited previous displays. The year finished with George overwhelmed with work after the successful exhibition. He was working on eight 7-inch vases and other exhibits for a forthcoming exhibition in Turin. By Christmas he had finished GW130 *A Message*, GW131 *Feathered Favourites* and GW132 *Ocean Gems*. In contrast, Thomas' year finished quietly with another of the Woodalls' dramatic entertainments in aid of libraries for Wordsley Council and Glynne Schools and a boot fund for the Council Schools' Benevolent and Orphan Fund.

By March 1909, George had completed GW133 *Seaweed* followed in August by GW139 *Morning* and GW140 *Night*, another set of companion vases. He finished the second version of the *Antarctic* vase and in January 1910, he and Pamela received an invitation to Jack's marriage to Annie Downes, a

GW12 *Penelope*, white on brown on flint flatsided vase 7ins, (18cms), signed Geo Woodall. (*Photograph by George Woodall*)

GW14 *The Message*, white on brown on flint vase, 7ins (18cms), signed Geo Woodall. (*Photograph by George Woodall*)

Right, W2767 *Sea Nymph* panel, 13ins x 10ins (33x25.5cms), signed Geo Woodall.
(*Photograph by George Woodall*)

Far right, GW32 *Calypso* panel, 12¹/₂ins (32cms), signed Geo Woodall.
(*Photograph by George Woodall*)

violinist (they subsequently had one child Thomas Granville John Woodall[71] but, by all accounts, the marriage was not a success). However, on learning that their daughter Amy was pregnant, George and Pamela declined their nephew's wedding invitation. Amy had been engaged to George Calloway for twelve years but when, at the age of thirty-eight, she became pregnant, Calloway fled to Ireland leaving her to cope as a single parent. The scandal could not be avoided and George and Pamela withdrew from much of Kingswinford's social life, making only rare public appearances. Consequently, they did not attend a presentation evening at the Bell Hotel, Stourbridge, on the 14th March, when Harry Woodall, Honorary Conductor, received 'a purse of gold in recognition of his services' and a silver baton from the Stourbridge Institute Male Voice Choir which had just returned from Blackpool as winners of the Grundy Shield. Despite his critical acclaim, Harry did not have a good income and would give piano lessons to many of his future nieces

The wedding of Jack and Annie Woodall. From left: back row, Thomas Woodall, unidentified man, Charles Roberts, unidentified man, Howard Pearson, Thomas Pass, two unidentified men; centre, May Woodall, Jack and Annie Woodall.

and nephews in order to make ends meet. Thomas Woodall was at the presentation having recently formed the Richardson Hall Orchestra to play at local engagements.

As details emerged about Amy's pregnancy, Thomas' side of the family kept a respectful distance, partly because they did not wish to be associated with the social disgrace but also because Thomas empathised with George's embarrassment. Sadly, for once they had been so close, the brothers never met again, though Harry continued to visit his uncle.

In August, George finished another *Aphrodite* plaque, GW146, and on the 29th September an *Origin of the Painting* plaque, GW145, was entered in the Webb's Price Book as available for sale, followed by GW148 *Idle Moments*. When the Brussels-Turin Exhibition opened in September, George did not make his customary appearance. He had chosen to stay at home and so could only read about the magnificent reception given to his work. Indeed, his work schedule had been so disrupted by Amy's disgrace, that he could provide just two major pieces of work, both of which had already been exhibited: *The Dance* and *Diana and Endymion*. Nonetheless, the Brussels International Exhibition awarded Thomas Webb & Sons a Grand Prix for their display. George was devastated by a telegraph from Congreve Jackson informing him that, 'four fine stands containing cut glass, gilt glass, engraved rock crystal glass and cameo work, ranging in price from £400 to £500 apiece' had been destroyed in a fire. Fortunately, the Belgians gave the Board of Trade the *Salle des Fêtes* concert hall to remount another display. Jackson was prevented from entering the ruins for several days until the building was declared safe, 'all that remained were twisted lumps of glass melted out of shape and intermingled with screws and bits of metal among the general debris of the ruins.'[72] From the wreckage, only a tiny fragment of *Diana and Endymion* survived (see page 36). George described the fire as 'the worst thing that has ever happened to my work.' It was soul destroying, he had spent hours carving the three girls in *The Dance*, after taking many photographs of dancing poses and watching live performances.

From left, GW131 *Feathered Favourites*, with companion vase GW130 *A Message*, 7ins (18cms), signed Geo Woodall, GW134 *Soppa* with companion vase GW135 *Tambourina*, white on brown, 7ins (18cms), signed Geo Woodall. (*Photographs by George Woodall*)

The year finished with the birth of George Calloway Woodall on the 6th December. Pamela had ordered Amy to leave Luton House but George was not prepared to put his daughter onto the streets. A compromise was reached whereby Amy and her son lived in the cramped and uncomfortable verandah of the house. Mother and child suffered the ignimony of village gossip and as a result of Amy's disgrace, Alice assumed a higher profile within the family. This proved a tremendous strain for her as she found it hard to condemn her sister, friend and mentor. Recognising this, George carved a portrait medallion, *The Armenian Girl*, as a private tribute to his staunchest supporter. He never explained the connection between Alice and the Armenians – was George expressing

sympathy for the plight of the Armenian people massacred in the atrocities of 1895, or was he simply inspired by the portrait of an Armenian girl which hung in Luton House? Nor did he offer a reason for inscribing Alice's name into a plaque of a siren. She had been the inspiration for many beautiful maidens, but the choice of a siren, a figure who lured men to their death, seems inappropriate.

Under constant pressure, George looked forward to his retirement when he could withdraw from the unwelcome gaze of the public. While he had carved the name 'Geo Woodall' into a symbol of success, appreciated by his peers, famous collectors and the public, his family's difficulties had caused scandal and distress.

Works outing: Congreve Jackson (centre, second row with bowler hat and bow tie), encouraged workers at Dennis Hall to take part in workers' outings. Among the many faces are Albert Saunders (first row, standing fourth from right), and William Hicks (front row, sitting sixth from left). Saunders and Hicks were part of Webb's best glassblowing team. (*Photograph by George Woodall*)

63 After Harry's death Bernice Woodall sold her home and moved in with her son and daughter, Beryl and Frank. After she died in 1964, Frank married his long time love, May Perks, and the couple lived in Bowling Green Road until his death in 1983. They had no children, and May Woodall is still alive. Beryl Rogers Woodall married Samuel Skidmore Hambrey, a glasscutter at the Dennis Hall Works, on 8th September 1936. After their marriage they moved to London and 'Skid' became foreman of Webb's industrial glassworks in Walthamstow. The couple retired to North Wales in 1967. They had one son, Martin Hambrey, born 16th June 1937. Beryl died on the 21st March 1978 and 'Skid' died on the 5th March 1991. There is little known about Geoffrey Woodall other than he married Anne Dorothy Walter on the 24th September 1969. The couple lived in East Sussex and are now dead.

64 Luton House as described by Pam Eldred, George Woodall's granddaughter: 'I remember the house. The front was an antique shop... inside was an open area... The sitting room had a piano, velvet sofa, Victorian flock paper, drapes and a fireplace. The kitchen had an enormous table, bench and chairs. There was a magnificent sideboard, Chippendale, and an old blackened range...used to heat up wrapped-up bricks as hot water bottles...Grandpa's studio was end on – the left side of the garden. You went down a garden path to a lane behind. The studio was built when he retired. The workshop was never touched after George died. Twenty-five years untouched.'

65 The workshop was demolished in 1947. George Calloway Woodall rescued many glass negatives and the studio tools. The latter can now be seen at Broadfield House Glass Museum. A further set of engraving tools is in the author's possession. Eyewitness accounts and parish records confirm that more glass plates were recycled during the Second World War when glass was at a premium. A few have gone into private collections or were sold to Broadfield House Glass Museum in September 1978 by Florence Woodall. Geoffrey Beard, in *Nineteenth Century Cameo Glass*, records: 'The lathe was a treadle machine being operated by foot pressure. A lubricant was fed to the copper wheel by the effective yet primitive feather suspended near to it. In a rack to his left hand, Woodall had arranged a set of about fifty copper wheels ranging from three inches to a mere pinpoint. Classical casts are on the walls and plater moulds of a human figure, leaves, feet, hands and arms. A bran pad lies on the oil-soaked table to take the vase seen on the stand, entitled *Undine*. Oil cans, a battered hat and a clay pipe can also be seen.' The engraver's lathe was removed in May 1940, current whereabouts unknown.

66 Percy Scriven (1880-1948) rose from being a glassblower at Stevens & Williams to become works manager and eventually a company director, before the firm was acquired as Royal Brierley Crystal. He died in 1948 and left his widow without a pension. She sold off many pieces of cameo glass left to her by her father; the American collector, Philip Budrose, visited the house and purchased several pieces, including an unfinished vase with lilies. Janet Scriven died on 7th January 1958 and

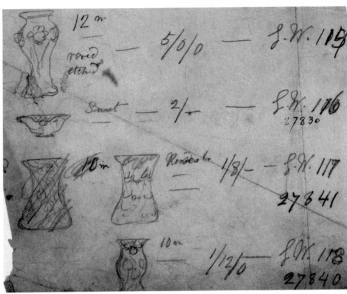

Sketches of the 'lost' pieces by George Woodall. These GW numbers were allocated to different pieces in Webb's Price Book. *(Family Collection)*

had three children: Marjorie Woodall Scriven, Roger Scriven and the youngest , Joan, who is still alive.

67 The couple's children were: Beryl, Herbert, Barbara, Daphne, Laurie, David and Alice. Herbert married Nancy McPhee and had a son, Herbert John Holds. Daphne married L. Mould and had two daughters, Pamela and Margot. Laurie married Enid Andrews and had two sons, Ken and Geoff and a daughter, Ruth. David married Margaret and had three daughters. Alice married Edward Pick and had a son and a daughter.

68 *The Connoisseur*, Vol 19, No.76, December 1907.

69 Lionel Pearce (b1852) was the son of Daniel Pearce – they joined Webb's in 1884. Daniel's engraving had been praised at the 1862 International Health Exhibition. The Pearce's specialised in imitation ivory pieces and for the Franco-British Exhibition in 1908, Lionel designed two cut-glass cannons, models of the famous gun 'Skipping Sally', with which Major General Baden-Powell defended Mafeking.

70 *The County Express*, 13th June 1908.

71 Thomas Granville John Woodall (1911-1987) worked for the Great Western Railway. He was survived by his wife, Marie, and son, Malcolm John Woodall (b1943).

72 *The County Express*, 24th September 1910.

From left, Harry Woodall, Percy Scriven, Janet Woodall, Kate Woodall. *(Author's collection)*

1911 – 1920

COMMISSIONS AT LUTON HOUSE

GW144 *Flora Surprise*, 8ins (20.5cms), signed Geo Woodall.
(*Photograph by George Woodall*)

On the 11th March 1911, Nora May Woodall married Howard George Pearson at the Church of Our Lady and All Saints, New Road, Stourbridge. Thomas had given the marriage his blessing, despite Howard's Catholicism, and the couple had two children, Norman Thomas Pearson (born 22nd October 1911), and Kathleen Ena Pearson (born 16th June 1913).[73] Norman was Thomas' favourite grandson and a frequent visitor to Rose

Cottage. Legend has it that while playing football in the hall with his cousins, he broke pieces of Thomas' family cameo – but, apparently, his grandparents never seemed to mind.

Preparations were well underway for the coronation of George V but George and Pamela took no part in the Kingswinford celebrations. They also stayed away from a garden party at their local church, St Mary's, too shamed by Amy's conduct to face George's brother and the social dignitaries. (In poignant contrast, Thomas conducted the Richardson Hall Orchestral Band at the garden party, playing light music in the afternoon and dance music in the evening.) Nationally, however, George's social position remained intact, and his cameo work continued to be praised. In May 1911, Webb's shipped a number of new pieces to the Turin Exhibition for display and sale: GW146 *Aphrodite*, GW147 *Sea Shells*, GW148 *Idle Moments*, GW149 *Seaweeds*, GW150 *Nautilus*, GW151 *Springtime* and *Cupid's Bower* (also known as *At Cupid's Shrine*). These were well received and the trade magazines were complimentary:

> Thomas Webb & Sons, Ltd., make a brave show with their four cases of art glassware. In one are shown some exquisite vases and plaques of cameo executed by Mr George Woodhall (sic). The subject of one of the largest is *Cupid's Bower*, with beautifully sculptured figures of the little archer and his mother, Venus. Certain details of the background – the water of a fountain, the mane of a lion, the foliage of some trees – are perfect marvels of careful execution. Among the smaller pieces I noted a girl swinging – a spirited piece of work; the graceful floating drapery of her dress had been cut away in some places to such a thin film that the blue tone of the body of the ware showed plainly through its transparency.[74]

Other cases included cut-glass vases, electrical fittings and a coronation set of wineglasses on which blank spaces were left for the insertion of the purchaser's monogram. The glass light-fittings proved very popular and George was commissioned to produce another four immediately, making it unlikely that he would finish before leaving Webb's at the end of the year. So, Jackson and he agreed that George should continue to make pieces for Webb's after his retirement, but on better terms and working from home. The Turin Exhibition passed unnoticed by Thomas whose daughter, Kate, was preparing to marry Harry Green[75], who also took part in the musical evenings.

Records kept by Thomas Webb & Sons reveal that thousands of commercial cameo pieces were made for sale before Thomas' and George's retirement in 1908 and 1911 respectively, but only twenty-eight were jointly marked 'T & G Woodall'. This record of work is almost certainly incomplete and the issue is further complicated by the possibility of occasional forgeries. Cameo glass had lost its market due to high production and selling costs and changing fashions. Interest in cheaper commercial cameo, plus an upturn in other forms of glassmaking, led to a steady decline in the amount of cameo produced by Webb's. It became a flagship for quality, but not quantity or great profit. Indeed, as retirement approached, George Woodall knew that his financial security could not depend on his freelance production of vases and plaques.

From left, top row: GW148 *Idle Moments*, white on red slab, 4ins (10cms); GW147 *Sea Shells*, white on red slab, 5ins (12.5cms); middle row, GW145 *Origin of the Painting*, white on blue on cinnamon brown plaque, 11ins (28cms); GW160 *Aphrodite*, white on red on brown plaque, 10³/4ins (27.5cms), for another version in Broadfield House Glass Museum, see page 75; bottom row, GW150 *Nautilus*, white on red slab, 4ins (10cms); GW149 *Seaweeds*, white on red slab, 4ins (10cms). All signed Geo Woodall. *(Photographs by G Woodall)*

GW159 *Undine*, white on brown vase, 11¹/₂ins (29cms), signed Geo Woodall. (*Photograph by George Woodall*)

In autumn 1911, George Woodall retired and set up as an independent cameo artist. Pamela also left the millinery trade, and Alice took control of the organisation of George's business. She was the natural choice for this as, unlike her brothers and sisters, she had no suitors and devoted her life to her parents. Luton House was now run as a business through which George sold cameo pieces engraved on the premises, using blanks left over from Richardson's. He also traded in antique furniture, negotiated property deals, rented houses and arranged funerals. A careful businessman who took no risks, George paid the Royal

Members of the Woodall family: from left, George Parkes Woodall, May Woodall, Arthur and Connie, Dora holding Reginald Bott Woodall, Thomas Bott Woodall, seated Pamela and George Woodall. (*Photograph by George Woodall*)

Insurance Company Ltd., 10s 9d per annum to insure his house and business in the event of a fire for four hundred pounds.

During the latter months at Webb's, George had been accompanied by his two sons, who were learning the trade. After work, the brothers would take their father for a drink in the local pub in Audnam. There, Thomas Bott Woodall met Gertrude May Goring[76], an attractive girl with aspirations to marry well and live like a 'lady'. Pamela Woodall objected to the match, dismissing May as 'common'. However, the more his mother objected, the more determined Thomas became and, after many bitter arguments, on the 8th January 1912 he and May married at St Mary's Church, Kingswinford. Almost immediately, the couple moved to Canada where Thomas Bott Jnr had been offered work as a glass decorator. However, on their arrival, he discovered that his business partner was dishonest. He was asked to persuade his father to send out cameo blanks that he would then carve and sign 'Geo. Woodall'. Thomas refused and returned to England immediately. By this time, May was expecting their child and, unable to renew his employment with Webb's, Thomas Bott Jnr went to work for Messrs Joseph Fleming and Co.

The week following his son's marriage, George gave an interview to a reporter from *The County Express*. Pleased by an article about his work and believing that it would help his business if people read that he was now making commissions to order, George spoke about the highs and lows of his career:

> I am going to rest for a time. Then I have many commissions from friends in many parts which I want to execute. I have also to do something for myself, for I have not anything of my own work to hand on to my children. Several times I have done work for Mrs Woodall, but friends come in and will not be satisfied without buying what they see and one by one the pieces go. So now I shall have to replenish our store. [He then showed the reporter a tiny plaque of a maiden's head, 1¹/₂ins square.] That is not finished yet, but it is already bespoken; I shall receive five guineas for it.

George mentioned that his daughter Pamela, had seen *Moorish Bathers* on display at the Adelaide Museum and Public Library in Australia, and had written home reporting that the 'sight of the beautiful plaque... brought a very big lump into my throat.'[77] So, even though it was only Connie who corresponded with her, clearly George was reading Pamela's letters, despite their estrangement.

By July the cameo lampshades were finished and Webb's commissioned George to produce a further five lamps and body pieces. Other freelance work followed including the *Mischief* vase and a plaque of *Perseus* and *Andromeda*. (As Alice had grown older, Connie had replaced her as George's principal model.) He completed two major vases for Webb's on the 29th July 1913: GW152 *Caught* and GW153 *Sea Gulls*. On the domestic front, May Woodall gave birth to Reginald Clifford Bott Woodall on the 8th October 1912 and, by Christmas, George's eldest son, George Parkes Woodall, returned home from an ill-judged move to Canada. George was beginning to suffer financial problems – land prices had plummeted, he owned land that he was unable to sell, and there were few orders for cameo pieces. These difficulties were exacerbated by the declaration of war, leading not only to a dearth of orders from the Continent, but also a scarcity of glass ingredients. George was unsuccessful in his attempts to find a partner for the land dealings. Nonetheless, he kept the facts from his wife, pretending that finances were secure.

Thomas' son, Harry, continued to enjoy success in his musical career but his schedule was exhausting and he suffered ill health. During the war he experienced the horrific trench conditions in France, which left him emotionally and physically scarred. (It was about this time that Thomas began to write his memoirs, which have been such a valuable source of information.)

In 1915, a year after his marriage to Dora Bourne, and to the great disappointment of his parents, George Parkes Woodall once again emigrated to Canada. The young couple had a turbulent marriage, and lived an impoverished life in the dominion. Because of their disapproval, father and mother refused to write to their son and, as was the case with Pamela, it was left to Connie to keep contact. An extract from Pamela's letter to her parents conveys her pain and sadness:

> Bert [Herbert Holds] feels it very much that you do not answer his letters... To Dad will you try to let us have a little of Bert's rents or if you cannot, say no and we will put all thoughts of it out of our minds... I suppose Alice will never write to us, I don't know why... Have I really lived these eight years out here or shall I wake up and find myself safely home with you again. I cannot write further without upsetting myself. [Sunday 6th February 1916]

The arrival of this letter must have been particularly poignant for Connie as she prepared for her marriage to Arthur Wood[78] on the 24th April 1916. Connie moved to Arthur's home in Sutton Coldfield but she regularly wrote to, and visited, her parents. The key communicator in the family, she remained on good terms with Alice (who was highly critical of her siblings for damaging the family's reputation), and kept George Parkes and Pamela Woodall in the family's thoughts. She also remained in touch with her cousin Kate Green and her husband when they lived in Erdington after the war, but lost contact after the couple's move to Pedmore.

George carved a small cameo oval, *Perseus and Andromeda*, for Connie's wedding present. Perseus was depicted as a bird, Andromeda as a naked figure wrapped in a piece of drapery, with her hands tied behind her back to a rock (see page 74). George intended to mount it as a pendant for Connie to wear at the ceremony but, because Andromeda was naked, she considered it indelicate. Instead, it was put into an inscribed silver box with a beautiful enamel lid designed by the jeweller, Claydon, which was commissioned by her sister, Amy, now engaged to Frank Meese. (The couple attended Connie's wedding and, in the interests of 'respectability' the guests were told that Amy and Frank had already been quietly married although they didn't actually wed until the 2nd January 1917.)

George Parkes wrote frequently for news, unable to cope with his isolation from Luton House. In 1916, Alice sent a letter telling him of his father's ill health and his response shows that he found the rift with his family hard to bear:

> We felt shut out of the family circle especially as you had dropped us altogether... after all I committed no crime. Please write often as if I were your brother. I have sad memories enough to look back on without adding. Tell Dad if there is <u>need</u> any time to bend his pride to let me know and what I can do will be done willingly... you will never know what it means to lose <u>all</u>. [24th January 1917]

Eventually, George and Dora returned to England where, using his contacts in Webb-Corbetts[79], George became a self-employed glass trader. Pamela persisted in her attempts to communicate with her parents, appealing to them to send the rents owed on Herbert Holds' properties:

Thomas Bott Woodall at the engraver's wheel. *(Family collection)*

> I have written a lot of letters but I don't get many answers and it seems useless to ask anything about the shops, but perhaps Dad will be well enough to write to me soon. [To Connie, 8th April 1917]

George *was* unwell, but it is clear that Connie used this to excuse his behaviour – he had, after all, owed rents to his son-in-law since 1907, and had never offered an explanation for withholding them.

On the 7th February, George finished his final commission from Webb's: GW163 *The Origin of the Harp* was based on Moore's *Irish Melodies*:

> 'Tis believed that this Harp, which I wake now for thee,
> Was a siren of old who sung under the sea;
> And who often at eve through the bright billow roved,
> To meet, on the green shore, a youth whom she loved...

In December 1907, *The Connoisseur* had stated, 'A future generation may well see a fight of millionaires for the possession of a Woodall plaque.' This generation proved to be some thirty years too late as far as George was concerned. While Thomas' music interests kept his household solvent, George's options were running out. His money was gone and there was to be no more income from work.

Portrait plaque of *Mrs Martin*, the wife of Dr Martin who was Alice Woodall's personal physician, signed Geo Woodall. *(Photograph by George Woodall)*

George and Pamela Woodall in retirement. *(Family collection)*

From left, George Woodall with his grandson, Reginald Bott Woodall and son, Thomas Bott Woodall.*(Family collection)*

[73] Howard Pearson manufactured glass until his death on 10th October 1950. May Pearson died on the 24th October 1966. Norman Pearson became an engineer. When Cis Woodall died, her husband offered Norman her cameo collection but Norman refused, and took some family fishing rods instead. He married, aged eighty, and is still alive. Ena Pearson worked for Stevens & Williams in Brierley Hill until her retirement. On 6th November 1970, she married Edgar Vale, whom she met through her work on Brierley Hill Council. Both are now dead.

[74] *The County Express*, 5th August 1911.

[75] Their only daughter Kathleen Joyce Green was born on 16th August 1912. After Kate Green's death on 25th March 1945, Harry Green married Mary Beasley. He died in the late 1950s. Joyce Green married Norman Langford on 7th August 1939, they had two children Clare born 25th January 1941 and Stephen born 25th March 1944. Stephen married Valerie Southwell on the 7th September and they have two children, Jane and Sarah. Clare married Thomas James Thomas on the 18th January 1969. They are separated with no children. Joyce, Stephen and Clare are still alive.

[76] Gertrude May Goring was born on the 16th November 1888.

[77] *The County Express*, 20th January 1912. This may have been an exaggeration as Pamela told her children many times that *Moorish Bathers* was one of her least favourite pieces as George had used naked models for some figures, and she did not approve.

[78] Arthur Wood (1888-1943) and Connie (d 11th May 1957) had a daughter, Pamela, on the 23rd December 1926. She married Dr. Vernon Eldred in 1951 and they have three children, Andrew, Sally and John who are all married with children.

[79] George Parkes Woodall died on the 30th April 1938. His glass business had failed and his widow, Dora (1877-1959), was left in financial difficulties.

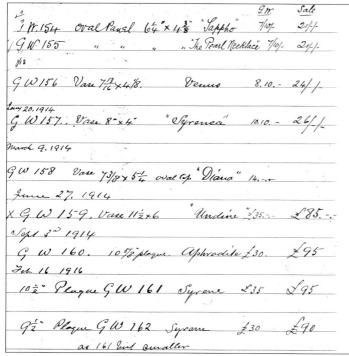

A page from the Thomas Webb & Sons' Woodall Price Book. *(Edinburgh Crystal Glass Co.)*

Marion Roberts plaque. *(Photograph by George Woodall)*

TROUBLED YEARS FOR THE WOODALL FAMILY

George's financial difficulties increased and small brooches were now his principal source of income. In 1921, Richardson's asked if he would remodel two cameo vases unsold after the 1878 Paris Exhibition: Alphonse Lechevrel's *Birth of Venus* and *Venus Rising from the Sea*. Initially, George was undecided. He had become used to working on his pieces only, also he was not well and the two vases in question were large and somewhat daunting. After some consideration, he agreed. The pairs of handles from each vase were to be removed and their connecting points polished away. Professional to the last, George not only removed the handles but also recarved borders and sharpened up the relief on the figure work. At Richardson's request, when completed, George signed both vases. However, his reworking had removed Lechevrel's signature from *Venus Rising for the Sea* so he scribed '*al 1877*' onto the base layer next to his signature. The Woodall signature aided the sale. (He had worked on *Love's Areo* earlier in his career and was to die before finishing a fourth piece, a second vase of Lechevrel's *Cupid on Panther*.)

George began work on a pedestal bowl and a tazza, but these were unfinished at his death. He already had five other pieces at different stages of completion including an $8^1/_2$-inch vase decorated with a petunia motif. An American buyer wanted these but George was unable to apply the concentration needed to carve accurately and, by mid-1923, he gave up. On the 20th December, Alice amended their insurance policy; the 'small glass engraver's lathe' was no longer on the premises and George's dark room, where he had spent so many hours

Aphrodite Walking from the Waves, signed Geo Woodall. (*Photograph by George Woodall*)

Aphrodite Rising from the Waves, plaque $8^1/_4$ins (21cms), signed Geo Woodall. (*Photograph by George Woodall*)

developing his photography, was converted into a 'store for glass'. His typewritten name was crossed out on the policy and Alice's name was pencilled in. Records of the London & Midland Bank reveal that after 1922 the balance in George's deposit account remained unaltered, except for accrued interest payments. On the 31st December 1920, George had £265.19.3 and the final entry for the 21st August 1925 showed a balance of £65.13.3. The account was then merged with his current account to give a sum of £121.7.9.

In February 1922, the beleaguered Woodall family assembled for George and Pamela's golden wedding anniversary. It was a quiet affair attended by some of the family, but not Thomas who was too old to travel and too busy with his large family. He had celebrated his own golden wedding anniversary the year before, and that too had been a low-key celebration.

GW11 *Pluvia*, white on brown on flint vase, 7ins (18cms), signed Geo Woodall. The jug which Pluvia holds symbolises rainfall. (*Photograph by George Woodall*)

Undine, flint glass vase, 13¹/₂ins (34.5cms), signed Geo Woodall. (*Photograph courtesy of Geoffrey Beard*)

A later version of the *Calypso* plaque, signed Geo Woodall. (*Photograph by George Woodall*)

On the 27th February 1925, after a two-week illness, George, aged seventy-five, died from a brain haemorrhage. On the 3rd March, a quiet funeral took place at St Mary's Church in the presence of family and close friends. Pamela had 'Reunion our abiding hope' inscribed on the grave stone. Harry Woodall, as his father's representative, joined George Parkes and Thomas Bott Woodall as official mourners and Pamela, and his friend and colleague, J.T. Fereday, were executors of his will.

It soon became evident that George died an even poorer man than was suggested by his bank records. His widow was dismayed to discover that he owed Herbert Holds his back rents, and that there was a bank overdraft of £60. Upon advice she sold a piece of land that George owned to clear the overdraft and repay Herbert, to whom George's solicitor wrote, tactfully excusing the non-payment as an oversight:

> Mr Woodall's health has gradually been on the decline for the last two or three years and unfortunately for everyone concerned during the above period he was not very businesslike. As a matter of fact I do not think his head would stand any business strain.

The back rents were paid to the Holds who had achieved an affluent, respected position in Australia. (Herbert became Mayor of Devenport and a street was named after him.[80])

On the 2nd October 1925, Alice lodged an appeal with HM Inspector of Taxes – business was dire!:

From left, Harry Woodall, Charles Roberts and other members of The Stourbridge Institute Male Voice Choir. *(Author's collection)*

GW161 *Syrene*, white on brown plaque, 10¹/₂ins (26.5cms), signed Geo Woodall. *(Photograph by George Woodall)*

Amblecote a/c3577. The amount taxed as profit about represents my takings for the year.

On 2nd June 1926, Thomas Woodall died peacefully in his sleep surrounded by his wife, children and grandchildren. Many local dignitaries attended his funeral at Holy Trinity Church, on the 7th June. Martha had 'For so He giveth his beloved sleep', Psalm CXXVII, inscribed on the grave. Rose Cottage was sold and Martha stayed alternately with Charles and Cis Roberts, the Scrivens, and the Greens.[82] The family suffered a second loss when Jack Woodall died from tuberculosis on the 24th August 1926, at the early age of forty-seven. The tragedy was compounded by the early death of Harry Woodall on the 14th May 1929, aged only fifty-three. Although unwell for some years, as late as the 14th April, he had conducted the Stourbridge Male Voice Choir at the Sunday evening concert at the town hall. An obituary in *The County Express*, 18th May 1929 stated:

> Wordsley will mourn the best musician she has ever nurtured. Stourbridge, his adopted town, loses a worthy citizen and the whole musical world is the poorer by his passing.

The family wished to bury him at Holy Trinity, Amblecote, but the rector refused because of the incident some twenty-seven years before. Harry was eventually buried at Holy Trinity, Wordsley, and in disgust, Bernice and his children converted to Roman Catholicism.

[80] Herbert Holds died on the 21st October 1956, and Pamela on the 19th October 1972, in Port Augusta, Australia.

[81] Martha Woodall died on the 23rd December 1934 at the age of eighty-four. She was buried alongside her husband.

George Woodall's studio at the rear of Luton House. *(Photograph by George Woodall)*

POSTSCRIPT

Dennis Hall 1982, white on brown plaque. The blank made in 1893, was decorated and signed by C. David Smith in 1982. The eighteenth-century Dennis Hall, is surrounded by four medallions featuring two Woodall pieces, the *Elgin* claret jug by F.E. Kny and the *Fritsche Ewer*. (*Photograph courtesy of Stanley Eveson*)

Pamela Woodall nursed a firmly entrenched resentment towards her daughter-in-law May, and her grandson, Reginald. She believed that they were responsible for inhibiting Thomas Bott Jnr's potential and, without George's restraining influence, became increasingly bitter and manipulative. Reginald Woodall entered Wordsley Art and Technical Institute, winning an award for 'Second Drawing from the Antique' in 1929. In 1930, Thomas Bott Jnr emigrated to Canada leaving his wife and son destitute. However, the couple were eventually reunited in 1939, and settled in Dudley; Thomas Bott died in St. George's Hospital, Stafford, on the 20th March 1952.[82]

From 1920 the Webb's Crystal Glass Company (incorporating Thomas Webb & Sons), introduced a new management style emphasising glassblowing and technical innovation, much of it masterminded on the shop floor by Stanley Eveson and his managing director, Sven Fogelberg.

However, there still remained a considerable amount of unsold cameo. Interest was reawakened in July 1935 by an article in *Antiques*, a New York based periodical, which featured:

> 'a gourd shape vase in the Chinese style. Several skilled craftsmen were engaged in the production of this vase. The blank glass before decoration consisted of a rose-coloured glass cased with an 'ivory' glass all over. After acid resist etching, Kretschman carried out his work in the year 1888. Jules Barbe was responsible for the coloured enamel work and the gold dots.'

Webb's provided photographs of the pieces still for sale, and a résumé of George Woodall's work which was largely duplicated from the *Glass Sculpture* booklet written thirty-six years earlier. Among the pieces were two Lechevrel vases, *Raising an Altar to Bacchus* and *Hercules Restoring Alcestis to her Husband Admetus*, which had been bought with the Richardson business when it

120

was acquired by Webb's. Many of the important cameos were eventually placed in the Works Museum – amongst the exhibits were the *Polar Vase, Wild Waves, The Rose, Feathered Favourites,* a plaque of *Origin of the Painting* and the two panel portraits of *Mr and Mrs Winans*. In 1987, the company was bought by the Coloroll Group. Unfortunately, all the pieces of cameo in the museum were removed by an American dealer. Knowing that export licenses might not be granted for such famous and rare pieces, they were taken back to the United States hidden among the dealer's hand luggage. Questions were asked in the House of Commons but the works were never recovered. George Woodall's design book, a seventeenth-century folio of figure work, a selection of hand tools together with other pieces of documentation and cameo frames also disappeared. A similar fate nearly befell *The Pearl Necklace* in 1988 when bought by the same dealer at Sotheby's. The staff thought his behaviour unusual and asked him to produce the export licence. As he was unable to do so, Sotheby's retained the piece which is now in Broadfield House Glass Museum. In 1990, Coloroll went into receivership and Webb's was sold to Edinburgh Crystal. The Stourbridge factory was closed and the glassmaking processes transferred to Penicuik in Scotland.

Pamela Woodall died on the 28th September 1937, aged eighty-eight and all her children, except for Pamela Holds, were present at her funeral. *The County Express* described her as:

> exceptionally well known in the village, and in a quiet way took a keen interest in local affairs. To the poor she was very kind and many will remember with gratitude her acts of generosity.

Her will stated that Luton House was to be sold and the money raised left equally between her children. Alice appealed to be allowed to remain in Luton House – a reasonable request as she had lived there all her life and had provided her parents with much-needed support. Her siblings initially accepted £600 each from the estate in exchange for their share of the house. However, when they learned that they had been misled about the value of the house and the business, the figure was renegotiated and Alice had to pay £950 to each of the beneficiaries. She was bitter about this allegedly 'unfair' treatment and henceforth had very little to do with her family. The remainder of the estate was divided and on the 10th May 1938, each received £145.17.1.

Alice continued running the business and became a familiar sight at auctions in the area, pursued by collectors who often wooed her with bottles of champagne. Many cameos including 'ivory' cameo vases had been sold to the collections of Albert Revi, Philip Budrose and Bertram Wolfson, and Alice was negotiating the sale of three cameo pieces to the London dealer, Nyman, but before this was completed she was admitted to Ashwood House Nursing Home, Summerhill, where she died on the 12th August 1954. One of her last acts was to agree to help a young writer called Geoffrey W. Beard who was writing an article about George Woodall for *Country Life*. Following Alice's death, Beard was helped by George Calloway Woodall and Connie, who were also charged with clearing Luton House. In a scene reminiscent of Miss Haversham in *Great Expectations*, they describe discovering rotted ball gowns and curtains, and George's room untouched after twenty-nine years. Amongst the personal effects, a floor-safe contained the three pieces of cameo glass which Nyman had wished to purchase, valued at £450. Amy asked for two pieces (*Aphrodite* and *Origin of the Painting*), because they reminded her and George Calloway of the hours she spent

Aquatic Life, white on red vase, 9¼ins (23.5cms), signed Geo Woodall. (*Pilkington Glass Museum*)

White on red vase with peonies and a spider-web border, attributed to the Woodall team. (*The Metropolitan Museum of Art*)

modelling and watching her father at work. The third piece, *Sappho*, had been purchased jointly by Connie and Alice and so now belonged to Connie.[83] Amy, Pamela, Connie and May Woodall received £1999.7s when the estate was sold, but Amy and Connie chose to take the glass in lieu of some money. *Sappho* was valued at £100 and the other pieces at £350 jointly. [84]

The publication of *Nineteenth Century Cameo Glass* by Geoffrey Beard in 1956, reintroduced the world to the delights of cameo and interest has continued. Today, the work of Thomas and George Woodall is exhibited all over the world and attracts large bids at auction. Two of the three pieces kept by Alice at Luton House are now on display at Broadfield House Glass Museum and serve as a fitting tribute to the skill and talent of the Woodall brothers.

Above, detail from an unidentified vase.
(*Photograph by George Woodall*)

Left, unidentified vase with a girl and a seagull.
(*Photograph by George Woodall*)

Far left, W2402 *The Rose*, two-handled vase,
16ins (40.5cms), signed G Woodall.
(*Photograph courtesy of Geoffrey Beard*)

[82] May moved to Waterlooville, nr Portsmouth, in 1974 and died on 11th December 1979. Reginald Woodall (d 8th December 1981) worked in the printing trade and married Annie Rachel Brooks in 1940. Their son Keith, (b 1941) married Christine Taylor in 1971. Rachel is still alive.

[83] *Sappho* had been auctioned at Sotheby's on Wednesday 16th June 1926. Lot 26 was bought for £22 from Mr Clement Harris of Tettenhall a friend of George and a keen cameo collector.

[84] Amy and Frank Meese received their share from Pamela Woodall's estate and moved to Primrose Hill, Wordsley, where they lived with their son's wife and two children during the Second World War. When Frank died and George was demobbed, Amy moved into sheltered housing, and died on the 28th January 1957. Florence Payton (b 1911), married George Calloway Woodall in 1932. They had two daughters, Pamela (b 1933), and Jill (b 1939). George Calloway Woodall died on the 8th April 1975, and Florence on the 22nd April 1984. Pamela Woodall married John Hatch, they had two sons: Robert Hatch (b 1959), who has three daughters, Tessa (b 1990), Jane (b 1992, and Elizabeth (b 1996); and Gideon (b 1961), who has two children, Eliza (b 1994), and Alfred (b 1998). John Hatch died in June 1992, his widow Pamela married his brother, Ronald, in 1994. Jill Woodall married Godfrey Perry on 14th June 1958. They have two children: Christopher (b 1969), and Victoria (b 1974).

George Woodall in his
studio, c1915.
(*Photograph courtesy of
The Corning Museum of
Glass*)

Four random pages from a Webb's Pattern Book which illustrates a great many of the Woodall designs, usually with pattern numbers relating to the Webb's Price Book (see page 125). The Pattern Book is reproduced in its entirety as a separate publication by Richard Dennis Publications. *(Courtesy of Edinburgh Glass Co.)*

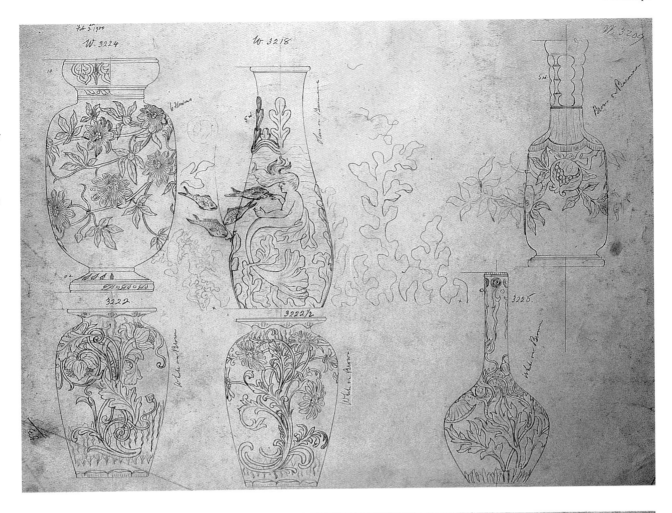

W3218
See page 67

GW6
See page 107

GW7
See page 101

W3260 &
W3261
See page 80

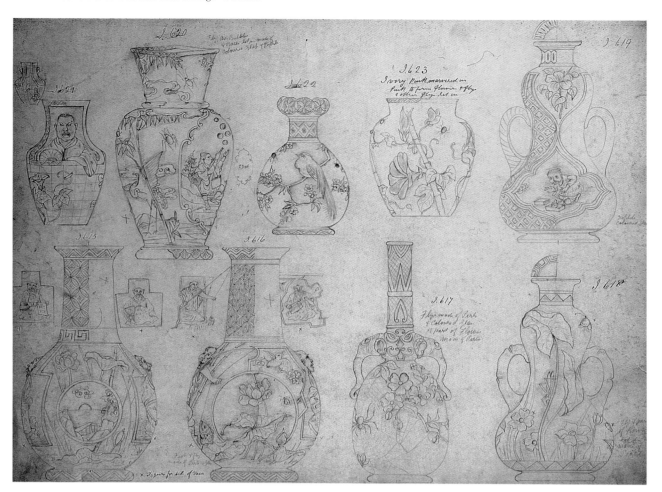

Pages from the Webb Pattern Book with I-numbers.

Above with typical 'ivory' Oriental subjects, below with more unusual floral designs.

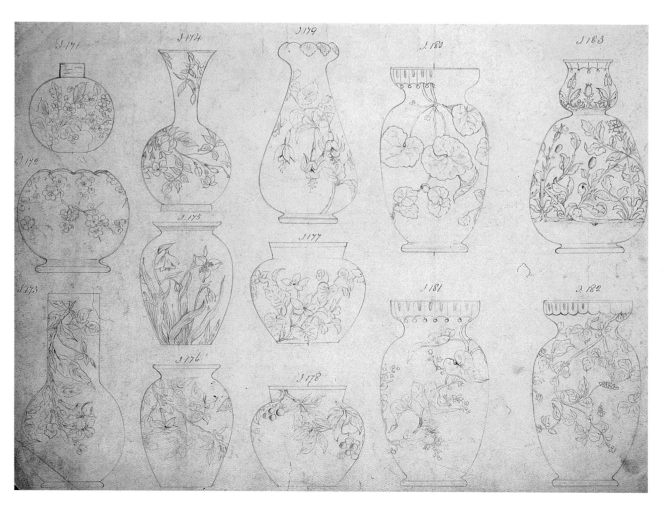

Thomas Webb & Sons' Price Book

The information in this Appendix is primarily taken from the Thomas Webb Price Book of the Woodall brothers' pieces, which allegedly records all their finished work for the firm. More cameo was produced as private enterprises, given away as seconds or completed as private commissions after George Woodall's retirement. Consequently, the Price Book has been checked with record held in museums, family archives and private collections. This combination of data has produced a more detailed guide to the work of the team who marked their pieces Gem Cameo. I have excluded pieces of 'ivory' cameo that were not made by the Woodalls. Work designed by Kretschman has been included when George Woodall also had an input. Below is Webb's pricing code as glass collectors may come across pieces which still bear the original price tag.

P R O V I D E N C H*	X	A
1 2 3 4 5 6 7 8 9 10	0	Repeat previous number

So, H/PA would be £10.11s or PX/PA was also £10.11s

*The 'H' replaced the second 'E' in the word PROVIDENCE to avoid confusion if two 'Es' were in the same word.

From the factory records and the amount of money paid for the work, it is possible to surmise the task of each member of the Woodall team: **Facer** was in charge of acid-resist work and his team would have prepared the cameo blank prior to carving; **Nash** would finish a piece as a punty, flatting off the base; **Barbe** was an enameller and gilder.

Key to text:

Carafe – a type of jug referred to as 'Croft' in the Price Book.
Clareteen – a type of decanter with no stopper and a wider neck.
Diaper – an ornamental design of diamond reticulation (i.e. a network pattern).
Italicised titles – titles recorded by the Woodalls.
Making – this refers to the amount of pieces made during a shift. Written in the Price Book as 'Make per turn'. A turn was the technical term used to refer to a six-hour shift. A move was half-a-shift, i.e. three hours. The smaller the pieces, the more were made by each glassblowing shift.
Non-italicised titles – adopted titles.
Private commission – George Woodall worked alone to specific instructions for a privately agreed price.
Toilet – pieces made as part of a toilet set designed for use in the bathroom. Toilet sets could include toothbrush holders, perfume sprayers and drinking cups
Unavailable – no information available at present.
Unlisted – space left empty in the Price Book or piece is not in the Price Book.
F = Fritsche GW = George Woodall **Gem** – a Woodall team piece where the works number is unknown **Gem Cameo** – the stamped mark on the base used to identify the work of the Woodall team **I** = 'ivory' pattern number **K** = Kretschman **TW** = Thomas Woodall **Rich** – a piece made by the Richardson factory, which was remodelled by George Woodall **Signed** – a piece signed by George Woodall where the works number is unknown **W** = Woodall team

Abbreviations:
B.H.G.M. – Broadfield House Glass Museum **C.M.G** – Corning Museum of Glass **Coll** – collection **Ex** – Exhibition **G.C.** – Gem Cameo **Mus** – Museum **PC** – private collection **Texas A&M** – MSC Forsyth Centre Galleries Texas A&M University

No.	Description of Piece	Costs of Workmen and Sale Price (SP)	History/Whereabouts
A1	5" cameo white on blue lampbody: *Apple Blossom*.	Unlisted SP 33/-	
B1	$4\frac{1}{2}$" cameo white on pink topaz lampbody: *Cori*… and *Butterfly*.	Unlisted SP 33/-	
C1	$5\frac{1}{2}$" cameo white on ruby on topaz lampbody: *Hawthorn*.	Unlisted SP 33/-	
D1	$5\frac{1}{2}$" cameo white on ruby on topaz lampbody with flowers.	Unlisted SP 33/-	
F100	$6\frac{1}{2}$" opal on dark green gilded vase with tadpoles with gilt enamelled neck.	Facer 15/-; Barbe 4/6; Nash 1/6; Engraving 2/6 SP 63/-	PC.
F100$\frac{1}{2}$	$7\frac{1}{2}$" opal on dark green gilded vase with tadpoles with gilt enamelled neck.	Facer 15/-; Barbe 4/6; Nash 1/6; Engraving 2/6 SP 60/-	
F101	7" green on Burmese coloured vase with bird and tree.	Facer 10/-; Barbe 2/6; Nash 9d; Engraving 20/- SP £5.5s	
F102	$8\frac{1}{2}$" flatsided flint on opal vase, carved and gilded with oriental bird and boat scene.	Facer 18/-; Barbe 5/6; Nash 2/-; Kretschman 45/- SP Unlisted	
F102$\frac{1}{2}$	$8\frac{1}{2}$" flatsided flint on opal vase, carved and gilded with oriental bird, mouse, man, parasol scene.	Facer 20/-; Barbe 15/-; Nash 2/1; Kretschman 45/- SP Unlisted	
F103	$5\frac{1}{2}$" Burmese on cameo vase, carved and gilded with bird and flowers, twisted neck effect.	Facer 3/-; Barbe 2/-; Nash 6d; Engraving 9/- SP 90/-	
F104	6" carved vase.	Facer 10/-; Barbe 21/-; Engraving 1/6 SP 35/-	
F105	$8\frac{1}{2}$" carved and gilded curio vase.	Facer 20/-; Barbe 12/6; Nash 1/6; Engraving 25/- SP £10	
F106	$4\frac{1}{2}$" carved and gilded curio bowl with birds and pattern.	Facer 40/-; Barbe 4/-; Engraving 2/6 SP £6	
F107	$8\frac{1}{2}$" carved and gilded curio vase with twists of pattern.	Facer 10/-; Barbe 8/-; Engraving 18/- SP 100/-	Damaged, reduced to $5\frac{3}{4}$"after repairs. In Webb's Museum until sold abroad. Now in PC.
F108	6" carved curio vase.	Facer 4/-; Engraving 8/- SP 25/-	
F109	$6\frac{1}{2}$" carved curio vase.	Facer 3/-; Engraving 6/- SP 25/-	
F110	7" carved and gilded curio vase.	Facer 25/-; Barbe 2/-; Engraving 15/- SP 100/-	
F111	$6\frac{1}{2}$" green mossled glass on flatsided jade curio vase with flowers and animal.	Facer 35/-; Nash 2/6; Plain blank 15/- SP £4.10	
F112	$11\frac{1}{2}$" gilded curio gourd ruby on brown on ivory vase with coloured metal leaves and green crockled ground.	Facer 10/-; Barbe 3/-; Nash 2/6; Engraving 24/- SP 90/-	
F113	9" opal on ruby curio vase with bird on stand with Cupid. Enamelled flint foot.	Facer 15/-; Barbe 5/6; Nash 1/6 SP 55/-	
F114	$5\frac{1}{2}$" carved jade vase.	Facer 12/-; Cutting 2/-; Engraving 40/- SP £6.10	
F114	7" gilded curio bowl.	Facer 10/-; Barbe 1/3; SP Unlisted	
F115	7" gilded curio vase with flowers. In Sketch Book F signified Fritsche.	Facer 15/-; Barbe 8/6; Nash 1/6; Engraving 15/- SP £5	
F115/2	9" flatsided curio vase.	Unlisted SP £18	
F116	8" gilded curio vase.	Facer 25/-; Barbe 8/- SP 100/-	
F118	10" white and light blue on ruby vase with bird and iris. Marked G.C.	Woodall estimate 75/- SP £10.10s	Formerly Parkington Coll, now B.H.G.M.
F119	White on ruby jug with flowers.	Woodall estimate 8/-, made for 15/- SP 42/-	Formerly in A.C. Revi Collection, now in PC.
F120	10" white on ruby vase with peony. Signed Geo Woodall.	Woodall estimate 30/- SP £5.10	Formerly in Arthur Knowles Collection now in PC.
F121	10" white on ruby vase with flowers.	Woodall estimate 12/- SP 55/- reduced to 45/-	

No.	Description of Piece	Costs of Workmen and Sale Price (SP)	History/Whereabouts
F122	6" white on ruby and white inside vase with flowers.	Woodall estimate 6/- SP 25/-	
F123	5" white and blue on ruby inside vase with flowers.	Woodall estimate 5/6 SP 18/-	
F124	2½" white on ruby vase with strawberries.	Woodall estimate 7/6 SP 20/-	
F125	5" white on topaz vase.	Woodall estimate 3/6 SP 12/6	
F126	5" white on blue on ruby vase.	Woodall estimate 6/- SP 21/-	
F127	8½" white on ruby on blue vase with flowers and oriental pattern neck.	Woodall estimate 25/- SP 84/-	
F128	8½" white on topaz vase with flowers.	Woodall estimate 16/- SP 50/-	
F129	White on topaz square bottle with jasmine.	Woodall estimate 12/- SP 30/-	
F130	8" white on blue on flint vase with flowers.	Woodall estimate 16/-, diaper extra 6/- SP 50/-, 63/- with diaper	
F131	7½" white on ruby on flint vase with flowers.	Woodall estimate 30/-, diaper extra 5/9 SP £4.10s	
F132	9" white on blue vase.	Woodall estimate 16/6 SP 63/-	
F133	7" white on blue on ruby vase with flowers.	Woodall estimate 10/6, diaper extra 5/- SP 42/-, 50/- with diaper	
F134	3½" white on pink on topaz vase with flowers.	Woodall estimate 1/6, diaper extra 1/1 SP 6/-, 8/6 with diaper	
F135	4½" red on ivory vase with flowers.	Woodall estimate 7/-, diaper extra 3/3 SP 20/-, 25/- with diaper	
F136	4½" white on red on ivory vase with flowers.	Woodall estimate 7/- SP 20/-	
F137	5½" white on ruby on topaz vase with flowers.	Woodall estimate 4/- SP 15/-	
F138	6" white on ruby on topaz vase with flowers.	Woodall estimate 5/- SP 18/-	
F139	6" white on blue vase with flowers.	Woodall estimate 3/-, diaper extra 2/9 SP 12/6, 18/- with diaper	
F140	8" white on topaz vase with flowers.	Woodall estimate 10/-, diaper extra 5/3 SP 32/-, 40/- with diaper	
F141	9½" white on topaz vase.	Woodall estimate 12/-, diaper extra 7/9 SP 42/-, 55/- with diaper	
F142	10" white on topaz vase with flowers. Marked G.C.	Woodall estimate 14/- SP 42/-	Sold by Joels Auctioneers, now in PC, Melbourne
F143	10" white on blue vase with flowers.	Woodall estimate 15/- SP 45/-	
F144	9" white on blue vase with wild roses.	Woodall estimate 30/- SP 88/-	
F145	6" flatsided ruby on green on rich yellow with opal inside vase with birds and stylised patterns.	Woodall £4 SP £15 reduced to £12.11	
F146	9" white on blue vase with narcissus.	Woodall estimate 35/-; Barbe 4/6 SP 95/-	
F146	Ivory on flint part cameo, part engraved vase with central flowering cup and stylised pattern surround.	Fritsche estimate 30/- SP £4	
F147	8" white on yellow body vase with roses	Woodall 10/-, diaper extra 5/6 SP 40/-	
F147	Flatsided jade vase with ovals of storks with flowers surround	Woodall estimate 24/- SP 63/-	
F148	4" white on blue vase with tapered neck with flowers	Woodall estimate 4/- SP 10/-	
F149	White on ruby on flint globe bowl with roses	Woodall estimate 3/-, diaper extra 3/6 SP 16/6	
F150	9" white on ruby vase with apple blossom.	Woodall estimate 13/6, diaper extra 7/1 SP 50/-	
F151	9" light blue on white on ruby vase with flowers.	Woodall estimate 20/- SP 50/-	
F152	9½" white on yellow vase with flowers.	Diaper extra 6/6 SP 60/-	
F153	9" white on ruby vase: *Flowers*.	Woodall estimate 13/6, diaper extra 6/6 SP 50/-	
F154	9" white on blue vase: *Flowers*.	Unlisted SP 40/-, later reduced	
F155	10" white on topaz vase with flowers.	Woodall estimate 16/-, diaper extra 5/6 SP 50/-	
F156	6" white on blue vase with flowers.	Woodall estimate 18/6 SP 45/-	
F157	7" white on blue vase with flowers.	Woodall estimate 9/- SP 30/-	
F158	4½" white on blue vase with mistletoe.	Diaper 2/6 SP 14/6	
F159	6" white on topaz vase with flowers.	Diaper 3/3 SP 30/-	
F160	7" white on topaz vase with grapes.	Diaper 3/9 SP 35/-	
F162	7½" white on blue vase with flowers.	Diaper 4/3 SP 38/-	
F163	White on ruby on topaz clareteen with passion flowers.	Diaper extra 3/6 SP 38/-	
F163½	Cut down version of F163, now a vase.	38/- to make SP unlisted	
F164	9" white on topaz vase: *Vine* with grapes.	Diaper extra 5/9 SP 50/-	
F165	9" white on topaz vase with phlox.	Diaper extra 5/9 SP 50/-	
F166	8" white on topaz vase with morning glory.	Diaper extra 4/6 SP 38/-	
F167	8" white on topaz vase.	Diaper extra 5/- SP 40/-	
F168	8" white on topaz vase with flowers.	Diaper extra 5/3 SP 45/-	
F169	10" white on brown vase with flowers.	Unlisted SP 60/-	
F170	White on pale claret vase with acorns.	Woodall 24/- SP unlisted	
F171	6" flint with green bottle with faked up enamelled flowers.	Barbe 10/6; PJ 30d; Cut 9d SP £4	
F172	White on blue globe toilet vase for mounting with flowers.	Unlisted SP 18/-	
F173	White on blue globe toilet vase for mounting with flowers.	Unlisted SP 18/-	
F174	White on topaz globe toilet vase for mounting.	Unlisted SP 12/-	
F175	7" white on blue salad bowl with morning glories. Marked G.C.	Unlisted SP 33/-	Formerly Bertram Wolfson Collection. Sold at Jackson's 1998 for $1680, now in PC.
F176	White on ruby salad bowl (white on blue at base) with honeysuckle.	Unlisted SP 36/-	
F177	White on brown on topaz salad bowl.	Unlisted SP 28/-	
F178	White on topaz biscuit jar.	Unlisted SP 18/6	
F179	White on ruby biscuit jar with flowers.	Unlisted SP 25/-	
F180	6" green bronze inside iridescent vase, faint outside with four peacock feathers. Enamel neck.	Barbe 3/6; Cutting 1/6; Engraving 4/6 SP 100/-	
F181	14" white on chinese yellow vase: *Figure playing tambourine and two children with flowers*.	George Woodall estimate £20 SP £45 (NB one of J. Locke's designs)	Sold for £25 in 1900.
Family	10" dark blue and white on aquamarine vase: *Phyllis at the Fountain*. Signed Geo Woodall.	Not intended for sale	Sold by Alice Woodall in 1938 to Mrs MW Holmes. Resold Sotheby's for £12000, now in PC.
Family	10" white on purple plaque: *Diana and Nymph Bathing*. Signed G Woodall 1878.	Not paid. Not for sale.	Experimental plaque given away c1900 Eventually in the Rakow Coll. Now in PC.

No.	Description of Piece	Costs of Workmen and Sale Price (SP)	History/Whereabouts
Family	13" white on light brown plaque: *The Favourite*. Signed T & G Woodall. (The second plaque with this title signed T & G Woodall was sold by Phillips 1984, £15,000-17,000).	Not for sale.	In Webb Museum until 1982. Sold at Phillips in 1982. Formerly in Runyon Family, now Texas A&M.
Family	3" white on amber vase, decorated with flowers.	Not for sale.	Given by Thos Woodall to daughter Ida when she married. Passed down the Petford family, now in FC.
Family	4" red slab: *Bird on a Branch*. Unsigned and unfinished.	Not for sale.	Rescued by Thomas Bott Woodall, passed to Reginald Woodall, then to son Keith, now in PC.
Family	4" white on blue oval brooch: *Perseus and Andromeda*. Signed GW.	Not for sale.	Given to to A Wood on their marriage, now in PC.
Family	4" white on red slab: Pamela Holds wearing a pearl necklace.	Not for sale	Given to Pamela, now in Family Collection.
Family	4" white on amber vase with oriental patterns and dragons.	Unfinished by T Woodall and taken by him when he retired. Not for sale	Given to Mrs J Scriven, passed to Mr & Mrs Wilday-Allin, passed to Miss J Scriven, then to Miss C Thomas. Now in PC.
Family	5" plaque: *Armenian Girl*. Signed Geo Woodall.	Not for sale.	Bequest from Lucas family, now B.H.G.M.
Family	6" white on red vase with a griffin and flowers.	Not for sale.	Given to cousin of Geo Woodall. Sold Sotheby's in Dec 1965 to W Chrysler Jr. Now in Chrysler Mus.
Family	6" white on red vase: *Nov 14th 1894*. Marked G.C.	Not for sale.	Formerly in Alice Woodall collection now in B.H.G.M.
Family	6¼" portrait medallions: *Dr and Mrs Samuel Parkes Cadman*. Signed Geo Woodall.	Not for sale.	Given to Parkes Cadman. Formerly in the Rakow Coll, now in the C.M.G.
Family	8" white on claret plaque without border: *Aphrodite*. Signed Geo Woodall.	Not for sale.	Alice Woodall collection, then GC Woodall, then J Perry & P Hatch. Now in PC. Exhibited at the B.H.G.M.
Family	9" white on raisin brown vase with cover: *The Origin of the Painting*. Signed Geo Woodall.	Not for sale.	Alice Woodall collection, then GC Woodall, then J Perry & P Hatch, now held by C &V Perry. Exhibited at B.H.G.M.
Family	Cut crystal brooch: *John the Baptist*.	Not for sale	Given to Dr & Mrs Parkes Cadman, now in PC.
Family	Pink on white tazza dish.	Unfinished SP Not for sale	Given to T Woodall, passed to members of family, now on loan to B.H.G.M.
GW001	12" panel: *Poetry*. Signed Geo Woodall.	Woodall £45 SP £130	Formerly with Leo Kaplan Ltd.
GW002	Vase: *Autumn*. Dated Nov 1899 in Price Book.	Woodall £30.10s SP £85	
GW003	13¼" white on brown vase: *Night*. Signed Geo Woodall.	Woodall £45 SP £120	Formerly in the Anna Wolfson Coll, now in PC.
GW004	See W2848		
GW004	Small panel: *Cleopatra*. Signed Geo Woodall.	Woodall £2.15s SP £6.10s	
GW005	White on brown vase: *Morning*. Signed Geo Woodall.	Woodall £45 SP £120	
GW006	10" flatsided white on brown vase: *Sea Foam*. Signed Geo Woodall.	Woodall £27.10.6 SP £63	
GW007	11" white on brown vase: *Pharoah's Daughter*. Signed G Woodall.	Woodall £40 SP £95	Sold to Adelaide Public Library. After being repaired it was de-accessed. Bought by Woodall descendant for $65 in Adelaide antique shop.
GW008	9" white on brown vase: *Luna*. Signed Geo Woodall.	Woodall £7 SP Unlisted	
GW009	7" white on brown vase: *Aurora*. Signed Geo Woodall.	Woodall £8 SP Unlisted	
GW010	7" white on brown on flint vase: *Flora*. Signed Geo Woodall.	Woodall £5.10s SP £14	Leo Kaplan Ltd.
GW011	7" white on brown on flint vase: *Pluvia*. Signed Geo Woodall.	Woodall £5.10s SP £14	Sold at Early's Auction Hse on 31.7.1998 for $30,800, now in PC.
GW012	6½" white on brown on flint flatsided vase: *Penelope*. Signed Geo Woodall.	Woodall £6.10s SP £!6	
GW013	6¾" white on brown vase: *Psyche*. Signed Geo Woodall.	Woodall £7 SP £16	Sold damaged at Phillips, 1997 for £2700 to London dealer, then purchased by B.H.G.M.
GW013a	7½" white on brown vase: *Psyche*. Signed Geo Woodall.	Woodall £7.10s SP £18	Sold Sotheby's 1985, £16,500 to Runyon Coll.
GW013a	Design folio 25 – no more details in Price Book.		
GW014	7" white on brown on flint vase: *The Message*. Signed Geo Woodall.	Woodall £6.15s SP £16	
GW015	6½" white on brown vase: *Chase*. Signed Geo Woodall.	Woodall £7 SP £17	GW15 and GW16 sold to Buckley Hall on 3.7. 1907 for £12 each.
GW016	6½" white on brown vase: *Caught*. Signed Geo Woodall.	Woodall £7 SP £17	GW15 and GW16 sold to Buckley Hall on 3.7. 1907 for £12 each.
GW017	7½" white on brown vase: *Terpsichore*. Signed G Woodall, Inv. et Sculpt.	Woodall £8 SP £18	
GW018	8" white on brown vase: *Juno*. Signed Geo Woodall.	Woodall £8 SP £18	
GW018	Amber, blue, ruby and white with amber inside vase with jasmine. From sketchbook.	Woodall 18/- SP Unlisted	
GW019	7½" white on brown vase: *Serpentina*. Signed Geo Woodall.	Woodall £8.5s SP £18.10s	
GW020	7½" white on brown vase: *Dawn*. Signed Geo Woodall.	Woodall £8.10s SP £18.10	
GW021	6¼ flatsided white on brown vase: *Ceramia*. Signed Geo Woodall.	Woodall £8 SP £18.10s	Sold at Phillips, 1997 for £16,000. Now in PC.
GW022	9" white on brown vase: *Painting*. Signed G Woodall.	Woodall £13.10s SP £35	Sold to Tiffany, NY, 13.6.1901. Now in PC.
GW023	8½" white on brown vase: *Night*. Signed Geo Woodall.	Woodall £8.5s SP £18.10s	Formerly in the AC Revi Collection. Now in PC.
GW024	8½" white on brown vase: *Morning*. Signed Geo Woodall.	Woodall £8.5s SP £18.10s	Sold to Tiffany, NY, 1901.
GW025	8¾" x 4¼" white on brown vase: *Sirene*. Signed Geo Woodall.	Woodall £11.10s SP £30	PC.
GW026	7" white on brown vase: *Diana*. Signed Geo Woodall.	Woodall £8.5s SP £18.10s	
GW26a	7¼" white on brown vase: *Diana*. Signed Geo Woodall.	Woodall £8.5s SP £21	Formerly Runyon Coll, now in Texas A&M.
GW027	7½" white on brown vase: *Hebe*. Signed Geo Woodall.	Woodall £8 SP £18	
GW028	See W2786	Woodall £73.10s SP £175	

No.	Description of Piece	Costs of Workmen and Sale Price (SP)	History/Whereabouts
GW029	7" white on brown vase: *Pomina*. Signed Geo Woodall.	Woodall £8.10s SP £18.10s	
GW030	20" plaque: *The Dance*. Signed Geo Woodall	Woodall £175 SP £450 reduced to `£350	Destroyed by fire in 1910.
GW031	6¾" white on blue on brown panel: *An Undine*. Signed Geo Woodall and A Choice Bit.	Woodall £35 SP £90	Sold 1917, formerly Runyon Coll, now Texas A&M.
GW032	12½" panel: *Calypso*. Signed Geo Woodall. Dated Oct 1902 in Price Book.	Woodall £35 SP £90 reduced to £60	At least 2 versions of this exist. Location unavailable.
GW033	12¼" white on brown panel: *Andromache*. Signed Geo Woodall.	Woodall £35 SP £90	Formerly Rakow Coll, now C.M.G.
GW034	13" white on claret on blue plaque: *Lord Kelvin*. Signed Geo Woodall.	Woodall £75 SP £180	Presented to Royal Soc, 1905. Now in RS Coll.
GW035	Plaque: *Sirene*. Signed Geo Woodall.	Unlisted SP £38	
GW113	Plaque on marble: *Aphrodite*. Signed Geo Woodall. Dated Nov 1904 in Price Book.	Woodall 63/- SP £7.7s	Customer later became British American Glass Co. Now in PC.
GW114	Green marble base, mounted like a mirror. For *Copal: Sirene*. Signed Geo Woodall.	Woodall 63/- SP £7.7s	Given to Webb's Australian agent, John Shorter. *Copal* signifies destination. Now in Shorter Coll.
GW115	5½" plaque mounted on a green marble base: *Sirene*. Signed Geo Woodall.	Woodall 63/- SP £7.10s	Exhibited in London prior to sale. Now in PC.
GW116	Vase: *Flora*.	Woodall 63/- SP £7.10s	
GW117	Oval brooch: *Greek Slave*.	Woodall 21/-; polishing 1/- SP £2.5s	
GW118	Oval brooch: *Nature's Mirror*.	Woodall 21/-; polishing 1/- SP £2.5s	
GW119	Oval brooch.	Woodall 21/- SP £2.5s	
GW119	Oval brooch: *Sea Nymph*.	Woodall 21/- SP £2.5s	
GW119	Oval brooch: *The Dove*. Dated Feb 23rd in Price Book.	Woodall 21/- SP £2.5s	
GW120	Oval brooch: *Gathering Pearls*.	Woodall 21/- SP £2.5s	
GW120-	Oval brooch: *Venus Rising from the Sea*.	Woodall 21/- SP £2.5s	
GW120	Oval brooch: *The Dance*. Dated March in Price Book.	Woodall 21/- SP £2.5s	
GW121	Oval brooch: *A Syrene*.	Woodall 21/- SP £2.5s	
GW121	Oval brooch: *Penelope*.	Woodall 21/- SP £2.5s	
GW121	Oval brooch: *Sappho*. Dated 30th March in Price Book.	Woodall 21/- SP £2.5s	
GW122	Oval brooch: *Bacchanate*	Woodall 21/- SP £2.5s	
GW122	Oval brooch: *Diana*.	Woodall 21/- SP £2.5s	
GW122	Oval brooch: *Girl in the Clouds*.	Woodall 21/- SP £2.5s	
GW122	Oval brooch: *Nature's Mirror*.	Woodall 21/- SP £2.5s	
GW122	Oval brooch: *Pandora*.	Woodall 21/- SP £2.5s	
GW122	Oval brooch: *Venus Rising from the Sea*.	Woodall 21/- SP £2.5s	
GW123	13" red plaque: *Wild Waves*. Signed Geo Woodall. Dated 6th May 1908 in Price Book.	Woodall £40 SP £120	Exhibited in Turin 1911.
GW124	16" white on green flint vase: *The Polar Vase*. Signed Geo Woodall. Dated 9th May 1908 in Price Book	Vase £3; Lionel Pearce's etching 40/-; Woodall £10.10s SP £35	Exhibited in Webb's Museum, then Runyon Coll, now Texas A&M.
GW125	18" white on deep amethyst plaque: *At Cupid's Shrine*. Signed Geo Woodall. Dated 9th May 1908 in Price Bk.	Woodall £110 SP £450, reduced to £300	Sold to Finnigans, 1917, £250, then to C.W. Harris. Resold Sotheby's, 1926, £140, then Sotheby's 1965, £7600 to Rakow Coll, now C.M.G.
GW126	10" white on blue vase: *Phyllis*. Signed Geo Woodall.	Unlisted SP Unlisted	Leo Kaplan Ltd.
GW129	6" white on brown panel: *Vestal*. Signed Geo Woodall.	Unlisted SP Unlisted	Ellman Coll.
GW130	7" white on brown vase: *A Message*. Signed Geo Woodall.	Woodall £4.10s SP £12	
GW131	7" white on brown vase: *Feathered Favourites*. Signed Geo Woodall	Woodall £4.10s SP £12	Formerly Ash Coll, now in PC.
GW132	7¾" white on brown vase: *Ocean Gems*. Signed Geo Woodall.	Woodall £4.10s SP £14	
GW133	7¾" white on brown vase: *Seaweed*. Signed Geo Woodall.	Woodall £4.10s SP £14	
GW134	7" white on brown vase: *Soppa*. Signed Geo Woodall.	Woodall £4.10s SP £12	
GW135	7" white on brown vase: *Tambourina*. Signed Geo Woodall.	Woodall £4.10s SP £12	
GW136	6" white on brown vase: *Nautilus*. Signed Geo Woodall.	Woodall £4.10s SP £12	
GW137	6" white on brown vase: *Dolphin*. Signed Geo Woodall.	Woodall £4.10s SP £12	
GW138	White inside brown and flint vase with roughly cameoed coloured flowers.	Woodall £2.10s SP Unlisted	At Turin Exhibition, 1909.
GW139	7" white on brown vase: *Morning*. Signed Geo Woodall.	Woodall 100/- SP £15	
GW140	7" white on brown vase: *Night*. Signed Geo Woodall. Dated August 1909 in Price Book.	Woodall 100/- SP £15	
GW141	14" vase: *The Antarctic*. Signed Geo Woodall.	Unlisted SP £42	Exhibited at Turin, 1909, for £63.
GW142	9" plaque: *Edin*. Signed Geo Woodall.	Woodall 40/- SP £90	Exhibited at Turin 1909, for £135. At Brussels Ex. for £120, destroyed by fire in 1910.
GW143	8" vase: *Flora Captive*. Signed Geo Woodall.	Woodall 10/- SP £23	Exhibited at Turin, 1909, for £55. At Brussels Ex. for £120, destroyed by fire in 1910.
GW144	8" vase: *Flora Surprise*. Signed Geo Woodall.	Woodall 10/- SP £23	Exhibited at Turin, 1909, for £35. At Brussels Ex. for £120, destroyed by fire in 1910.
GW145	11" white on blue on cinnamon brown plaque: *Origin of the Painting*. Signed Geo Woodall.	Woodall £30 SP £80	At Brussels Ex. for £120, destroyed by fire, 1910.
GW145b	10" white on blue cinnamon brown plaque: *Origin of the Painting*. Unsigned.	Unlisted SP Piece unfinished	Commissioned with the insurance money from GW145. Webb's Mus until 1982, formerly in Runyon Coll. now in Texas A&M.
GW146	11" plaque: *Aphrodite*. Signed Geo Woodall.	Woodall £120 SP £400	At Turin Ex., now in PC.
GW147	5" red slab: *Sea Shells*. Signed Geo Woodall.	Woodall 90/- SP £12	At Turin Ex.
GW148	5" red slab: *Idle Moments*. Signed Geo Woodall.	Woodall 90/- SP £12	At Turin Ex., then F. Smith Coll, now in PC.
GW149	4" red slab: *Seaweeds*. Signed Geo Woodall.	Woodall 60/- SP £9	At Turin Ex.
GW150	4" red slab: *Nautilus*. Signed Geo Woodall.	Woodall 60/- SP £9	At Turin Ex.
GW151	7" white on brown vase: *Springtime*. Signed Geo Woodall.	Woodall £6 SP £15	At Turin Ex.

No.	Description of Piece	Costs of Workmen and Sale Price (SP)	History/Whereabouts
GW152	7½" white on brown vase: *Caught*. Dated 29th July 1913 in Price Book.	Woodall £8 SP £20	
GW153	7½" white on brown vase: *Sea Gulls*. Signed Geo Woodall.	Woodall £8 SP £20	Formerly Runyon Coll, now Texas A&M.
GW154	6¼"x5" white on claret oval panel: *Sappho*. Signed Geo Woodall.	Woodall £7.10s SP £21	Bought by C. Harris, sold, Sotheby's 1926, to Alice and Connie Woodall. Now in Family Coll.
GW155	6¼"x5" white on claret oval panel: *The Pearl Necklace*. Signed Geo Woodall.	Woodall £7.10s SP £21	Sold Sotheby's, 1988 for £16000, acquired by MBC, now in B.H.G.M..
Dudley			
GW156	8"x4" white on brown vase: *Venus* with naked girl standing upright in waves. Signed Geo Woodall.	Woodall £8.10s SP £42	Made in 1913, sold 1915, now Leo Kaplan Ltd.
GW157	8¼"x4" white on purple vase: *Syrena*. Signed Geo Woodall. Dated 20th January 1914 in Price Book.	Woodall £10.10s SP £26	Completed in Jan 1914, formerly in Mitman Coll, sold, Sotheby's, 1995, £8500, now in PC.
GW158	8"x5¼" white on plum vase with oval top: *Diana*. Signed Geo Woodall. Dated 9th March 1914 in Price Book.	Woodall £14 SP Unlisted	Sold, Sotheby's, £14500.
GW159	12" white on blue on raisin brown vase: *Undine*. Signed Geo Woodall. Dated 27th June 1914 in Price Book.	Woodall £35 SP £85	Sold Sotheby's, 1979, £25000, bought by Runyon Coll, now in Texas A&M.
GW160	10¾" plaque: *Aphrodite*. Signed Geo Woodall. Dated 3rd September 1914 in Price Book.	Woodall £30 SP £95	Sold Sotheby's, 1977, £11500. Formerly in Runyon Coll, now in Texas A&M.
GW161	10½" white on brown plaque: *Syrene*. Signed Geo Woodall.	Woodall £35 SP £95	Sold to Edward's Glasgow, 1916, sold Sotheby's, 1970s to A Tilman for £6500, now in PC.
GW162	9½" white on brown plaque: *Syrene*. Signed Alice Woodall, A Song of the Sea. Geo Woodall.	Woodall £30 SP £90	Formerly Wolfson Coll, now in PC.
GW163	7" oval white on purple vase, body 5¼"x4½": *The Origin of the Harp*. Dated 7th February 1918 in Price Book.	Woodall £12.10s SP £40	Sold to Phillips, 1918.
GW164	14" white on citrine vase: *Antarctic Vase*.	Woodall figure illegible; Etching 100/-; Fereday £5 SP £50	Sold to Phillips, £45, then in Revi, then Chrysler Colls, now in the Chrysler Museum, USA.
GW189	7" vase: *Night*. Signed Geo Woodall.	Unlisted SP Unlisted	
GW?	2" oval brooch with unfinished *Undine* design.	Unlisted SP Unlisted	Formerly in Grover Coll. Texas A&M.
Gem	8" white on topaz vase with Mars. Marked G.C.	Unlisted SP £15	Offered for sale at Buckley House on 21.1.1885.
Gem	9¼" 3-layered plate with two dragons and patterns. Marked G.C.	Unlisted SP Unlisted	Formerly in Bertram Wolfson Coll. Now in PC.
Gem	10" topaz vase with padded on red glass and enamel decoration. Marked G.C..	Unlisted SP Unlisted	Formerly in Runyon Coll. Texas A&M.
Gem	10½" white and pale yellow on brown vase, vertical pine cones, stylised orange peel reserve. Marked G.C.	Unlisted. but photographed by George Woodall SP Unlisted	Sold Sotheby's 1991, £5280. Now in PC.
Gem	10¾" aubergine on white and blue flask vase with rosette in Oriental style, reverse, bat with peach. Marked G.C.	Unlisted SP Unlisted	Sold Christie's 1978, $14300. Now in PC.
Gem	11" two-handled blue on blue vase, stylised oriental patterns. Signed Theodore B Starr, New York and G.C.	Unlisted SP Unlisted	PC.
Gem	11¼" pink on blue on white vase with stylised oriental patterns. Signed Tiffany & Co Paris Ex 1899 & G.C.	Unlisted SP Unlisted	PC.
Gem	11¼" two-handled white on ruby amphora vase, acanthus around stand of fruit, reverse griffin head. Marked G.C.	Unlisted SP Unlisted	Formerly in Rakow Coll. Now, C.M.G.
Gem	11½" white on pink vase, passion flowers with stippled background on top border. Marked G.C..	Unlisted SP Unlisted	PC.
Gem	12" red on white on citron on flashed white on ivory vase. Marked G.C.	Unlisted SP Unlisted	Formerly Runyon Coll. Now Texas A&M.
Gem	12" three-layered vase, stylised oriental patterns. Marked G.C.	Unlisted SP Unlisted	PC.
Gem	13¾" white on ruby vase, dahlias, bees, sunflowers, dragonflies. Signed Paris Exhibition 1889 and G.C.	Unlisted SP Unlisted	PC.
Gem	14¾" white on amber vase, geraniums. Marked G.C.	Unlisted SP Unlisted	PC.
Gem	16" two-handled white on blue vase, winged females hanging garlands on urn with decoration. Marked G.C.	Unlisted SP Unlisted	Dtd to 1888-9 from photograph of G Woodall carving on it. Formerly Blount Coll. Now in PC.
Gem	16¾" light blue on peacock blue vase, foxglove with foliage with bee and butterfly. Marked G.C.	Unlisted SP Unlisted	Sold Early's Auction Hse, 1994, $25300. Now PC.
Gem	19" white on pink on blue vase, oriental stylised flowers. Signed Tiffany & Co Paris Exhibition 1889 and G.C.	Unlisted SP Unlisted	PC.
Gem	23½" white on ruby vase, foxgloves. Signed Tiffany & Co Paris Exhibition 1889 G.C.	Unlisted SP Unlisted	PC.
Gem	3" white on emerald green vase, parrot perched upon pine bough. Marked G.C.	Unlisted SP Unlisted	Sold Early's 1996, $3520. Now in PC.
Gem	3½" rainbow glass on red vase, rose. Marked G.C.	Unlisted SP Unlisted	Formerly Runyon Coll. Now Texas A&M.
Gem	4¼" white on ruby bowl with a rose spray with forget-me-not on reverse. Marked G.C.	Unlisted SP Unlisted	Sold, Sotheby's, 1979, £1200, now in PC.
Gem	5" ruby cologne vase, three floral panels and stylised decoration. Marked G.C.	Unlisted SP Unlisted	Sold Early's 1999, $4510. Now in PC.
Gem	6½" white on aquamarine vase, honeysuckles. Marked G.C.	Unlisted SP Unlisted	PC.
Gem	6¾" white on satin blue vase, lily of the valley, spring blossom, butterfly. Marked Tiffany & Co Paris Exhibition 1889 & G.C.	Unlisted SP Unlisted	PC.
Gem	7" white on blue bell form vase, gloxinias, foliage and grasses. Marked G.C.	Unlisted SP Unlisted	Sold Early's 1998 , $2475 Now in PC.
Gem	7¾" red on flint vase with cameo tulips and intaglio roses. Gold enamel on rim. Marked G.C.	Unavailable SP Unavailable	Formerly Runyon Coll, now Texas A&M.
Gem	8" vase, flowers with cameo-cutting on blown-out neck. Signed George Woodall and G.C.	Unlisted SP Unlisted	PC.
Gem	8" white on blue on stippled emerald green vase, cherries. Marked G.C.	Unlisted SP Unlisted	PC.
Gem	8" white on blue vase, pensive girl seated by lily pond, one hand holding lamp. Marked G.C.	Unlisted SP Unlisted	Sold Sotheby's 1975, £1400. In PC. A similar vase signed G Woodall also exists in a PC.
Gem	8" white on flint on red vase, dahlias. Marked G.C.	Unlisted SP Unlisted	Formerly Runyon Coll. Now Texas A&M.
Gem	9" four colours on green bulbous vase, grey/green & pink fans with cords, surrounded by leaves, dark pink daisies and fernery held with cord, bow and tassels. Marked G.C.	Unlisted SP Unlisted	Sold Early's 1994, $30,800. Now in PC.
Gem	9" white on lemon vase, flowers. Marked G.C.	Unlisted SP Unlisted	PC.
Gem	9¼" white on aquamarine vase, foxgloves. Marked G.C.	Unlisted SP Unlisted	PC.
Gem	Pink on white on green vase, oriental patterns. Marked G.C.	Unlisted SP Unlisted	Sold 1980 for £3000. Now in PC.
Gem	Red on jade vase, octopus and dragons. Marked Tiffany & Co Paris Exhibition 1889 and G.C.	Unlisted SP Unlisted	PC.
Gem	White on blue vase, rose sprays and thorny borders. Marked Tiffany & Co Paris Exhibition 1889 and G.C.	Unlisted SP Unlisted	Sold Sotheby's 1980, £2600. Now in PC.
Gift	11½" two-handled white on cobalt blue vase: *Crane and Palm*. Signed Geo Woodall.	Unlisted Not for sale	Gift to Richardson family, presented in 1953 to Brierley Hill Library. B.H.G.M.
Gift	13" cut crystal vase, vine branch, blossom with butterfly. Signed Geo Woodall.	Unlisted Not for sale	Given to Stourbridge family, sold Sotheby's 1998 £1300. Now in PC.
Gift	5" white on pale green vase, roses.	Unlisted SP Unlisted	Gift from G Woodall to daughter Alice. Now in PC.
Gift	6" white on green vase, flower and etched leaves on reverse.	Unlisted Not for sale	To Davidson's on retirement, then to C Woodall,

No.	Description of Piece	Costs of Workmen and Sale Price (SP)	History/Whereabouts
K011	6" flatsided jade vase.	Kretschman 85/-; Facer 28/- SP £10.10s	Collection of Leo Kaplan Ltd
K100	5 1/4" flatsided vase, shoreline of houses, boat on lake, town in background.	Kretschman 84/-; Facer 30/- SP Unlisted	Held by owner, then sold to Webb's Mus, then abroad. Formerly Runyon Coll. Now Texas A&M.
K102	4 1/2" mossled glass cameo gilded vase, rocks, pot and small person.	Kretschman 15/-; Facer 7/6; Barbe 6/6 SP 80/-	Made for Webb's after 1911. Exhibited in Webb's Mus then sold abroad. Formerly Runyon Coll now Texas A&M.
K103	7" green on Burmese coloured vase, two birds, one on a tree branch.	Illegible 12/-; Nash 9d; Engraving 25/- SP £6 reduced later	
K105	3 1/2" curio vase.	Kretschman 18/- SP 35/-	Formerly Budrose Coll. Now, Currier Gallery of Art.
K107	6" flatsided cameo vase, Chinese man staring in mirror. Marked G.C.	Kretschman figure illegible SP £6.15s	Commissioned for Thos Goode & Co. Formerly Rakow Coll. Now, C.M.G.
K109	5" jade vase.	Kretschman 25/-; Facer 7/6; Nash 1s SP £3.10s	
K110	6" flatsided jade vase, grapes. Woodall did leafage.	Kretschman 42/-; Woodall 11/-; Nash 1/6; Facer 7/6 SP £7.7s	
K111	5" black on ivory curio bowl, rings of birds, hunters with spears, large cats..	Kretschman 18/6; Nash 3/-; Facer 15/- SP 85/-	
Private	11" x 8 1/2" white on brown portrait panel: *Mr James Winans*. Signed G Woodall 1885.	Unlisted SP Unlisted	
Private	12" white on cobalt blue two-handled vase: *Wild Waves*. Signed Wild Waves By Geo Woodall.	Unlisted SP Unlisted	
Private	13" flatsided cut and engraved flint glass vase with *Undine*. Signed Geo Woodall.	Unlisted SP Unlisted	As *Mr James Winans*, above.
Private	15" red on white on yellow-green on white on dark green dish: *The Great Tazza*. Marked G.C.	Unlisted SP Unlisted	Commissioned privately. PC, USA.
Private	11" x 8 1/2" white on brown portrait panel: *Mrs James Winans*.	Unlisted SP Unlisted	With F Smith, then Runyon Coll, now Texas A&M. Collection Leo Kaplan Ltd.
Private	2 1/2" white on red portrait medallion: *William E Gladstone*. Signed G Woodall & G.C.	Unlisted SP Unlisted	Formerly in Wiggin-Davies Coll, then Mrs J Lewis. Exhibited B'ham Art Gallery, sold 1996. Now in PC.
Private	6" white on blue on brown panel: *Feathered Favourites*. Signed Geo Woodall.	Unlisted SP Unlisted	Sold Sotheby's 1971, £2500, then Runyon Coll. Now, Texas A&M.
Private	6" white on blue plaque: *Syrene*. Signed Geo Woodall.	Unlisted SP Unlisted	
Private	6 1/2" white on cinnamon brown plaque: *Perseus and Andromeda*. Signed Geo Woodall	Unlisted SP Unlisted	
Private	8" white on blue on raisin brown vase: *A Siren*. Signed Geo Woodall.	Unlisted SP Unlisted	Comm by CW Harris, sold Sotheby's 1926, now PC. Formerly Wiggins-Davies Coll, then to son. Exhibited B'ham Art Gallery, sold Sotheby's 1975 for £5800 into Grover Collection. Now in PC.
Private	8 1/4" white on amber vase, cupids and butterflies. Signed Geo Woodall.	Unlisted SP Unlisted	
Private	8 1/2" white on red vase: *Mischief*. Signed Geo Woodall.	Unlisted SP Unlisted	
Private	8 3/4" white on red pedestal bowl.	Unfinished Unlisted SP Unlisted	Passed to Alice Woodall, sold later. Now in PC.
Private	Plaque: *Marion Roberts*. Signed Geo Woodall.	Unlisted SP Unlisted	Commissioned by Mr Roberts, friend of the Parkes Cadman family. Now in PC.
Private	Plaque: *Mrs Martin*. Signed Geo Woodall.	Unlisted SP Unlisted	Commissioned by Dr Martin as gift for his wife.
Rich	10 1/2" white on cobalt blue vase: *Cupid on Panther*.	2 versions by Lechevral, later one exhibited Paris 1878. SP Unlisted	First version remodelled by Woodall, unfinished. Sold by A Woodall 1938 to Mrs M.Holmes; resold at Sotheby's 1976, £600. In Rakow Coll, now in PC.
Rich	11" white on blue vase: *The Birth of Venus*. Signed Geo Woodall and AL 1877.	Originally made 2-handled by Lechevral, exhibited Paris 1878. SP Unlisted	Remodelled by Woodall for Richardson's. Bought by former Rakow Coll, now in the C.M.G.
Rich	7" white on cobalt blue vase: *Love's Area*. Signed Geo Woodall and Tiffany & Co, Paris 1889 and G.C.	Originally made by Lechevral, exhibited Paris 1878. SP Unlisted	Remodelled by Woodall to aid its sale. Sold to Tiffany & Co who stamped it incorrectly believing...
Rich	8" white on blue vase: *Venus Arising from the Sea*. Signed Geo Woodall and AL 1877.	Originally made 2-handled by Lechevral, exhibited Paris 1878. SP Unlisted	Remodelled by Woodall for Richardson's who left it to Brierley Hill Glass Collection.
S100	5 1/4" cameo vase with mount.	Unlisted SP 30/-	Sent in July 1912 to Paul Mohmann.
S101	5" cameo vase with mount. Dated July 1912 in price book.	Unlisted SP 30/-	Sent in July 1912 to Paul Mohmann.
S102	3 3/4" cameo white on flint on ruby lampbody.	Unlisted SP 20/-	Sent in July 1912 to Paul Mohmann.
S103	5 1/2" cameo topaz on ruby on white lampbody.	Unlisted SP 33/-	Sent in July 1912 to Paul Mohmann.
S104	4 1/2" cameo blue on white on flint lampbody.	Unlisted SP 44/-	
Signed	10" white on blue vase with cupid seated on rocks, head bowed. Signed G Woodall and G.C.	Unlisted SP Unlisted	PC.
Signed	10 1/2" white on red vase with roses, Canterbury bells, carnations etc. Signed G Woodall and G.C.	Unlisted SP Unlisted	PC.
Signed	12" white on pink vase with stylised oriental flowers. Signed G Woodall.	Unlisted SP Unlisted	Formerly in Bertram Wolfson Coll. Now in PC.
Signed	12" companion vase, to similar white on pink vase.	Unlisted SP Unlisted	Formerly in Bertram Wolfson Coll. Now in PC.
Signed	12" white on blue vase with seated girl holding her shoulder, facing left. Signed G Woodall and G.C.	Unlisted SP Unlisted	PC.
Signed	16" 2-handled white on brown vase with flowers. Sig G Woodall & Tiffany & Co Paris Ex 1889 & G.C.	Unlisted SP Unlisted	PC.
Signed	3" white on emerald green tapered vase with cherub sitting on a branch. Signed Woodall.	Unlisted SP Unlisted	Similar to W2296, though sig is doubtful. Sold At Early's Auction in 1995 for $8250. Now in PC.
Signed	6" white on blue on aquamarine bowl-vase with butterfly and strawberries. Signed Geo Woodall	Unlisted SP Unlisted	Bought by A Hordern & Sons, Sydney, then by the Powerhouse Museum, Sydney in 1912.
Signed	8" white on amber vase with reindeer. Signed G Woodall and G.C.	Unlisted SP Unlisted	PC.
Signed	8 1/4" white on blue vase, lady against a wall, head in hand, looking to right. Signed G Woodall & G.C.	Unlisted SP Unlisted	
Signed	Shell-shaped plaque: *Aphrodite* with her walking out of the waves onto beach. Signed G Woodall.	Unlisted SP Unlisted	
Signed	6 1/4" white on amber vase with stylised bird. Signed G Woodall	Unlisted SP Unlisted	
TW001	17" white on cobalt blue vase in 3 pieces: *Aurora*. (5 air bubbles, crack on rear.) Unmarked	Thomas Woodall worked alone, wage unknown.	Sold Sotheby's 1965 to Chrysler Museum of Art. Exhibited at Paris1878 and Melbourne Int. Ex 1880. Sold to Art Gallery of New South Wales, £250. From 1987, on loan to Powerhouse Museum Sydney.

No.	Description of Piece	Costs of Workmen and Sale Price (SP)	History/Whereabouts
TW033	White on amber vase.	Unlisted SP £55	Offered for sale at Buckley House on 21.1.1885.
TW043	White on dark blue complete lamp.	Unlisted SP £16.16s	Offered for sale at Buckley House on 21.1.1885.
TW048	White on dark blue vase.	Unlisted SP £18	Offered for sale at Buckley House on 21.1.1885.
TW330	White and green on amber vase.	Unlisted SP £24	Offered for sale at Buckley House on 21.1.1885.
TW371	White on ruby plate.	Unlisted SP £8.8s	Offered for sale at Buckley House on 21.1.1885.
TW379	Lemon on ruby complete lamp.	Unlisted SP £45	Offered for sale at Buckley House on 21.1.1885.
TW404	Lemon on ruby vase.	Unlisted SP £22.10s	Offered for sale at Buckley House on 21.1.1885.
TW467	Vase decorated with symmetrical patterns.	60gns SP £50	
TW489	White on ruby vase.	Unlisted SP £12.15s	Offered for sale at Buckley House on 21.1.1885.
TW568	White on green on brown vase.	Unlisted SP £14	Offered for sale at Buckley House on 21.1.1885.
TW569	7" white on amber vase with giraffes. Signed G Woodall and G.C.	Unlisted SP 60/-	Offered for sale at Buckley House on 21.1.1885. Formerly in Wolfson Coll., now in PC
TW681	White on ruby vase.	Unlisted SP £35	Offered for sale at Buckley House on 21.1.1885.
TW692	White on green complete lamp.	Unlisted SP £30	Offered for sale at Buckley House on 21.1.1885.
TW701	11½" pink on white on blue vase with stylised floral patterns. Marked G.C.	Unlisted SP £75	Offered for sale at Buckley House on 21.1.1885. Formerly in Runyon Coll., now in Texas A&M.
TW723	8" white on amber vase with stag. Signed G Woodall and G.C.	Unlisted SP 84/-	Offered for sale at Buckley House on 21.1.1885.
TW733	13¼" white on brown plaque: Dancers. Signed G Woodall 1886.	Unlisted SP £63	Offered for sale at Buckley House on 21.1.1885. In Nyman Coll; sold Sotheby's, 1989 £11000. Now in PC.
TW780	Amber and white on brown vase.	Unlisted SP £50	Offered for sale at Buckley House on 21.1.1885.
TW788	Vase decorated with flowers.	£50 SP £76	
TW841	White on amber vase decorated with flowers in a symmetrical pattern.	Unlisted SP £85.5s	Offered for sale at Buckley House on 21.1.1885.
TW853	White on topaz vase.	Unlisted SP 84/-	Offered for sale at Buckley House on 21.1.1885.
TW880	White on ruby vase.	Unlisted SP £5.1s	Offered for sale at Buckley House on 21.1.1885.
TW881	White on ruby vase.	Unlisted SP £28	Offered for sale at Buckley House on 21.1.1885.
TW882	Amber and white on brown vase.	Unlisted SP £25	Offered for sale at Buckley House on 21.1.1885.
TW884	13" white on claret plaque: Water Nymph. Signed G Woodall 1884.	Unlisted SP £75	Offered for sale at Buckley House on 21.1.1885. Formerly Rakow Coll. now in C.M.G.
TW855	Vase decorated with flowers.	65/-	
TW904	White on topaz vase.	Unlisted SP £7	Offered for sale at Buckley House on 21.1.1885.
TW906	7½" white on ruby vase with passion flowers. Marked G.C.	Unlisted SP £8	Offered for sale at Buckley House on 21.1.1885. Sold at Sotheby's, 1996, now in PC.
TW907	White on ruby vase.	Unlisted SP £15	Offered for sale at Buckley House on 21.1.1885.
TW908	White on ruby vase.	Unlisted SP £15	Offered for sale at Buckley House on 21.1.1885. Formerly in Runyon Coll., now in Texas A&M.
TW914	Vase decorated with flowers.	Unlisted SP £85	Offered for sale at Buckley House on 21.1.1885.
TW918	Amber vase.	Unlisted SP 21/-	Offered for sale at Buckley House on 21.1.1885.
TW919	Ruby vase.	Unlisted SP 22/6	Offered for sale at Buckley House on 21.1.1885.
TW926	White on ruby vase.	Unlisted SP £16.16s	Offered for sale at Buckley House on 21.1.1885.
TW927	Blue vase.	Unlisted SP 17/6	Offered for sale at Buckley House on 21.1.1885.
TW929	White on brown vase.	Unlisted SP £9.9s	Offered for sale at Buckley House on 21.1.1885.
TW935	Vase decorated with ferns.	Unlisted SP £25	Offered for sale at Buckley House on 21.1.1885.
TW950	White on topaz vase.	Unlisted SP £18.18s	Offered for sale at Buckley House on 21.1.1885.
TW959	White on amber vase.	Unlisted SP 65/-	Offered for sale at Buckley House on 21.1.1885.
TW960	White on ruby vase.	Unlisted SP 65/-	Offered for sale at Buckley House on 21.1.1885.
TW961	White on topaz vase.	Unlisted SP 60/-	Offered for sale at Buckley House on 21.1.1885.
TW985	White on ruby vase decorated with flowers and a baby butterfly.	65/-	
TW989	White on ruby vase decorated with foxgloves.	Unlisted SP £45 (an imperfect vase sold for £35)	
W069	Vase decorated with stylised flowers.	£30 SP £45	
W388	3" carved and gilded curio vase.	Woodall 16/-; Barbe 6/6 SP 40/-	
W406	Green on lemon vase with flowers.	22/6 SP 60/-	Sent to buyer on 9th June 1898.
W434	Light blue on opal vase with flowers.	28/- SP 70/-	Sent to buyer on 9th June 1898.
W489	4" acid-etched ruby over opal over blue vase with floral patterns.	Unlisted SP 80/-	Bought by Taylor, Son & Gosnells, sold at Clarke Gammon in 1996. Now in PC.
W489	8¼" mallet form opal over pink/ruby vase with foliage.	Unlisted SP £9.10s	Bought by Taylor, Son & Gosnells, sold at Clarke Gammon in 1996. Now in PC.
W647	Vase decorated with oriental patterns.	£15.15s	
W655	Vase decorated with strawberries.	£8	Given to National Coll. of Washington Mus., 1937.
W680	Cameo hock.	Unlisted SP 84/-	B.H.G.M.
W701	9" ivory gourd vase with gilded dots. The pink top layer was removed, only the opal layer was carved.	Woodall £8.10s; Barbe figure illegible SP £8.10s	
W706	Vase decorated with flowers.	75/- SP Unlisted	
W723	Vase decorated with tulips.	75/- SP £40	
W823	Cameo hock.	84/- SP Unlisted	
W907	Vase decorated with flowers.	65/-	
W908	Vase decorated with birds on a basket of flowers.	Unlisted SP£75	

No.	Description of Piece	Costs of Workmen and Sale Price (SP)	History/Whereabouts
W926	Pair of vases decorated with butterfly and flowers one side, and flowers on the other.	Unlisted SP £26.10s each	
W949	Vase decorated in a Japanese style with flowers.	Unlisted SP £26	
W950	Pair of vases with flowers one side, and blackberries on the other.	Unlisted SP £27.10s each	
W972	Vase decorated with flowers.	Unlisted SP 70/-	
W978	Vase with flowers.	Unlisted SP 70/-	
W981	Vase with ferns.	£7 SP £14	
W982	Vase decorated in Islamic style.	£8 SP £10	
W983	Vase decorated with Islamic patterns.	£8 SP £16.10s	
W984	Vase decorated with flowers.	84/- SP £6.6s	
W1055	Vase decorated with flowers.	£5.5s	
W1062	Vase with flowers.	Unlisted SP £34.10s	
W1148	3" acid-etched ruby on clear citron on opal vase with oriental patterns.	Unlisted SP 80/-	Bought by Taylor, Son & Gosnells, sold at Clarke Gammon, 1996. Now in PC.
W1183	6" white on red vase with laburnams and sweet peas.	Unlisted SP £9.9s	Bought by Taylor, Son & Gosnells, sold at Clarke Gammon, 1996. Now in PC.
W1254	5½" ivory bottle with enamelled flowers each side. I83	Brushing 1/-; Cameo 1/6; Painting 1/6 SP 16/6	Formerly in Runyon Coll., now in Texas A&M.
W1300	10" plaque: *Origin of the Painting*. Signed G Woodall 1884.	Unlisted SP Unlisted	Formerly in Rakow Coll., now in C.M.G.
W1322	Small vase	Cameo 6/-; Barbe 3/6 SP 12/6	
W1346	Plaque with bird with blossoms.	Unlisted SP Unlisted	PC.
W1350	4½" white on blue vase with girl holding a branch. Marked G.C.	Unlisted SP Unlisted	Formerly in Geo Russell Coll., now Milan Historical Mus, Ohio.
W1356	4" white on amethyst vase with various flowers.	Unlisted SP £4.10s	Bought by Taylor, Son & Gosnells, sold at Clarke Gammon, 1996. Now in PC.
W1400	10¼" white on blue on cinnamon brown plaque with five cherubs. Signed G Woodall.	Unlisted SP Unlisted	Formerly in Runyon Coll., now in Texas A&M.
W1444	9½ins white on ruby vase. Marked Gem Cameo.	Unavailable SP Unavailable	PC, Melbourne.
W1538	8¼" vase: *Cloches with* standing Greek woman, tying her hair. Signed G Woodall and G.C.	Unlisted SP Unlisted	The Metropolitan Museum of Art.
W1598	12¾" white on blue one-handled ewer with Minerva. Signed G Woodall 1885.	Unlisted SP Unlisted	Formerly in Runyon Coll., now in Texas A&M.
W1624	16" white on blue vase: *The Water Iris*. Marked G.C.	Unavailable SP £18.18s	Sold to Adelaide Public Library, now in Art Gallery of South Australia.
W1709	12½" white on topaz vase with flowers on one side only.	Unlisted SP 75/-	
W1721a	9" white on ruby on Chinese yellow body vase with honeysuckle.	Woodall 16/6; SP 55/-	
W1737	Paperweights: white, red and white on flint.	Woodall 20/-; Nash 6d SP 50/-	
W1753	12" vase with two dancing girls, signed G Woodall.	Unlisted SP Unlisted	Formerly in Mrs C. Udell Coll., now in PC.
W1776	12" two-handled light blue on white on dark blue vase: *The Milkmaid*. Signed G Woodall.	£2.12s SP Unlisted	Bought by Melbourne Tennis Club, 1891, sold at Christie's, 1975, £8925 to Mr Tillman. Now in PC.
W1781	12½" white on blue two-handled vase with floral bouquet design. Signed G Woodall & G.C.	Unlisted SP Unlisted	Formerly in Runyon Coll., now in Texas A&M.
W1797	9½" white on blue vase with cover: *Origin of the Painting*. Signed G. Woodall 1887.	Unlisted SP Unlisted	Frambers Collection.
W1810	6" flatsided white on red vase, carved and gilded.	Woodall 14/6; Barbe 10/- SP Unlisted	
W1833	4" vase. I3	Unlisted SP 22/6	
W1834	3½" scent bottle. I57	Making 100; Cameo 11/6; Barbe 1/6 SP 25/-	
W1846	6½" ivory vase. I29	Making 70; Brushing 1/4; Cameo 7/6; Barbe 2/- SP 21/-	
W1848	6" ivory vase. I469	Etching 19/-; Painting 2/6 SP 45/-	
W1849	6" flatsided vase. I1	Unlisted SP 65/-	
W1861	7½" ivory vase. I468	Making 30/-; Etching 29/6; Painting 3/6 SP 63/-	
W1862	2½" scent bottle. I54	Cameo 5/3; Barbe 4/- SP 15/6	
W1863	3" scent bottle. I55	Making 130; Cameo 5/6; Barbe 4/6 SP 21/-	
W1868	3½" two-handled vase. I14	Unlisted SP 32/-	
W1875	10" ivory scent bottle.	Making 18; Cameo 2/-; Barbe 38/- SP 84/-	
W1875	6¼" two-handled ivory vase.	Making 24; Brushing 1/3; Cameo 18/6; Barbe 4/- SP 50/-	
W1875	8" two-handled ivory vase with Persian patterns. I44	Making 20; Brushing 1/6; Cameo 23/6; Barbe 5/6 SP 65/-	
W1876	8½" ivory vase with bird in panel surrounded by stylised flower patterns. I458	Making 35; Brushing 1/3; Etching 29/-; Painting 3/6 SP 70/-	
W1888	5" ivory vase with stylised flowers. I485	Brushing 2/-; Etching 17/6; Painting 3/- SP 50/-	
W1889	6" flatsided ivory vase with apple blossom. I85	Unlisted SP 60/-	Sold to A.C. Revi, now in PC.
W1890	8" ivory tusk with stylised flowers. I70	Making 24; Brushing 1/6; Cameo 36/6; Barbe 6/6 SP 100/-	
W1891	5" vase. I21	Unlisted SP 32/-	
W1893	4½" ivory vase. I4	Making 60 SP 10/6	
W1894	4½" ivory vase. I5	Making 60 SP 11/6	
W1897	2¼" round bottle. I106	Cameo 1/-; Painting 8d SP 5/6	
W1898	3½" ivory globe toilet. I492	Etching 2/4; Painting 1/- SP Unlisted	
W1900	3½" two-handled vase. I15	Cameo 4/3; Barbe 1/6 SP 12/6	
W1902	10" ivory vase. I31	Making 50; Brushing 1/6; Cameo 17/6; Barbe 3/6 SP 45/-	
W1903	Triangular top ivory bowl, tinted black with birds in panels. I35 & I136	Making 18; Brushing 1/6; Cameo 17/-; Barbe 3/6 SP 45/-	
W1904	Small ivory jug with flowers. I38	Making 45; Brushing 1/6; Cameo 6/-; Barbe 2/- SP 21/-	
W1905	Triangular top ivory bowl. I37	Making 18; Brushing 1/6; Cameo 13/6 SP 40/-	
W1906	5" vase. I8	Unlisted SP 12/-	
W1907	4½" ivory vase with leaves. I45	Making 60; Brushing 1/2; Cameo 4/-; Barbe 1/6 SP 14/-	
W1908	4" ivory bowl with flowers. I11	Making 72; Brushing 1/4; Cameo 17/6; Barbe 3/- SP 42/-	

No.	Description of Piece	Costs of Workmen and Sale Price (SP)	History/Whereabouts
W1910	5½" ivory vase with light body with fruit in panel. I36	Making 36; Brushing 1/3; Cameo 11/6; Barbe 1/6 SP 27/6	
W1911	8" ivory vase with flowers. I23	Making 30; Brushing 2/-; Cameo 24/6; Barbe 2/- SP 60/-	
W1912	8" ivory bowl with flowers. I34	Making 28; Brushing 2/-; Cameo 25/-; Barbe 5/- SP 65/-	
W1913	8" two-handled ivory bowl with dark brown patterns. I48	Making 14; Brushing 2/6; Cameo 25/6; Barbe 5/- SP 70/-	
W1914	14" ivory vase with flowers. I197	Making ; Brushing 1/6; Cameo 19/-; Barbe 5/- SP 50/-	
W1915	6" two-handled ivory vase with light brown body and dark brown handles. I24	Making 20; Brushing 1/6; Cameo 19/6; Barbe 3/6 SP 45/-	
W1916	5" ivory vase with hexagonal top with Persian patterns. I46	Making 40; Brushing 1/6; Cameo 15/6; Barbe 2/- SP 36/-	
W1917	9" ivory vase with light brown body and dark brown top. I32	Making 30; Brushing 1/6; Cameo 17/-; Barbe 4/- SP 45/-	
W1923	8½" ivory bowl with light brown body and dark brown ornamented top. I26	Making 30; Brushing 2/-; Cameo 35/6; Barbe 6/6 SP 84/-	
W1924	5" ivory bowl with dark brown inside with flowers inside panels. I27	Making 72; Brushing 1/6; Cameo 23/- Barbe 3/6 SP 54/-	
W1925	4" ivory bowl with flowers. I16	Making 60; Brushing 1/3; Cameo 12/6; Barbe 1/6 SP 30/-	
W1925	5" ivory vase with flowers. I71	Making 45; Brushing 1/4; Cameo 12/6; Barbe 3/6 SP 36/-	
W1926	8" ivory bowl with dark brown inside the pattern panels. I75	Making 30; Brushing 2/3; Cameo 26/6; Barbe 7/- SP 80/-	
W1927	9" ivory vase with stylised patterns and flowers. I68	Making 30; Brushing 2/-; Barbe 7/- SP 130/-	
W1928	6½" ivory, white and amber vase with fruit on branches. I59 & I60	Making 70; Brushing 1/6; Cameo 11/6; Barbe 3/6 SP 32/-	
W1929	5½" ivory vase with flowers. I62	Making 40; Brushing 1/6; Cameo 20/-; Barbe 3/6 SP 50/-	
W1930	4½" ivory vase with perforated top with stylised flowers. I114	Making 80; Brushing 1/6; Cameo 15/6; Painting 2/6 SP 36/-	
W1931	5" ivory vase with perforated top with stylised flowers. I113	Making 40; Brushing 1/6; Cameo 20/-; Painting 3/6 SP 50/-	
W1932	4" vase. I72	Cameo 16/6; Barbe 3/6; SP 45/-	
W1933	8½" ivory vase with fruit on branches. I69	Making 30; Brushing 1/6; Cameo 22/6; Barbe 5/- SP 57/6	
W1934	8" two-handled oval ivory vase with Persian patterns. I79	Making 24; Brushing 2/-; Cameo 21/6; Painting 5/6 SP 60/-	
W1935	8½" two-handled red ivory vase. I82	Making 24; Brushing 2/-; Cameo 22/6; Painting 5/6 SP 60/-	
W1936	5¼" ivory, white and dark brown vase with flowers. I95	Making 50; Brushing 1/3; Cameo 5/6; Painting 1/9 SP 17/6	
W1937	8" ivory bowl with flowers. I101	Making 30; Brushing 2/3; Cameo 60/-; Painting 7/- SP 140/-	
W1938	5½" ivory bowl with flowers. I105	Making 35; Brushing 1/6; Cameo 36/6; Painting 5/6 SP 84/-	
W1939	5¼" ivory vase with plums on branches. I178	Making 30; Brushing 1/6; Cameo 30/-; Painting 4/6 SP 68/-	
W1940	10" ivory bowl with flowers. I102	Making 22; Brushing 3/-; Cameo 50/-; Painting 10/6 SP 130/-	
W1941	4" ivory vase with flowers. I73	Making 80; Brushing 1/6; Cameo 8/-; Barbe 3/6 SP 24/-	
W1942	4" ivory vase with flowers. I74	Making 80; Brushing 1/6; Cameo 7/-; Barbe 3/6 SP 22/6	
W1943	4" ivory vase with flowers. I77	Making 60; Brushing 1/4; Cameo 3/6; Painting 1/- SP 12/-	
W1944	4½" ivory vase with flowers. I93	Making 60; Brushing 1/2; Cameo 10/-; Painting 1/- SP 22/6	
W1945	5½" ivory vase with flowers. I92	Making 72; Brushing 1/3; Cameo 9/6; Painting 2/- SP 22/-	
W1948	8¼" white on clear jug with flowering branches. Marked G.C.	Unlisted SP Unlisted	Silver mount and handle added 1904. Sold at Sotheby's, 1996. Now in PC.
W1951	Cup.	Woodall 1/9 SP 5/-	
W1951	Lancer Cup.	Woodall 1/9 SP 5/-	
W1956	6¾" two-handled ivory vase with girl's face in panel. I76	Brushing 1/3; Cameo 68/-; Barbe 6/6 SP 147/-	
W1957	6" flatsided ivory vase with stylised flower patterns. I84	Making 60; Brushing 6/6; Cameo 31/6; Painting 4/6 SP 84/-	
W1958	6" flatsided ivory vase with house and tree on cliff's edge. I90	Making 60; Brushing 1/6; Cameo 27/6; Painting 4/6 SP 80/-	
W1959	Ivory scent bottle with flowers. I198	Making 100; Brushing 3/-; Cameo 1/10; Painting 6d SP 5/-	Sold to A.C. Revi, Dallas, Texas.
W1960	Ivory scent bottle with flowers. I197	Brushing 4/-; Cameo 6/-; Painting 6d SP 12/-	
W1961	10" ivory vase with flowers. I103	Making 18; Brushing 2/3; Cameo 49/-; Painting 7/6 SP 168/-	
W1962	13½" ivory vase with flowers. I128	Making 16; Brushing 2/6; Cameo 89/-; Painting 10/- SP £10	
W1962	Small ivory tankard jug with flowers. I132	Making 45; Cameo 32/-; Painting 2/- SP £3	
W1966	2½" round ivory bottle with flowers. I107 & I108	Cameo 2/9; Painting 10d SP 8/6	
W1967	7¼" ivory vase with stylised flowers. I116	Making 30; Brushing 1/6; Cameo 20/6; Painting 3/- SP 50/-	
W1968	7¼" ivory vase with stylised flowers and patterns. I115	Making 30; Brushing 1/6; Cameo 24/6; Painting 3/- SP 56/-	
W1972	10" two-handled ivory vase. I130	Making 18; Brushing 2/3; Cameo 40/-; Painting 7/6 SP 6 gns	
W1973	10" two-handled ivory vase. I129	Making 18; Brushing 2/3; Cameo 43/6; Painting 7/6 SP £8	
W1982	7½" ivory vase. I211	Making 60; Brushing 1/-; Cameo 20/-; Barbe 4/- SP 60/-	
W1983	5" white on blue bowl with pears, branches, blossom and berries. Marked G.C.	Unlisted SP Unlisted	Sold, Sotheby's 1996, now in PC.
W1984	5" ivory bowl. I194	Making 45; Brushing 1/-; Cameo 11/6; Barbe 3/- SP 30/-	
W1986	4" ivory bowl. I193	Making 60; Brushing 9d; Cameo 18/-; Barbe 2/- SP 21/-	
W1987	5½" ivory vase. I188	Making 72; Brushing 1/4; Cameo 16/-; Painting 3/- SP 40/-	
W1992	5" ivory bowl. I195	Making 45; Brushing 1/-; Cameo 14/-; Barbe 3/- SP 34/-	
W1993	5" ivory bowl. I196	Making 45; Brushing 1/-; Cameo 9/6; Barbe 3/- SP 27/6	
W1994	15½" ivory vase with flowers. I377	Making 14; Brushing 3/-; Etching 70/-; Painting 14/- SP 8gns	
W1995	12" ivory tusk. I160	Making 18; Brushing 2/6; Cameo 77/-; Painting 10/6 SP 180/-	
W1997	6½" ivory and blue vase. I166	Making 40; Brushing 1/-; Cameo 2/6; Painting 1/3 SP 12/-	
W1997	6½" ivory and blue vase with flowers. I168	Making 40; Brushing 1/-; Etching 2/6; Barbe 1/3 SP 12/6 (10/6 unpolished)	
W1997	6½" ivory vase. I353	Making 40; Brushing 1/-; Cameo 2/6; Painting 1/3; unpolished 10/6 SP 12/-	
W2000	6½" ivory and ruby vase with flowers. I180	Making 40; Brushing 1/-; Cameo 2/10; Painting 1/3 SP 12/6	
W2000	6½" ivory vase with flowers. I181	Making 40; Brushing 1/5; Cameo 2/10; Painting 1/3 SP 12/6	
W2001	6" ivory vase. I186	Making 48; Brushing 1/6; Cameo 7/-; Painting 2/- SP 24/-	
W2002	5½" ivory vase. I185	Making 40; Brushing 1/3; Cameo 15/6; Painting 1/6 SP 20/-	
W2003	6" ivory vase. I191	Making 40; Brushing 1/3; Cameo 4/6; Painting 1/6 SP 15/-	

No.	Description of Piece	Costs of Workmen and Sale Price (SP)	History/Whereabouts
W2004	3½" ivory vase. 1248	Making 50; Brushing 8d; Cameo 9/-; Barbe 1/6 SP 22/6	
W2005	8" ivory bowl. 1201	Making 24; Brushing 1/6; Cameo 7/-; Barbe 3/6 SP 26/-	
W2006	8" ivory bowl. 1203	Making 30; Brushing 1/6; Cameo 8/6; Barbe 4/6 SP 28/-	
W2010	12" ivory vase with elephant's head on bird's body with patterns surround. 1170	Making 18; Brushing 3/6; Cameo 78/-; Painting 20/- SP £12.10s	
W2013	8" ivory vase with flowers. 1199	Making 20; Brushing 1/-; Cameo 17/-; Barbe 4/- SP 48/-	
W2014	8" two-handled ivory vase. 1198	Making 20; Brushing 1/-; Cameo 13/6; Barbe 4/- SP 42/-	
W2015	7" ivory plate. 1520	Making 50; Etching 10/6; Painting 1/6 SP Unlisted	
W2016	8¼" ivory jug with flowers. 1204	Making 35; Brushing 1/4; Cameo 24/-; Barbe 3/6 SP 56/-	
W2017	10" ivory vase with flowers. 1200	Making 20; Brushing 2/-; Cameo 43/6; Barbe 5/6 SP 80/-	
W2018	8" ivory bowl. 1257	Making 30; Brushing 1/6; Cameo 6/-; Barbe 4/6 SP 30/-	
W2019	7" ivory vase. 1183	Making 28; Brushing 1/-; Cameo 18/6; Painting 2/- SP 42/-	
W2020	5½" ivory vase. 1240	Making 40; Brushing 8d; Cameo 6/-; Barbe 2/- SP 16/-	
W2022	3¾" ivory vase. 1231	Making 65; Brushing 6d; Cameo 3/6; Barbe 10d SP 10/-	
W2023	9¼" ivory vase. 1261	Making 50; Brushing 1/-; Cameo 7/6; Barbe 2/6 SP 22/6	
W2024	4" ivory bowl. 1226	Making 80; Brushing 8d; Cameo 2/2; Painting 10d SP 8/-	
W2025	6½" ivory vase. 1224	Making 70; Brushing 9d; Cameo 3/3; Barbe 1/6 SP 12/-	
W2026	6½" ivory vase. 1223	Making 70; Brushing 9d; Cameo 3/6; Barbe 1/6 SP 12/-	
W2027	4½" ivory, white on ruby toilet vase. 1234	Making 120; Brushing 6d; Cameo 3/-; Barbe 10d SP 8/-	
W2028	5¾" ivory vase. 1219	Making 50; Cameo 2/8; Barbe 1/3 SP 10/-	
W2029	4½" bowl. 1415	Making 60; Brushing 6d-; Etching 7/6; Painting 1/6 SP 18/6	
W2030	6¼" ivory vase. 1255	Making 24; Brushing 1/3; Cameo 8/6; Barbe 4/- SP 32/-	
W2030	9¾" ivory vase. 1318	Make per turn 30; Brushing 1/2; Cameo 24/6; Barbe 4/- SP 60/-	
W2031	5¾" ivory vase with bird and flowers. 1241	Brushing 8d; Cameo 16/-; Barbe 1/6 SP 37/6	
W2033	12½" snake-carved, two-handled ivory vase with storks in panel. 1379	Making 15; Brushing 3/-; Etching 78/-; Painting 10/- SP £10	
W2034	15½" ivory vase with flowers. 1425	Making 14; Brushing 2/3; Etching 36/-; Painting 8/6 SP 100/-	
W2035	7¼" ivory vase. 1254	Making 30; Brushing 1/3; Cameo 18/6; Barbe 4/- SP 50/-	
W2037	6¼" ivory vase. 1320	Make per turn 24; Brushing 9d; Cameo 8/6; Barbe 3/- SP 30/-	
W2038	9" ivory vase with Persian patterns. 1250	Make per turn 30; Brushing 1/3; Cameo 27/6; Barbe 4/6 SP 60/-	
W2039	6" ivory vase. 1276	Make per turn 40; Cameo 8/6; Barbe 1/6 SP 20/-	
W2040	10" ivory candlestick. 1298	Make per turn 30; Brushing 1/6; Cameo 20/6; Barbe 3/- SP Unlisted	
W2041	7" ivory vase with bird and stems in panel. 1466	Making 35; Etching 24/6; Painting 2/- SP 45/-	
W2042	8" two-handled ivory vase. 1309	Make per turn 20; Brushing 1/-; Cameo 15/6; Barbe 4/6 SP 42/-	
W2043	12" white on brown vase: *Before the Race*. Signed T & G Woodall and G.C	Woodall £7 SP Unlisted	Formerly in Nyman Coll., then Australia, sold at Christie's 1977, £20,000. Now in PC.
W2045	8" two-handled ivory vase. 1310	Make per turn 20; Brushing 1/-; Cameo 16/-; Barbe 4/6 SP 42/-	
W2047	7½" ivory tusk. 1290	Make per turn 18; Cameo 18/6; Barbe 3/6 SP 50/-	
W2048	5½" ivory globe. 1408	Brushing 1/4; Etching 16/6; Painting 3/6 SP 40/-	
W2049	5" ivory bowl. 1259	Making 72; Engraving 1/3; Cameo 10/-; Barbe 2/6 SP 27/6	
W2050	9" ivory vase. 1306	Make per turn 30; Brushing 1/9; Cameo 19/6; Barbe 4/6 SP 50/-	
W2051	9" ivory vase. 1307	Make per turn 30; Brushing 1/9; Cameo 17/-; Barbe 4/6 SP 48/-	
W2052	10" ivory vase with flowers in panels. 1428	Making 18; Brushing 2/-;Etching 20/6; Painting 5/- SP 50/-	
W2053	9" ivory vase with two men having a tug-of-war. 1426	Making 30; Etching 43/-; Painting 4/6 SP 5gns	
W2054	5" ivory sprinkler. 1299	Make per turn 60; Cameo 3/6; Barbe 1/6 SP 12/-	
W2054	Left-sided ivory bottle with flowers. 1391	Etching 3/6; Painting 1/6 SP 11/-	
W2054	Right-sided ivory bottle with flowers. 1391	Etching 3/6; Painting 1/- SP Unlisted	
W2055	13¾" white over dark brown vase: *Before the Race*. Marked G.C.	Unlisted SP Unlisted	Sold by Christie's to Tillman £22,000, now PC.
W2056	9" ivory candlestick. 1297	Make per turn 25; Cameo 13/6; Barbe 2/- SP 30/-	
W2057	8" ivory candlestick. 1295	Make per turn 18; Cameo 10/6; Barbe 2/- SP 25/-	
W2058	8" ivory candlestick. 1296	Make per turn 25; Cameo 11/6; Barbe 2/- SP 28/-	
W2059	10¾" ivory vase. 1268	Make per turn 50; Cameo 3/6; Barbe 2/6 SP 13/6	
W2060	6½" ivory vase. 1319	Make per turn 50; Cameo 3/-; Barbe 1/6 SP 10/6	
W2061	6½" ivory vase. 1311	Make per turn 50; Cameo 2/10; Barbe 1/6 SP 10/6	
W2063	9" ivory salad bowl with flowers. 1464	Make 20; Etching 5/6; Painting 3/- SP Unlisted	
W2064	2¾" ivory vase with flowers. 1346	Make 72; Etching 8d; Barbe 4d SP 3/-	
W2065	5½" ivory vase. 1337	Make 50; Etching 10d; Barbe 4d SP 4/-	
W2066	3½" ivory vase with flowers. 1345	Make 72; Etching 1/6; Barbe 4d SP 4/6	
W2068	6" ivory sprinkler. 1275	Make per turn 40; Cameo 2/4; Barbe 6/- SP 8/6	
W2068	6" ivory, white on ruby toilet-set scent bottle. 1293	Make per turn 40; Cameo 2/4; Barbe 1/- SP 8/6	
W2069	8½" ivory vase. 1331	Make per turn 40; Cameo 4/-; Barbe 2/- SP 15/-	
W2070	9" ivory vase. 1330	Make per turn 30; Cameo 6/-; Barbe 2/- SP 22/-	
W2071	9" ivory vase. 1329	Make per turn 30; Cameo 7/6; Barbe 2/- SP 22/-	
W2072	9" ivory card tray. 1519	Make per turn 40; Brushing 1/6; Etching 15/-; Painting 3/- SP 36/-	
W2073	4" ivory and ruby vase with five flowers and two butterflies. 1457	Brushing 8d; Etching 5/6; Painting 9d SP 14/-	
W2075	2" watch bottle. 1336	Make 100; Etching 1/-; Colour 1/3 SP 3/6	
W2078	4¾" ivory sprinkler. 1303	Make per turn 60; Cameo 1/3; Barbe 8d SP 5/-	
W2078	4¾" ivory sprinkler. 1304	Make per turn 60; Cameo 1/3; Barbe 8d SP 5/-	

No.	Description of Piece	Costs of Workmen and Sale Price (SP)	History/Whereabouts
W2078	4 3/4" ivory sprinkler. I305	Make per turn 60; Cameo 1/3; Barbe 8d SP 5/-	
W2079	5" ivory sprinkler. I285	Make per turn 60; Cameo 2/-; Barbe 10d SP 7/-	
W2079	5" ivory sprinkler. I302	Make per turn 60; Cameo 2/-; Barbe 10d SP 7/-	
W2080	2 3/4" ivory sprinkler. I286	Make per turn 72; Cameo 1/3; Barbe 4d SP 3/9	
W2080	2 3/4" ivory sprinkler. I287	Make per turn 72; Cameo 1/3; Barbe 4d SP 3/9	
W2082	6 3/4" ivory vase. I312	Make per turn 50; Cameo 4/-; Barbe 1/6 SP 12/-	
W2083	6 1/4" ivory vase. I314	Make per turn 50; Cameo 5/3; Barbe 1/6 SP 13/6	
W2084	8" ivory vase. I335	Make 45; Etching 5/9; Barbe 1/- SP 15/-	
W2085	6" ivory vase. I333	Make per turn 70; Cameo 10/-; Barbe 5/- SP 26/-	
W2086	8 1/2" ivory vase with flowers. I359	Make 50; Etching 6/3; Barbe 2/6 SP 18/-	
W2087	8 1/2" ivory vase with flowers. I351	Make 50; Etching 7/4; Barbe 2/6 SP 20/-	
W2088	7" two-handled, flatsided ivory bowl with flowers. I369	Make 20; Etching 8/6; Barbe 4/6 SP 30/-	
W2089	7" two-handled, flatsided ivory bowl with flowers. I370	Make 20; Etching 10/-; Barbe 4/6 SP 33/-	
W2090	1 1/2" ivory jug with pumpkin tree. I429	Make 35; Etching 7/6; Painting 1/6 SP 20/-	
W2091	1 1/2" ivory jug.	Make 35; Etching 7/6; Painting 1/6 SP 20/-	
W2092	8" ivory vase with birds on branches. I322	Make 30; Etching 7/9; Barbe 1/6 SP 21/-	
W2092	8" ivory vase with birds on branches. I323	Make per turn 30; Cameo 7/9; Barbe 2/- SP 22/-	
W2092	8" ivory vase with flowers. I342	Make per turn 30; Cameo 7/9; Barbe 2/- SP 22/-	Sold Sotheby's 2000, now in PC.
W2092	8" ivory vase with grapes. I343	Make 30; Etching 7/9; Barbe 1/6 SP 21/-	
W2093	15" ivory candlesticks. I500	Make 18; Brushing 2/6; Etching 27/-; Painting 5/6 SP 841/-	May have been sold as DP1340, now in PC.
W2094	10" ivory vase with flowers. I420	Make 30; Brushing 1/3; Etching 8/6; Painting 3/- SP 26/-	
W2094	6 1/4" ivory vase. I325	Make per turn 50; Cameo 4/2; Barbe 1/6 SP 12/-	
W2095	10" ivory vase with flowers. I453	Make 30; Brushing 1/3; Etching 6/3; Painting 3/- SP 22/-	
W2095a	10" ivory vase with flowers. I452	Make 30; Brushing 1/3; Etching 6/3; Painting 3/- SP 22/-	
W2096	12 1/2" ivory vase with flowers. I376	Make 24; Brushing 1/6; Etching 19/6; Painting 5/- SP 50/-	
W2097	12" ivory vase with flowers. I421	Make 24; Brushing 1/6; Etching 10/6; Painting 5/- SP 40/-	
W2098	12 1/2" ivory vase with flowers. I375	Make 24; Brushing 1/6; Etching 10/-; Painting 5/- SP 40/-	
W2099	Ivory tusk jug with a peacock feather. I398	Make 30; Brushing 2/-; Etching 9/6; Painting 2/6 SP 28/-	
W2100	5 1/2" flatsided ivory vase. I340	Make 60; Etching 13/-; Barbe 4/6 SP 32/-	
W2101	12" ivory vase with berries on a branch. I381	Brushing 1/6; Etching 11/-; Painting 3/6 SP 32/-	
W2102	7" ivory bamboo vase. I324	Make per turn 70; Cameo 5/9; Barbe 1/- SP 13/6	
W2102	7" ivory vase with flowers. I360	Make 70; Etching 5/9; Barbe 1/6 SP 14/-	
W2103	6" oval ivory bowl with flowers. I348	Make 60; Brushing 1/-; Etching 5/-; Barbe 1/5 SP 16/6	
W2104	5 1/2" flatsided ivory vase with patterns of lines. I352	Make 72; Etching 13/6; Barbe 4/- SP 33/-	
W2106	5" ivory vase. I339	Make 40; Etching 4/3; Barbe 1/6 SP 12/6	
W2107	7" ivory vase with stylised flowers. I451	Make 72; Brushing 1/3; Etching 13/6; Painting 2/3 SP 28/-	
W2108	7" ivory vase with bamboo on one side. I368	Make 72; Brushing 1/3; Etching 13/-; Barbe 3/6 SP 34/-	
W2109	7" ivory vase with flowers. I366	Make 80; Etching 7/3; Barbe 2/- SP 18/6	
W2110	8" ivory vase of bamboo shoots. I363	Make 80; Etching 9/-; Barbe 2/6 SP 21/-	Sent to Australia in February 1891.
W2111	5 1/2" ivory vase. I338	Make 72; Etching 10d; Barbe 1/- SP 5/-	
W2112	4" ivory bowl. I327	Make per turn 80; Cameo 9d; Barbe 1/- SP 4/6	
W2113	Left-sided ivory violer. I334	Make per turn 110; Cameo 6d; Barbe 4d SP 2/3	
W2113	Right-sided ivory violer. I334	Make 120; Etching 4/6; Barbe 3d SP 1/10	
W2113a	2" ivory bottle. I639	Etching 41/2; Painting 3d SP Unlisted	
W2114	1 1/2" ivory candle piece. I373	Make 130; Etching 1/8; Painting 4d SP 4/-	
W2114	2 1/2"ivory candle piece. I374	Make 120; Etching 1/6; Painting 4d SP 4/-	
W2114	3" ivory candle piece. I372	Make 72; Etching 1/8; Painting 4d SP 4/-	
W2115	9 1/2" ivory vase with flowers. I424	Make 30; Brushing 1/6; Etching 6/-; Painting 3/- SP 25/-	
W2124	8 1/2" ivory vase with flowers. I416	Make 50; Brushing 1/-; Etching 7/4; Painting 2/6 SP 20/-	
W2125	4 1/2" ivory bowl with bamboo fence. I417	Make 60; Brushing 1/-; Etching 5/-; Painting 1/3 SP 14/-	
W2126	4 1/2" ivory bowl. I474	Etching 5/-; Painting 10d SP 5/-	
W2127	Ivory rose jar with flowers. I434	Make 18; Etching 9/6; Painting 3/6 SP 30/-	
W2129	Ivory rose jar with flowers. I433	Make 18_2; Etching 10/6; Painting 3/6 SP 30/-	
W2130	Ivory rose jar with flowers. I431	Make 18_2; Etching 19/6; Painting 5/- SP 50/-	
W2131	9" ivory bamboo with forget-me-not flowers, bamboo shoots and butterflies. I364	Make 80; Etching 5/3; Barbe 2/- SP 14/6	Sent to Australia in 1891.
W2132	9" ivory bamboo. I365	Make 80; Etching 6/3; Barbe 2/- SP 16/6	
W2136	Ivory tusk jug with flowers. I413	Make 30; Engraving 6d; Etching 3/3; Painting 1/6 SP 14/-	
W2138	5"two-handled ivory vase with birds in panel. I409	Etching 14/-; Painting 2/6 SP 35/-	
W2139	4 1/2" ivory vase with bamboo shoots and flowers. I472	Etching 1/9; Painting 1/- SP 8/6	
W2141	3 3/4" ivory vase with bamboo shoots and flowers. I473	Make 80; Etching 1/9; Painting 1/- SP 10/6	
W2142	5" two-handled ivory vase with sun effect pattern. I387	Make 30; Brushing 1/6; Etching 7/6; Painting 2/6 SP 30/-	
W2143	7" ivory bowl with flowers. I399	Etching 9/6; Painting 3/- SP 32/-	
W2143	7" ivory vase with flowers. I396	Make 60; Etching 6/3; Painting 1/3 SP 16/-	
W2144	8" ivory bowl with blossom on tree. I412	Etching 8/3; Painting 3/- SP 32/-	
W2150	6 1/2" ivory vase with flowers. I354	Make 40; Brushing 1/-; Etching 2/10; Barbe 1/3 SP 12/6 (10/6 unpolished)	
W2151	12" ivory candelabra. I499	Brushing 1/6; Etching 24/6; Painting 5/- SP 90/-	Bought as part dessert service, now in PC.

No.	Description of Piece	Costs of Workmen and Sale Price (SP)	History/Whereabouts
W2152	8 1/4" stained ivory glass tusk vase, painted with watercolours. 1414	Engraving 6d; Etching 3/3; Painting 1/3 SP 12/-	Formerly in Runyon Coll., now Texas A&M.
W2153	L/S ivory inks with flowers. 1478	Make 65; Brushing 1/-; Etching 2/10; Painting 10d SP 9/6	
W2154	R/S ivory bottle with stork in a panel. 1423	Make 60; Brushing 6d; Etching 4/-; Painting 1/3 SP 12/-	
W2155	L/S ivory bottle with flowers. 1422	Make 50; Etching 4/8; Painting 1/6 SP 13/-	
W2156	S/S ivory ink with acorns on branches. 1479	Make 60; Brushing 1/-; Etching 2/2; Painting 8d SP 8/-	
W2157	L/S ivory ink with flowers. 1479	Make 65; Brushing 1/-; Etching 2/6; Painting 10d SP 9/6	
W2157	S/S ivory inks with flowers. 1478	Make 60; Brushing 1/-; Etching 2/-; Painting 8d SP 8/-	
W2158	Ivory ink with flowers. 1491	Etching 2/9; Painting 1/3 SP 9/-	
W2159	2 1/2" ivory bottle with floral patterns. 1475	Etching 1/7; Painting 5d SP 4/-	
W2159	3" ivory bottle with flowers. 1475	Make 130; Etching 1/10; Painting 6d SP 5/-	Formerly in Nyman Coll., now in PC.
W2160	3" figure shaded ivory bottle with flowers. 1402	Etching 9d; Painting 5d SP 3/3	
W2160	3" figure shaded ivory bottle with flowers. 1404	Etching 9d; Painting 5d SP 3/3	
W2161	2" watch bottle with flowers. 1406	Make 100; Etching 8d; Painting 5d SP 3/3	
W2161	3" figure shaded ivory bottle with flowers. 1405	Etching 8d; Painting 5d SP 4/-	
W2161	3" ivory figure bottle with flowers. 1406	Etching 7d; Painting 5d SP Unlisted	
W2162	2" watch bottle with floral patterns. 1403	Make 100; Etching 1/2; Painting 5d SP 4/-	Formerly in Runyon Coll., now in Texas A&M.
W2163	2" watch bottle with people on a bridge. 1401	Make 100; Etching 10d; Painting 5d SP 3/6	
W2178	Yellow and pink on white vase with flowers.	Unlisted SP Unlisted	
W2179	12" white on brown vase: *The Race*. Signed T & G Woodall.	Woodall £6.10.6 SP Unlisted	Rebought by Webb's Museum, now in PC.
W2182	9" ivory vase with stylised floral patterns. 1495	Make 30; Brushing 1/9; Etching 9/9; Painting 4/- SP 35/-	
W2187	7 1/2" ivory vase with flowers. 1521	Make 70; Brushing 1/-; Etching 6/6; Painting 1/6 SP 20/-	
W2191	Ivory rose jar with flowers. 1435	Make 18; Etching 6/6; Painting 3/6 SP 24/- (jar and lid)	
W2192	12" ivory vase with carved and gilded fish. Marked G.C.	Brushing 2/-; Etching 8/-; Painting 3/6 SP 35/-	
W2192	6" two-handled ivory vase. 1526	Make 24; Brushing 1/5; Etching 3/3; Painting 4/- SP 15/-	
W2192	8" ivory vase. 1526	Make 20; Brushing 1/6; Etching 5/-; Painting 2/6 SP 21/-	
W2192a	3" ivory bottle. 1477	Etching 2/6; Painting 6d SP Unlisted	
W2195	8" ivory vase with flowers. 1517	Brushing 1/6; Etching 5/3; Painting 2/- SP 18/6	
W2196	7" ivory vase with flowers. 1524	Make 35; Brushing 1/5; Etching 4/2; Painting 1/6 SP 14/-	
W2198	9 1/2" ivory vase with berried Virginia creeper. 1525	Make 30; Brushing 6/3; Etching 6/6 SP 22/6	
W2200	4" ivory vase.	Brushing 6d; Etching 5/6; Painting 2/6 SP 20/-	
W2201	9" ivory vase with flowers. 1708	Nash 1/6; Engraving 3/6; Etching 4/3; Painting 3/- SP 25/-	
W2202	9" ivory vase with papion and yellow flowers. 1707	Nash 1/6; Engraving 4/6; Etching 4/6; Painting 3/- SP 26/-	
W2202 1/2	9" ivory vase with flowers. 1709	Nash 1/6; Engraving 3/6; Etching 4/3; Painting 3/- SP 25/-	
W2203	9" ivory vase with flowers. 1674	Brushing 1/6; Etching 5/6; Painting 2/6 SP 21/-	
W2205	8" ivory vase with flowers. 1534	Make 45; Brushing 9d; Etching 1/8; Painting 1/6 SP 8/6	
W2206	8" ivory vase with flowers. 1533	Make 45; Brushing 9d; Etching 3/-; Painting 1/6 SP 10/6	
W2212	5 1/4" ivory candlestick with flowers. 1537	Brushing 4d; Etching 1/10; Painting 1/- SP 7/-	
W2212	5 1/4" ivory candlestick with flowers. 1538	Brushing 4d; Etching 1/10; Painting 1/- SP 7/6	
W2213	5 1/4" ivory candlestick with flowers. 1539	Brushing 5d; Etching 2/4; Painting 1/- SP 8/6	
W2214	7" ivory candlestick with flowers. 1541	Brushing 6d; Etching 2/2; Painting 1/- SP 8/6	
W2215	7" ivory candlestick with flowers. 1544	Brushing 6d; Etching 1/10; Painting 1/- SP 8/-	
W2216	5 1/4" ivory candlestick with flowers. 1546	Brushing 5d; Etching 2/4; Painting 1/- SP 8/6	
W2216	5 1/4" ivory candlestick with flowers. 1547	Brushing 5d; Etching 2/4; Painting 1/- SP 8/6	
W2217	5 1/4" ivory candlestick with flowers. 1543	Brushing 5d; Etching 1/2; Painting 1/- SP 7/-	
W2218	5 1/4" handled ivory candlestick with flowers. 1548	Brushing 7d; Etching 2/2; Painting 1/- SP 8/6	
W2218	5 1/4" ivory candlestick with flowers. 1542	Brushing 5d; Etching 2/2; Painting 1/- SP 8/-	
W2219	5 1/2" handled ivory candlestick with flowers. 1549	Brushing 7d; Etching 1/7; Painting 1/- SP 8/-	
W2220	5 1/4" handled ivory candlestick with flowers. 1550	Brushing 7d; Etching 2/7; Painting 1/- SP 10/-	
W2221	7" ivory candlestick with flowers. 1540	Brushing 6d; Etching 2/3; Painting 1/- SP 8/6	
W2222	6 1/4" ivory candlestick with flowers. 1545	Brushing 6d; Etching 2/10; Painting 1/- SP 15/-	
W2226	Blue and ruby on flint bowl.	Unlisted SP Unlisted	
W2226	Fingerplates: blue and red on flint.	Woodall 13/6 SP 32/-	At International Health Ex., 1885. Now, V&A Mus.
W2233	6 1/2" ivory vase. 1592	Make 50; Etching 11/-; Painting 2/- SP 30/-	Sold at Skinner's, 1998, now in PC.
W2233	8 1/2" ivory urn vase with bird serpent in arabesque frame with floral background. 1592	Maker 40; Etching 23/-; Painting 3/6 SP £3	Sold at Skinner's, 1998, now in PC.
W2233	8 1/2" ivory urn vase with bird serpent in arabesque frame with floral background.	Maker 40; Etching 23/-; Painting 3/6 SP £3	Sold Phillips, 1996, £20,000 to Leo Kaplan Ltd, now Chrysler Mus.
W2237	12 1/2" white on brown vase: *The Race*. Marked Gem Cameo.	Unlisted SP Unlisted	
W2243	5" coloured cameo vase.	Woodall 3/6; purple body work by Barbe 6/- SP 30/-	
W2273	4 1/2" Burmese on opal vase with forget-me-not flowers and butterfly. 1594	16/9 SP 32/-	
W2273	6 1/2" Burmese on topaz vase.	Woodall 9/6 SP 28/-	
W2281	6" green, pink and white bowl with flowers.	Unlisted SP Unlisted	
W2282	Flatsided vase, carved and gilded	Woodall 82/-; Barbe 30/- SP £12	
W2286	7" ivory vase, tinted gold with panels. 1726	Nash 13/-; Painting 5/6 SP 50/-	
W2287	5" ivory globe bowl with panels of flowers and stylised patterns. 1653	Make 12; Brushing 2/-; Etching 46/-; Painting 12/6 SP £7	
W2291	Square plaque of rich colours.	60/- SP £10	
W2300	6" white on pale amber plate with two youths fishing. Signed T & G Woodall.	Unlisted SP Unlisted	Sold at Early's Auction 1998, $9350, now in PC.

No.	Description of Piece	Costs of Workmen and Sale Price (SP)	History/Whereabouts
W2312	9" ivory double gourd vase with Persian panels of hunters, animals, birds and figures. 1604	Brushing 2/6; Etching 95/-; Painting 4/6 SP £12	In auction Sotheby's 1998, unsold, now Leo Kaplan.
W2312a	9" ivory double gourd vase with Persian panels of hunters, animals, birds and figures.	Brushing 2/6; Etching 95/-; Painting 55/- SP Unlisted	In auction Sotheby's 1998, unsold, now Leo Kaplan.
W2312d	7½" ivory vase. 1604a	Brushing 2/6; Etching 92/-; Painting 23/6 SP £12	
W2313	8¾" two-handled ivory vase with dragon in Persian panel surround. 1212	Making 28; Engraving 20/-; Brushing 1/3; Cameo 8/-; Barbe 3/6 SP 63/-	Sold Sotheby's NY, 1991, for $1500-2000.
W2316	10" ivory bowl with panels of walking upright animals in a Persian style. 1605	Make 14; Brushing 3/6; Etching £7.3s; Painting £5.5s SP £26.10	
W2317	16" ivory vase with gilded outlines to imitate iron with coloured flowers and ornaments. 1612	Make 12; Brushing 4/6; Etching £8.14s; Painting 70/- SP £26	
W2318	Large ivory vase and cover. 1609	Make 8; Brushing 5/6; Etching £11.13s; Painting £6.10s SP £42	
W2321	Cameo hock.	Woodall 40/- SP 76/-	
W2322	5¼" white on light green hock glass with flowers.	Woodall 36/- SP 70/-	Formerly in Runyon Coll., now in Texas A&M.
W2323	6½" two-handled (carved as snakes) ivory bowl with animals among arabesque foliage. 1632	Make 20; Brushing 2/-; Etching 82/-; Painting 4/6 SP £7.10s	
W2324	5½" dark ivory vase with reclining man and Persian animals and birds. 1649	Brushing 1/-; Etching 28/-; Painting 12/6 SP 80/-	
W2324	5½" ivory vase with Persian style elephant and birds. 1650	Brushing 1/-; Etching 28/-; Painting 2/6 SP 80/-	Sold, Sotheby's, 1976 for £660.
W2325	6½" ivory vase with Persian-style panels of a bird on a branch and stylised flowers. 1630	Make 35; Etching 34/-; Painting 3/- SP £4.4s	
W2327	6½" ivory vase with various panels including a man sitting on a chair and an upright animal. 1606	Make 40; Etching 34/-; Painting 15/- SP £5.15s	
W2328	7" ivory vase with panels of birds. 1627	Make 30; Brushing 1/6; Etching 30/-; Painting 1/6 SP £4.5s	
W2330	9" flatsided ivory vase with arabesque panels of antelope walking upright. 1608	Make 40; Brushing 3/6; Etching £6.4s; Painting 5/- SP £8.8s	
W2331	7½" ivory vase with Persian panels of a stork, man and birds. 1624	Make 30; Etching 31/-; Painting 2/- SP £4.10s	
W2332	6" ivory vase with panels of mice, animals, rats and birds. 1631	Make 40; Brushing 1/-; Etching 34/-; Painting 3/- SP £4.4s	
W2335	6" white on topaz vase with frog, tree and rocks.	Woodall 11/6 SP 35/-	
W2336	6" opal on flint vase with stylised flowers. 1610	Woodall 37/6; Nash 1/6 SP £4.17	
W2340	Cameo hock.	Woodall 27/6 SP 55/-	
W2341	Cameo hock.	Woodall 34/6 SP 70/-	
W2342	6½" ruby on opal on flint vase with stylised flowers.	Woodall 33/-; Nash 1/6 SP £5	
W2345	5½" ivory vase with small panels of elephants. 1629	Make 30; Brushing 1/-; Etching 36/-; Painting 1/10 SP £4	
W2346	6½" ivory vase with a panel of an elephant. 1626	Make 30; Brushing 1/6; Etching 32/-; Painting 1/10 SP £4.10s	
W2347	8" ivory vase with a panel of a man on horseback. 1625	Make 30; Brushing 2/-; Etching 50/-; Painting 3/- SP £6.6s	
W2350	6" ivory vase with blossom on a branch. 1666	Brushing 9d; Etching 8/6; Painting 1/6 SP 25/-	
W2352	6½" ivory vase. 1633	Brushing 8d; Etching 20/-; Painting 1/6 SP 50/-	
W2356	4½" ivory bowl with perforated ruby.	Brushing 1/-; Etching 41/- SP £6	PC.
W2358	15¼" white on blue on brown two-handled vase known as *Industry*. Signed G Woodall & G.C.	Woodall £38.10s SP £100	Sold, Sotheby's NY 1988, $60,500 Runyon Coll, now Texas A&M.
W2365	7" curio vase.	Woodall 18/6 SP 42/-	
W2377	6" white on ruby vase with jasmine.	Unlisted SP 35/-	
W2381	6½" white on yellow Burmese/cameo vase with flowers and insect.	Woodall 6/3 SP 25/- increased to 45/-	
W2382	5" cameo vase.	Woodall 5/3 SP 25/-	
W2383	Vase.	Woodall 4/6 SP 50/-	
W2384	10" white and red on Burmese vase with budding and leafy branches.	Unlisted SP Unlisted	Sold at Phillips 1998, now in PC.
W2385	6½" white on tricolour on Burmese vase with flowers.	Woodall 23/9 SP 80/-	
W2386	3½" ivory bottle. 1638	Brushing 9d; Etching 7/-; Painting 6d SP 16/-	
W2387	8½" ivory bottle. 1636	Brushing 1/6; Etching 18/6; Painting 2/- SP 40/-	
W2388	6½" ivory bottle with birds and animals. 1637	Brushing 1/-; Etching 10/-; Painting 1/- SP 22/6	
W2390	6½" red and white on rich yellow (white outer) vase with flowers.	Woodall 25/- SP 80/-	
W2400	4" white on yellow vase with flower in oval shape with flower surround.	Woodall 12/- SP £3	
W2402	16" two-handled vase: *The Rose*. Signed G Woodall.	Woodall £28 SP £60	Exhibited in Webb's Museum then sold to PC.
W2403	15¾" two-handled white on raisin brown vase: *The Fruit Seller*. Signed G Woodall 1889 and G.C.	Woodall £28.10s SP £60 reduced to £50	Formerly in the Grover Coll., now in PC.
W2404	6" ivory vase. 1641	Brushing 1/-; Etching 25/6; Painting 2/6 SP 65/-	
W2412	7" ivory vase with green on ivory flowers. 1645	Etching 27/-; Painting 2/6 SP 80/-	
W2412a	5½" ivory vase with green on ivory blossom on branches. 1644	Brushing 6d; Etching 17/- SP 45/- (60/- with case)	
W2413	6" green on Burmese ground, ruby brown on top, with birdhouse.	Woodall 40/-; Barbe 2/-; Nash 6d SP £6.6s	
W2413b	5½" ivory vase with green on ivory flowers. 1643	Brushing 6d; Etching 17/- SP 42/-	
W2415	6" green on Burmese ground with ruby and brown fish and waves.	Woodall 38/-; Barbe 2/-; Nash 6d SP Unlisted, sold with W2413	
W2417	9" cameo on flint vase with a sea foam scene.	Unlisted SP £8.8s	
W2420	4" small jade gourd vase with stylised patterns.	Woodall 20/- SP Unlisted	
W2421	4" small jade gourd vase with stylised patterns (to match W2420).	Woodall 24/6 SP Unlisted	
W2422	Vase	Woodall 58/-; Barbe 6/6; Nash 1/6 SP £12	Sold to Mr Nett.
W2423	6" green on Burmese body with ruby and brown fish and waves on vase.	Woodall 45/-; Barbe 2/-; Nash 6d SP Unlisted	
W2426	7½" carved and coloured metal vase.	Woodall 24/6; Barbe 5/-; Nash 1/3; SP 70/-	
W2427	6½" jade vase.	Woodall 42/-; Barbe 6d; Nash 9d SP 100/-	
W2428	6½" flatsided jade-coloured vase with flat rim with mouse and marrow.	Woodall 46/-; Barbe 6d; Nash 1/- SP £5	
W2429	4¾" jade vase with fruit on a branch.	Woodall 19/6; Nash 6d SP 46/-	
W2430	5½" jade vase with two sections of stylised patterns.	Woodall 23/-; Nash 9d SP 50/-	
W2431	9" ivory vase with flowers. 1654	Brushing 1/6; Etching 66/-; Painting 33/- SP £10.10s	
W2431	Curio vase with flowers.	Unlisted SP £12	
W2438	Ivory and gilded dessert plate with stylised floral patterns. 1662	Etching 2/6; Painting 5/6 SP 16/-	
W2438	Ivory flask. 1662	Etching 3/-; Painting 6/6 SP 21/-	
W2438	Tall ivory flask 1662	Etching 3/6; Painting 7/6 SP 30/-	

No.	Description of Piece	Costs of Workmen and Sale Price (SP)	History/Whereabouts
W2440	9" flatsided ivory vase with six bird and floral Persian patterns.	Woodall £6.15s; Nash 2/- SP illegible	In G Woodall's collection, sold by Alice Woodall 1949. Auctioned Skinner's $9775, now in PC.
W2441	5" flatsided vase with flowers in a tortoiseshell motif.	Woodall 34/- SP 75/-	
W2442	3½" bowl with flowers.	Woodall 37/6; Nash 1/- SP £4.16.6	
W2444	2 flatsided cups.	Woodall 33/6; Nash 1/- SP £3.12.6	
W2445	6" flint carved bowl with roses.	Woodall 82/-; Nash 3/-; Plain 5/6 SP £10.10	
W2445	6" jade bowl.	Woodall 92/-; Nash 1/6 SP £10	
W2446	6" jade bowl.	Woodall 90/-; Nash 1/6 SP £10	
W2447a	9" cameo vase with convolvulus.	Woodall 32/-; SP 70/-	
W2447b	9" cameo vase with geraniums.	Woodall 32/-; SP 70/-	
W2447c	9" cameo vase with flowers.	Woodall 32/-; SP 70/-	
W2448	3½" all jade bowl with flowers and a bat carved in the Chinese style.	Woodall 29/6; Nash 9d SP 70/-	Bought at antiques fair as Chinese glass, now in PC.
W2449	6½" ivory vase with butterfly, birds and blossom on tree branches. I657	Make 14; Brushing 1/6; Etching 21/6; Painting 5/- SP 60/-	
W2451	6½" ivory vase and cover with a topaz birdcage and opal birds. I659	Make 14; Brushing 1/6; Etching 34/6; Painting 5/- SP 84/-	
W2454	8" two-handled ivory vase with sage sitting on a wicker chair. I652	Brushing 1/6; Etching 56/-; Painting 35/- SP £8.15s	
W2456	4" ivory bowl with perforated ruby top and stylised flowers. I611	Etching 40/- SP £7.10s	
W2457	9½" white on brown vase with cover: *Origin of the Painting*. Signed G Woodall & G.C.	Woodall 42/6; Nash 6d SP £4.10s (£6.10s with case)	Sold to Mr Nett, cover destroyed, now in PC.
W2458	Vase: *Pomegranate*.	Woodall 37/-; Nash 6d SP £4.10s (£6.10s with case)	Sold to Mr Nett.
W2459	9" flatsided jade vase.	Woodall £6.2s; Polishing 2/-; price of blank if sold plain 10/- SP £14	
W2462	5¾" carved and gilded vase with man in panel.	Woodall 40/6; Barbe 5/-; Nash 1/- SP £4.4s	
W2463	6" ivory vase. I655	Brushing 1/6; Etching 25/-; Painting 5/- SP 45/-	
W2464	7" ivory carved and painted bowl with flowers in bullring border. I665	Painting 18/-; Brushing 1/6; Etching 38/6 SP £5.10s	
W2465	7" ivory and gilded bowl with exotic bird and flowers. I664	Brushing 1/6; Etching 60/-; Painting 29/6 SP £7.10s	
W2466	4" ivory ground mossled colours and gilded curio vase with bird on branch in scene.	Woodall 24/6; Nash 9d; price of blank per turn 14d; Barbe 2/6 SP 75/-	
W2467	3½" ivory vase with flowers. I660	Brushing 1/-; Etching 28/6; Painting 15/6 SP £5	
W2467	5" curio vase with a duck on a pond with fish underwater.	Woodall 24/-; Nash 6d SP 60/-	
W2468	5½" two-handled ivory on ruby curio vase with oriental patterning and flower.	Woodall 14/6 SP 40/-	
W2469	3" mottled body yellow and ruby on white curio vase. Ground painted green and gilded with flower.	Woodall 8/6; Barbe 1/3; 72d price of blank per turn SP 21/-	
W2470	6½" carved and gilded curio vase.	Woodall 50/-; Barbe 5/6; Nash 1/6 SP £8	
W2471	7½" flint ground with brown and ivory inside curio vase with window/diamond shapes against wall.	Woodall £5.15s; Barbe 3/- SP £10.10s	
W2472	6" carved and gilded curio vase with ruby fish and ivory shells.	Woodall 82/-; price of blank per turn 10d; Nash 2/6; Barbe 1/6 SP £15	
W2473	5½" flatsided flint body with coloured flowers curio vase.	Woodall 38/-; Barbe 4/- SP £7	
W2475	5½" flint ground with mossled colours curio vase with seaweed and water scene.	Woodall 56/-; price of blank per turn 14d; Nash 8d SP £7.7s	
W2476	10" white on red on blue vase with lovers on a swing. Marked Tiffany & Co Paris Exhibition 1889.	Unlisted SP Unlisted	Mark was added later. In Nyman Coll., then Runyon Coll., now in Texas A&M.
W2477	6½" jade and coloured metal vase with birds.	Woodall 76/-; price of blank per turn 10d; Nash 2/- SP £12	
W2478	5½" flint ground colours mossled curio vase with flowers and pot.	Woodall 63/-; price of blank per turn 14d; Nash 6d SP £7.7s	
W2479	7" ivory vase with birds and a goldfish in a bowl. I658	Make 14; Brushing 1/6; Etching 37/6; Painting 5/- SP £6	
W2480	6" curio carved vase with flint ground and fish.	Woodall 90/-; price of blank per turn 10d; Nash 6d SP £12	
W2481	6" coloured body vase.	Woodall 72/-; price of blank per turn 10d; Nash 2/- SP £12	
W2482	5½" curio carved vase with horizontal birds and flowers.	Woodall 45/-; price of blank per turn 10d; Nash 9d SP £5.5s	
W2483	7" ivory ground with green outside curio vase with bird in birdcage plus other birds and trees.	Woodall 68/-; Barbe 4/- SP 140/-	
W2484	6" ivory vase with topaz and ruby birds and insects. I656	Make 14; Brushing 1/6; Etching 44/6; Painting 3/6 SP 105/-	
W2484	7½" ivory vase with flowers and a fish in a bowl. I661	Brushing 1/6; Etching 46/6; Painting 9/6 SP £6	
W2485	4½" carved curio vase.	Woodall 36/6 SP 105/-	
W2486	4½" flint ground with mossled colours curio vase with ruby fish, green seaweed & ivory shells.	Woodall 34/- SP 100/-	
W2487	4" curio carved vase with upper pattern of flowers, lower pattern of other flower variety.	Woodall 12/6; Nash 1/- SP 32/-	
W2488	4¼" carved curio blue and brown on flint bowl with fish.	Woodall 59/6; Nash 1/6 SP £10	
W2489	8" curio carved vase with rocks, leaves and flowers.	Woodall 62/-; price of blank per turn 10d; Nash 2/- SP £8.8s including case	
W2490	5½" carved and gilded curio vase with Burmese body and coloured sprays.	Woodall 56/-; Barbe 3/6 SP £7	
W2491	4½" carved and gilded curio vase.	Woodall 28/-; Barbe 15/6 SP £9	
W2492	6½" gilded vase with two blue knobs with a bird cage in topaz with dark green leaves on Burmese.	Woodall 40/-; Barbe 16/6 SP £8	Exhibited in Webb's Mus, sold abroad, now in PC.
W2493	4" light brown on opal on flint bowl.	Woodall 21/6; Painting 1/6 SP 55/-	
W2494	5½" carved and gilded curio vase.	Woodall 43/6; Barbe 7/6; Nash 1/9 SP £7	
W2495	5½" flatsided gilded vase with coloured knobs, Burmese body with dark green outside.	Woodall 39/-; Barbe 3/6 SP £5.5s	
W2496	5½" carved and gilded curio vase.	Woodall 43/6; Barbe 7/6 SP 140/-	
W2497	6½" carved curio vase.	Woodall 32/6 SP 66/-	
W2498	3½" carved and gilded curio bowl with scene in panel.	Woodall 41/- SP £4	
W2499	8½" flint on white, blue, white, turquoise coloured vase.	Woodall 58/-; Barbe 6/6; Nash 1/6 SP Unlisted	
W2500	3½" brown on ivory on flint bowl.	Woodall 25/- SP 60/-	
W2501	8½" white on dark topaz vase: *Pandora*. Signed Tiffany & Co Paris Ex 1889 & G Woodall & G.C.	Woodall £5 SP £25	The signature Paris Exhibition 1889 was added later. Now in The Currier Gallery of Art.
W2502	4" ivory and ruby bowl with stylised floral patterns. I663	Brushing 1/6; Etching 46/6 SP £6.10s	
W2503	16" white & pink on matt clr tint vase with lion mask and acanthus pattern. Signed Tiffany & Co Paris Ex 1889 & G Woodall & G.C.	Woodall £8.10s SP £18	The signature Tiffany & Co Paris Ex. 1889 was added later. Sold, Sotheby's 1994, £27,000, now in PC.
W2504	No details	Woodall £8.5s SP £18	
W2505	4" ivory globe bowl with an upright bull with gilding and perforated ruby layer. I680	Brushing 1/-; Etching 44/-; Painting 11/6 SP £17.10s	

No.	Description of Piece	Costs of Workmen and Sale Price (SP)	History/Whereabouts
W2506	4" ivory on pink globe bowl with man in patterns. 1669	Brushing 1/-; Etching 80/-; Painting 5/6 SP £11.11s	
W2507	4" ivory on ruby on ivory on pink globe bowl showing perforated ruby flowers. 1682	Etching 80/- SP £10.10s	
W2508	4" ivory on ruby globe bowl with perforalia. 1668	Brushing 1/-; Etching 68/6 SP £7.12s	
W2509	4" ivory globe bowl with fruit and scrolls. 1667	Brushing 1/-; Etching 36/6; Painting frosted SP £6.10s	
W2510	8½" two-handled white on light brown vase: Ceres Receiving from Bacchus a Restorative Cup. Marked G.C.	Unlisted SP £35 reduced to £27.10s	Sold 1902, then Grover Coll., now in Texas A&M.
W2512	8" green on white on flint curio vase with flowers.	Woodall 45/-; Nash 1/- SP 120/-	
W2513	6" vase: Flower Girl. Signed G Woodall. (Similar design to W2803).	Woodall £16.10s SP £45	Formerly in Mrs Van Name Coll., now in PC.
W2514	6" vase: Fairies Spring.	Woodall £16.15s SP £42	
W2515	3½" green and brown on flint curio bowl with panels of flowers.	Woodall 26/6; Nash 1/- SP 60/-	
W2516	9" carved curio vase.	Woodall 12/6 SP 34/-	
W2517	9" carved curio vase with apple blossom.	Woodall 13/- SP 34/-	
W2518	6" carved curio vase.	Woodall 14/6 SP 35/-	
W2519	6½" carved curio vase.	Woodall 13/6; SP 33/-	
W2520	6½" carved curio vase.	Woodall 13/6 SP 33/-	
W2521	5" carved curio vase.	Woodall 12/6 SP 30/-	
W2522	6½" carved curio vase with fruit and leaves using flint on coloured metal effect.	Woodall 8/- SP 21/-	
W2523	6½" carved curio vase.	Woodall 8/- SP 21/-	
W2524	6" carved curio vase with flowers using flint on coloured metal effect.	Woodall 8/6 SP 30/-	
W2525	6¼" carved curio vase.	Woodall 8/6 SP 22/-	
W2526	6" carved curio vase with ruby flowers and grass using flint on coloured metal effect.	Woodall 13/- SP 30/-	
W2527	6" flint, ivory and base topaz curio vase with flowers.	Woodall 13/- SP 30/-	
W2529	3½" carved curio bowl.	Woodall 28/6; Nash 1/- SP 60/-	
W2530	11" carved curio vase: Flora.	Woodall £7.6s; Nash 2/6 SP £18 reduced to £10	
W2531	11" carved curio vase with flowers and stylised pattern.	Woodall £5.10s; Nash 2/6 SP £15 reduced to £12.10s	
W2532	White on citron lampbody with goddess holding owl on lampbase. Marked G.C.	Unlisted SP Unlisted	Formerly in Runyon Coll., now Texas A&M.
W2533	3½" brown on ivory on flint curio bowl with pattern with sea effect.	Woodall 22/6; Nash 1/- SP 80/-	
W2534	5" carved and gilded on dark brown curio vase with stylised flowers.	Woodall 42/-; Barbe 8/6 SP £5	In Knowles Coll., B.H.G.M.
W2535	White on ivory lampbody with stylised flowers. 1686	Brushing 6d; Etching 10/-; Painting 2/6 SP 25/-	
W2536	Lampbody with stylised flowers. 1685	Brushing 6d; Etching 12/6; Painting 2/6 SP 28/-	
W2537	3¾" carved curio bowl with bird on a ledge.	Woodall 25/- SP 63/-	
W2538	6" flint curio vase with flowers.	Woodall 12/6 SP 33/-	
W2539	6" carved curio vase.	Woodall 12/6 SP 33/-	
W2540	6" coloured pieces on flint vase, black metal on bottom with flowers.	Woodall 17/- SP 45/-	
W2541	6" coloured metal on flint body base with pears.	Woodall 39/- SP 100/-	
W2542	3½" black on ivory vase with a leopard and snake fighting.	Woodall 32/6 SP 80/-	Exhibited in Webb's Mus, then sold abroad. Then
W2543	9" carved curio vase using flint with coloured metal effect to create ruby and blue flowers.	Woodall 14/9 SP 34/-	Sold at Skinner's, 1998, $4500.
W2544	5¾" carved and gilded curio vase with orchids & daisies on scrollwork gold ground. Marked G.C.	Unlisted SP £7	
W2545	6¾" coloured metal on flint body vase with black plums.	Woodall 36/- SP £6	
W2546	6" coloured metal on flint body vase with topaz flowers, birds and fruit.	Woodall 52/- SP 120/-	
W2549	10½" white on ruby vase with cabbage roses and other flowers. Signed G Woodall & G.C.	Unlisted SP £10.10s	
W2550	Globe black on red curio bowl with canary, stylised Chinese patterns and gilded rim and outlines.	Unlisted SP £10	
W2551	Carved curio tumbler.	Woodall 10/6 SP 25/-	
W2551	Handled carved curio carafe.	Woodall 28/- SP £4	
W2552	Carved curio tumbler with flowers.	Woodall 9/6 SP 25/-	
W2552	Two-handled curio carafe.	Woodall 26/- SP 70/-	
W2552d	3½" white on topaz globe bowl with flowers.	Woodall 7/6; Nash 1/6 SP 21/-	
W2553	4" ivory on flint bowl.	Woodall 8/6 SP 30/-	
W2554	4" brown on flint curio bowl with cockerel in oval panel on one side.	Woodall 32/- SP 70/-	
W2555	Decanter and stopper with coloured grapes and fly.	Woodall 28/6 SP 70/-	
W2556	Carved curio clareteen with vine and grapes on horizontal lines.	Woodall 58/- SP 120/-	
W2566	6½" carved curio oval in case.	Woodall 144/-; Plain 20/-; Case 45/- SP £25	
W2567	9½" white on brown vase and cover: Night. Signed G Woodall 1890.	Woodall £29 SP £80	Formerly Revi Coll., then Runyon, now Texas A&M.
W2568	Carved curio clareteen.	Woodall 50/- SP 95/-	
W2569	Brown jug with ivory on flint with figs.	Woodall 44/- SP 95/-	
W256?	Handled jug with grapes.	Unlisted SP Unlisted	
W2570	9" black metal on ivory vase with four horses/riders and two figures. 1715	Brushing 1/6; Etching 72/- SP £12	
W2571	6½" white on green vase with oriental house with central window.	Woodall 42/- SP £5.5s	
W2572	Decanter and stopper with coloured grapes and fly.	Woodall 46/- SP £5.5s	
W2573	6" flatsided ruby, opal, ivory and brown on flint curio vase with flowers.	Woodall 62/- SP £10.10s	
W2574	Curio paperweight.	Woodall 16/- SP 38/-	
W2575	9" white and flint outside vase with stylised flowers.	Woodall 58/- SP £6.6s	
W2576	10" white on brown vase with Chinese dogs. Dated to Oct 1890 in Sketch Book.	Woodall £5.10s SP £15	
W2577	Curio paperweight.	Woodall 20/- SP 45/-	
W2578	8" white on blue on red ground cameo vase, dancing girl and a spray on obverse side.	Woodall £5.10s SP £12.10s	Bght by S Buckley & Co, now Cincinnati Art Mus.
W2579	8" white, topaz and light blue on a red ground cameo vase: dancing girl with a spray on reverse.	Woodall £5.10s SP £12.10s	Formerly Grover Coll, then Runyon now Texas .A&M. Sold Sotheby's NY 1988, $29,700, Runyon Coll.

No.	Description of Piece	Costs of Workmen and Sale Price (SP)	History/Whereabouts
W2580	8" white on blue on red cameo vase with nude listening to a bird with a spray on reverse.	Woodall £6 SP £12.10s	Formerly Armitage, then Revi, Texas has similar vase signed G.C.
W2581	8" white on red on light blue cameo vase with woman holding branch. Signed G Woodall.	Woodall £5.5s SP £12.10s	Formerly Armitage Coll, now in PC.
W2582	10" white on brown cameo vase with cupids on the upper half, flowers below. Signed G Woodall.	Woodall £11.12s; SP £25	Formerly Rakow Coll, now C.M.G.
W2582	12" cameo figure vase: *The Dancing Girl*. Signed G Woodall and G.C.	Woodall £11.15s; 10FT SP £30	
W2584	Small cameo tube.	Woodall 2/- SP 4/6	
W2585	Small white on ruby tube with pattern decoration.	Woodall 2/3 SP 5/-	
W2586	Small cameo tube with pattern decoration.	Woodall 1/9 SP 4/-	
W2588	12" cameo ginger jar and cover with scrollwork patterns. Marked G.C.	Woodall £25.5s SP £65	Sold Sotheby's, 1980, £4400 to Leo Kaplan Ltd, now in PC.
W2590	White on topaz on flint basin.	Woodall 2/6 SP 7/-	
W2591	White and topaz-on flint basin with stylised flowers.	Woodall 2/4 SP 7/-	
W2593	4" carved and gilded curio globe bowl.	Woodall 19/6; Barbe 4/- SP 63/-	
W2595	7" flint body with red, blue and opal patterns.	Woodall 70/-; Nash 4/- SP £10	
W2597	7½" ivory vase with a gilded lip and coloured flowers, pince cup effect on lower vase. 1723	Etching 5/-; Painting 10/6 SP 42/-	
W2598	9" cupid red on turquoise on ivory vase with flowers.	Cup 3/6; Barbe 21/-; Woodall 5/- SP £4.10s	
W2599	7" flint body vase with black metal and green, black and turquoise flowers.	Plain blank 15/-; Nash 4/- SP £6.10s	
W2600	8½" vase with a house with a face at the window. 1687	Etching 98/-; Painting 18/- SP £15	
W2601	White on blue honey cameo pot with flowers.	Unlisted SP Unlisted	
W2602	9" white on on a light yellow vase with flowers as requested by Charles Webb.	Woodall 64/- SP £8.8s	
W2604	6½" jade curio vase with black boy on ivory background and ivory bird on black.	Woodall 73/- SP £10	
W2605	8½" flatsided curio vase.	Woodall 108/-; Cut 3/6; Plain blank 30/- SP £14.14s	
W2609	15½" two-handled white on brown vase: *Cupid and Psyche*. Signed G Woodall & Tiffany and Co, Paris Ex 1889.	Woodall £25; 3PT; foot cost 25/6 SP £65 reduced to £55	Formerly Budrose Coll, then Grover Coll, now PC.
W2610	Decanter and stopper with flowers and spider's web.	Woodall 42/- SP 88/-	
W2613	Ivory salad bowl. 1683	Etching 7/6; Painting 6/6 SP 35/-	
W2613	Ivory tankard with flowers. 1716	Brushing 1/6; Etching 4/6; Painting 8/6 SP 30/-	
W2613	Ivory tankard with flowers. 1717	Etching 4/6; Painting 8/6 SP 30/-	
W2615	8" gilded curio vase.	Plain blank 30/-; Woodall 58/-; Barbe 2/6; Nash 4/6 SP £8.8s	Gift of Mrs H McLellan, now Currier Gallery of Art.
W2616	8½" gilded jade curio vase with oriental man in leaf-shape. Gilded and enamelled on neck.	Woodall 35/-; Barbe 16/6; Nash 3/6 SP £5.10s	
W2617	3½" curio globe toilet.	Woodall 22/6; Nash 1/6 SP 45/-	
W2618	3½" curio globe toilet	Woodall 19/6; Nash 1/6 SP 45/-	
W2619	8" melon-shaped ivory and gilded jug. Marked G.C. 1718	Etching 4/6; Painting 6/6 SP 28/-	PC.
W2621a	3½" ivory globe toilet with three patterns of flowers. 1719	Etching 2/-; Painting 2/6 SP 12/-	
W2622	Ivory S/S mug and L/S mug with flint bottom, etched and gilded. 1714	Etching 2/6 & 3/-; Painting 3/6 & 5/- SP 13/6 & 18/-	
W2626	9" cameo vase.	Woodall 56/- SP £9.9.9	
W2627	Cover for bowl.	Woodall and Nash paid SP incl. with price of bowl	
W2627	Cover for vase.	Woodall and Nash paid SP incl. with price of vase	
W2627	L/S partly engraved and partly cameo vase in ruby and white for vase, cover and stand.	Woodall and Nash paid £13.10	
W2627	S/S partly engraved and partly cameo bowl.	Woodall and Nash paid £12.10s	
W2627	Stand for bowl.	Woodall 17/6 incl; Nash 3/6 incl. SP £2.10s	
W2627	Stand for vase.	Woodall 19/6 incl; Nash 5/- incl. SP £3	
W2630	4" gilded ivory on flint on ruby globe bowl with six flies and ruby ladybirds.	Woodall 52/-; Barbe 1/-; Nash 1/9 SP 110/-	
W2635	S/S dark brown on white pearl scent jar and cover with winged lady holding fan.	Unlisted SP 63/-	Formerly Rakow Coll, now C.M.G.
W2636	Flint jar and cover. with flowers and beehive.	Unlisted SP £2.2s	
W2637	Flint curio pearl jar and cover with flowers.	Unlisted SP 33/-	
W2638	4" curio globe.	Woodall 18/6; Nash 1/6 SP 45/-	
W2643	Flint blue curio pearl jar and cover with flowers.	Unlisted SP45/-	
W2644	Curio pearl jar and cover with flowers.	Unlisted SP 45/-	
W2651	S/S flint cameo pearl jar and cover.	Woodall 12/6 SP 40/-	
W2652	Curio pearl jar and cover.	Unlisted SP 18/-	
W2654	Light jade ground curio pearl jar and cover with flowers.	Unlisted SP 50/-	
W2655	8" two-handled blue and opal on brown vase with white on brown handles with cherub descending.	Unlisted SP Unlisted	Formerly Runyon Coll, now Texas A&M.
W2656	Curio pearl jar and cover.	Unlisted SP Unlisted	
W2658	Light brown on white on black on flint body curio pearl jar and cover with stylised flowers.	Woodall 23/-; Nash 1/3; plain blank 7/6; Lining 2/6 SP 60/-	
W2659	5" curio vase ruby on ivory on flint body with eighteen flutes, five rings and flowers.	Woodall 12/6; Nash 2/6; plain blank 7/6 SP 40/-	
W2660	12" white on blue on brown vase, white on brown cover: *Loves Awakening*. Signed G Woodall & G.C.	Woodall £28.10s SP £80	*Cupid* in factory pattern book. Formerly in Budrose and then Runyon Colls, now Texas A&M.
W2661	Two-handled flint cameo scent jar and cover with hunter with spear and animal.	Woodall 19/6 SP 45/-	
W2662	Two-handled blue flint cameo pearl jar and cover with roses.	Woodall 10/6 SP 30/-	
W2669	8¾" white on blue vase with lady on wall with elbow on tambourine. Signed G Woodall and G.C.	Woodall 16/6 SP 63/-	
W2671	Lq toilette.	Woodall 5/- SP 21/-	
W2677	11½" white on dark brown vase and cover: *Dancing Girls*. Signed T & G Woodall.	Woodall £25.10s SP £63	
W2679	Flint body decanter and stopper with red and metal coloured sprays.	Woodall 11/6 SP 30/-	
W2681	Flint body decanter and stopper with red and metal coloured sprays.	Woodall 10/6 SP 22/6	
W2682	Curio.	Woodall 25/- SP 70/-	
W2682	Flint body vase with white flowers.	Woodall 28/6; Nash 2/- SP 63/-	PC.

No.	Description of Piece	Costs of Workmen and Sale Price (SP)	History/Whereabouts
W2684	Flint body vase with flowers.	Woodall 20/6; Nash 2/6 SP 50/-	
W2685	Cameo jar and cover: *Pompeian Maidens*.	Woodall £32.70s SP £100	
W2688	Flatsided flint claret decanter and stopper with flowers.	Woodall 20/6; Nash 4/6 SP 50/-	
W2690	Clareteen curio vase with flowers.	Woodall 14/6 SP 46/-	
W2691	6½" ivory polished vase with birds. 1724	Etching 4/6 SP 12/-	
W2692	12" black on flint vase with cut and engraved pillars with stylised floral pattern.	Woodall 100/-; Nash 25/- SP £21	Sold £25, Adelaide Pub Lib, now Art Gall of Sth Australia.
W2693	10" opal on six layers including light brown & flint vase and a foot for mounting with iris & convolvulus.	Woodall 90/- SP £24	
W2702	White on ruby on topaz on flint jar with flowers.	Woodall 29/-; Nash 4/6 SP 70/-	Bght by Taylor, Son & Gosnells, sold from HR Taylor Coll 1996, now in PC. Cover broken.
W2710	White on brown oval for brush back cameo.	Woodall 22/- revised to 21/- SP 60/- revised to £3.10s	
W2711	White on topaz oval for brush back cameo.	Woodall 21/- SP 60/-	
W2712	6½" white on dark blue vase and cover with three panels of storks.	Woodall £5 SP £15.15s reduced to £12.12s	Ordered by Mr Goode, 1891, formerly owned by B. Wolfson, now in PC.
W2713	9" ruby and white on blue on white hock vase with five panels of patterns (to match W2715).	Woodall £5.5s SP £15	Formerly Runyon Coll, now Texas A&M. Sold Adelaide Pub Lib, now Art Gall, Sth Australia.
W2714	9" opal on dark brown cameo vase: *Dancing Girl*. Signed G Woodall and G.C.	Woodall £6 SP £15	Grover Coll, then Runyon Coll, now Texas A&M.
W2715	15" white on flint vase with fish in storm. Marked G.C. (Sketch Bk lists W2715 as grapes on decanter/stopper.)	Woodall 50/- estimated SP £6.10s	Sold Phillips, 1910, now Currier Gallery of Art.
W2716	7½" flatsided white on topaz vase: *Flower Gatherer*. Signed G Woodall and G.C.	Woodall £9.15s SP £30	Formerly Goode & Co, 1956, now in PC.
W2717	6½" vase with cover with Ganymede and Zeus as an eagle. Marked G.C.	Woodall £8.9s SP £10.10s	
W2718	10" white on brown vase with cover: *Diana and Nymph*.	Woodall £33.5s SP £105	
W2719	15" white on sea green vase: *Sea Scene* aka *The Storm* with fish and seaweed, marked G.C.	Woodall £20; Nash 5/-; Plain 40/- SP £65	Formerly Grover Coll, now in PC.
W2720	Two-handled white on brown vase with the minuet.	Woodall £15 SP £45	Now Dr and Mrs J B Foote.
W2721	10" white on brown vase: *Psyche*. Signed G Woodall and G.C.	Woodall £10.5s SP £31.10s	Formerly Revi and Rakow Colls, now C.M.G.
W2722	10" white on brown vase: *Phyllis at the Fountain*. Signed T & G Woodall.	Woodall £11.5s SP £31.10s	Formerly Nyman Coll, now C.M.G.
W2723	10" white on brown vase: *A Maid of Athens*. Signed T & G Woodall and G.C.	Woodall £11.5s SP £31.10s	Formerly Budrose & Runyon Colls now Texas A&M.
W2724	12" white on brown vase: *Inspiration* with a dancing girl. Signed G Woodall.	Woodall £19.10s SP £55	
W2725	15" two-handled white on blue vase, foot fitted by Nash & Pearce with Icarus and Cupid. Signed G Woodall and G.C.	Woodall £22.10s; Nash & Daniel Pearce 5/- SP £75 reduced to £50	Formerly Budrose Coll, another version Revi Coll. Both now in PC.
W2726	7" white on brown jar with cover: *A Quiet Nook*. Signed Geo Woodall.	Woodall £17.5s SP £50 reduced to £42.10s	Formerly Budrose and Grover Colls, now in PC.
W2728	11" white on brown vase: *Nature's Mirror*. Signed T & G Woodall.	Woodall £15.5s SP £45	Formerly Ash Coll, now on loan to V & A Museum. Now in PC.
W2729	Brown on green on flint champagne glass with grapes.	Woodall 18s SP 50s	
W2730	13½" white on brown (dark topaz) vase: *Pandora*. Signed T & G Woodall.	Woodall £38.10s SP £100	Formerly in Nettlefold, Revi & Rakow Colls, now C.M.G.
W2731	12¾" white on brown vase: *Feathered Favourites*. Signed T & G Woodall.	Woodall £20.10s SP £55	
W2732	13¼" white on puce plaque: *Aphrodite*. Signed G Woodall 1892 and G.C.	Woodall £42 SP £125	
W2733	13" white on brown plaque: *Floralia*. Signed G Woodall 1892 and G.C.	Woodall £37 SP £110	Formerly Runyon Coll, now Texas A&M.
W2734	13" plaque: *Cupid in Disgrace*. Signed G Woodall 1892 and G.C.	Woodall £40 SP £120	Formerly Harris Coll, sold Phillips 1983, now in PC.
W2741	5"x3½" white on gold brown menu with top/bottom borders joined by flowers at either side.	Unlisted SP Unlisted	Sold Sotheby's 1970, £3250, Rakow Coll, now in PC.
W2746	5"x3½" opal on deep blue on light blue vase with boy helping girl over stream. Signed G Woodall & G.C.	Unlisted SP Unlisted	
W2747	5"x3½" white on gold brown menu with diamonds within border, dated 3.11 in Sketch Book.	Unlisted SP Unlisted	
W2748	5"x3½" white on gold brown menu with occasional flowers in border and corners.	Unlisted SP Unlisted	
W2749	5"x3½" white on gold brown menu with small squares carved in border corners.	Unlisted SP Unlisted	
W2756	Ruby on white on topaz small egg-shaped scent bottle.	Woodall 3/- SP 7/-	
W2757	8" white on ruby on topaz vase with flowers.	Woodall estimate 17/9 SP 45/-	Formerly in Ash Coll, now on loan to V&A.
W2759	13" plaque: *Feathery Favourites*. Signed T & G Woodall 1892.	Woodall £48 SP £150	Formerly Revi & Runyon Colls, now Texas A & M.
W2760	9"x12" white on brown panel: *Flora*. Signed T & G Woodall.	Woodall £16.5s SP £35	Given to Mrs Parker by Wordsley Liberals, now PC.
W2765	White on brown on flint jar: *Penelope*. Signed T & G Woodall.	Woodall £15.10s SP £42	
W2767	13"x10" panel: *A Nymph of the Sea*. Signed Geo Woodall.	Woodall £32.10s; frame 15/- SP £63	
W2777	12" white on blue vase with aquilegia with two flies on reverse side.	Woodall estimate 25/- SP 90/-	
W2778	9½" white on blue vase with jasmine.	Woodall estimate 35/- SP 105/-	
W2779	8" white on blue vase: *Peacock Feather*.	Woodall estimate 6/- SP 25/-	
W2785	9"x12" white on brown panel: *Flora*. Signed T & G Woodall and G.C.	Woodall £16.15s SP £45	Formerly Nettlefold, Revi & Rakow Colls. Now, C.M.G.
W2786	17½" white on brown plaque: *Diana and Endymion*. Signed T & G Woodall	Woodall £58.10s SP £180 reduced to £150	Destroyed, surviving 1½" fragment in PC.
W2787	9" white on blue on topaz vase: *Jasmine*.	Woodall 14/6 SP 45/-	
W2788	9" white on pink on topaz vase: *Jasmine*.	Woodall 14/6 SP 50/-	
W2788	9" white on brown vase: *Begonia*.	Woodall 17/6 SP 50/-	
W2789	9" white on ruby on topaz vase: *Apple Blossom*.	Woodall 17/6 SP 65/-	Formerly owned by Robinson & Foster, then Nyman Coll, sold Bonhams 1999 £38000, now B.H.G.M.
W2790	12½"x7½" white on brown panel: *Sappho*. Signed T & G Woodall.	Woodall £23.10s SP £52.10s	
W2791	See W3172		
W2792	White on claret brown panel: *Pandora/Psyche*.	Woodall £13.5s; frame 7/6 SP £37.10s	
W2793	8¼" white on brown plaque: *Un Jour d'èté* (A Summer's Day).	Woodall £15.10s; frame cost 9/6 £42 reduced to £33	Formerly Ash Coll, bought from Leo Kaplan by Mr and Mrs Hitt, now Chrysler Museum.
W2794	16½" white on brown plaque: *Intruders*. Signed T & G Woodall.	Woodall £56.10s SP £160	

No.	Description of Piece	Costs of Workmen and Sale Price (SP)	History/Whereabouts
W2295	10" white on brown vase: *Pomona*. Signed T & G Woodall.	£23.10s SP £60	Now in PC. Damaged.
W2296	3" white on brown vase: *Cupid Dancing*.	Woodall 24/6 SP 70/-	
W2297	7½"x5" white on brown oval plaque: *Greek Girl with dancer*. Dated March 1894 in Sketch Book.	Woodall 95/- SP £15	
W2801	White on brown vase: *Corinna*.	Woodall £22.10s SP £60	Sold to Mrs Muller, Karlsruhe, £95, now in PC.
W2802	Panel: *Wandering Stars*.	£44.10s SP £120	PC.
W2803	7½" white on brown vase: *Cloches*. Signed T & G Woodall and G.C.	Woodall £5.7s6d SP £15.15s	Exhibited at Philadelphia Museum of Art in 1970s.
W2804	10" white on brown vase: *Psyche*. Signed G Woodall and G.C.	Woodall £10.5s SP £28	Formerly in Grover Coll, now in PC.
W2805	8"x5½" white on brown oval panel: *The Nymph of the Sea*. Signed Geo Woodall.	Woodall £7.15s SP £18	Sold at Finnigans. 1915 for 15gns, then in Smith Coll. Sold Phillips, 1976, $4200, now in PC. A version in Mus of Bombay labelled Wedgewood.
W2806	9" white on brown vase: *A Pompeian Girl*. Dated July 1894 in Price Book. Signed T & G Woodall.	Woodall £12.5s SP £30	Formerly in Ash Coll, on loan to V & A Museum.
W2807	8" white on brown vase: *Muses*. Signed T & G Woodall. Des & Sculpts and G.C.	Woodall £27.10s SP £65 reduced to £55	Formerly Rakow Coll, now C.M.G.
W2808	4½" white on flint vase with dragonfly on pond.	Woodall 8/- SP 21/-	
W2809	6" white on lavender on flint vase with fish and pond lily.	Woodall £1.16.6 SP 75/-	
W2810	7" white on sea green vase: *Duck etc*.	Woodall 28/6 SP 75/-	
W2811	8" white on sea green on flint vase with mermaid.	Woodall £4.8s SP £12.10s	Formerly Runyon Coll, now Texas A&M.
W2812	5" light brown on opal vase with antelope and other animals in two scrolls.	Woodall 7/9 SP 25/-	
W2815	4" white on blue on green bowl with face in scroll above a pillar and flower surround. Marked G.C.	Woodall 35/6 SP 90/-	Leo Kaplan Ltd.
W2816	5" white on sea green vase with stylised flower scrolls, part engraved, part cameo.	Woodall 14/6 SP 35/-	
W2817	8" white on brown vase: *Phyllis*.	Woodall £8.15s SP £25 reduced to £22.10s	Formerly Nyman Coll, now in PC.
W2818	White on ruby toilet vase for mounting with spider and web above flowers.	Woodall 8/- SP 20/-	
W2822	10" white on brown vase: *At the Portal*.	Woodall £18.15s SP £47.10s reduced to £40.	Formerly Nyman Coll, now in PC.
W2824	12"x9½" plaque in velvet frame: *Music*. Signed Geo Woodall.	Woodall £38.10s SP £110	Original photograph by G Woodall shows WOODALL signature. GEO must have been added later, now in PC.
W2826	11" two-handled white on dark brown vase: *The Minuet*. Signed Geo Woodall 1891.	Unlisted SP Unlisted	In PC near Corning, USA.
W2827	9" white on brown vase: *Hebe*. Signed Geo Woodall.	Woodall £10.10s SP £27	Signature added in 1907 to aid sale. Sold Finnigans, 1915, then Runyon Coll, now Texas A&M
W2828	7½" white on brown vase: *Dancing Girl*.	Woodall £6 SP £17.10s	Formerly Budrose Coll, now in PC.
W2830	9" white on brown vase: *Vestal*. Signed T & G Woodall. Dated April 1895 in Price Book.	Woodall £12.10s SP £35 reduced to £33	Formerly Ash Coll, on loan to V & A Museum.
W2831	7½" white on brown vase: *Psyche*. Signed T & G Woodall.	Woodall £5.15s SP £17.10s	PC.
W2832	8" white on brown vase: *Euterpe*.	Woodall £8.15s SP £25	
W2834	12¼"x 8½" white on blue on plum panel: *On the Terrace*. Signed T & G Woodall.	Woodall £43.10s SP £130	Formerly Ash then Grover Colls, now Texas A&M.
W2838	12¾" white on blue on brown vase with female looking left. Arms of Cure of London on reverse. Signed T & G Woodall & G.C.	Unlisted SP Unlisted	Made as special order for Capel Cure family. Passed to Edward Drummond Libbey, sold to Delomosne & Son Ltd., London, now in Toledo Mus of Art.
W2839	12¾" white on blue on brown vase with female looking right. Arms of Cure of London on reverse. Signed T & G Woodall & G.C.	Unlisted SP Unlisted	Made as special order for Capel Cure family. Passed to Edward Drummond Libbey, sold to Delomosne & Son Ltd., London, now in Toledo Mus of Art.
W2840	13" white on blue on brown vase: *Aurora*. Signed T & G Woodall.	Woodall £35 SP £90 reduced to £72.10s	Formerly in Budrose Coll, sold Sotheby's 1974, £5200 to Grover, then Runyon, now Texas A&M.
W2841	10" white on brown vase: *Harmony*.	Woodall £21.10s SP £55	Later mounted on marble base with silver mount dated London 1902. Sold, Joel's now PC.
W2842	7" white on brown plaque: *Adam and Eve*. Signed Geo Woodall, dated Nov 1895 in Price Book. Also listed as W2848.	Woodall £87.10s SP £210	Sold to Finnigans, 1915, £55, then Rakow Coll, now C.M.G.
W2843		Unlisted SP £85 reduced to £75	
W2845	6¼" white on amethyst oval plaque: *Perseus and Andromeda*. Signed Geo Woodall.	Unlisted SP Unlisted	
W2848	11" white over raisin brown vase: *Cleopatra*, *Egyptian Princess*. Signed Geo Woodall and G.C.	Woodall £35 SP £85 reduced to £70	
W3058	18" plaque: *Antony and Cleopatra*. Signed Geo Woodall. Dated 1897 in Price Book.	Woodall £195 SP £450	Formerly owned by Sir P McBride MP, auctioned T Bruce, Australia, 1971, bought restored, $600.
W3111	10¾" two-handled opal on brown vase: *Narcissus*. Signed Geo Woodall and G.C.	Woodall £23 SP £60	Sold to Buckley Hall, 1907, £40, now Wysor Coll.
W3111	10¾"x5½" two-handled opal on brown vase: *Iris*. Signed Geo Woodall and G.C.	Woodall £23 SP £60	Formerly Rakow Coll, now in PC.
W3120	9" white on red vase: *Aquatic Life*. Signed Geo Woodall.	Unlisted SP Unlisted	Held by C Andrea Gallery until liquidation in 1920s. Now in Pilkington Glass Mus.
W3125	3¼" flint cameo toilet vase.	Woodall 12/6 SP 30/-	
W3128	7" yellow, green and opal cameo and engraved vase with griffin pattern.	Woodall 54/6 SP £7	
W3139	18¼" opal on frosted deep amethyst plaque: *Moorish Bathers*. Signed Geo Woodall.	Woodall £222 SP £500	Sold to Hon G Brookman, Australia, then Rakow Coll, now C.M.G.
W3151	4½" ruby on topaz vase: *Flowers* (chrysanthemums).	3/9 (crossed out) SP 12/6 deleted, 30/- added	PC.
W3160	11" flatsided white on brown vase: *Autumn*. Signed Geo Woodall.	N/A SP N/A	
W3160	11" flatsided white on brown vase: *Spring*. Signed Geo Woodall.	Woodall £34 (£30 crossed out) SP £75 deleted by GW, £85 added	
W3164	3¼" white on light blue vase with flowers and patterns.	Woodall 28/- SP 70/-	Sent to buyer on 9.6.1898.
W3165	3¼" white on yellow on white vase: *Flowers*.	Woodall 18/- SP 50/-	Sent to buyer on 9.6.1898.
W3167	Green on flint finger bowl with flowers on bowl and plate.	Woodall 7/- SP 16/-	
W3167	Green on flint plate.	Woodall 7/6 SP 16/-	

No.	Description of Piece	Costs of Workmen and Sale Price (SP)	History/Whereabouts
W3168	Green on flint finger bowl with flowers.	Woodall 9/6 SP 20/-	Formerly Ash Coll, now in PC.
W3169	Olive on flint plate with a spray from the centre.	Woodall 12/- SP 25/-	
W3170	12" two-handled light blue on white vase with child's face within heavy floral pattern.	Woodall £5.15s SP £17.10s	
W3172	17¼" white on brown plaque: The Attack. Signed T & G Woodall. Title Pompian scrawled in Price Book.	Woodall £190 SP £350	Sold to Tiffany, NY, 1901, £350, then Runyon Coll, now Texas A&M.
W3173	6" ivory bowl with faked painted colour Morning Glory by L Pearce (Barbe credited on sketch).	Woodall 14/6; Pearce 10/-; Barbe 12/6 SP £10	
W3185	17¼" white on blue on plum plaque: Toilet of Venus. Signed Geo Woodall, dated June 1901 in Price Book.	Woodall £214.10s; frame £6 SP £500	
W3185a	The Roman Bath – working title for W3185. Abandoned after an air bubble burst.	Not paid SP Not paid	
W3186	6½" opal on ruby on opal vase: Mice and Trelliswork with three mice.	Woodall 17/6; Barbe 7/6 SP £4.10s	Formerly Runyon Coll, now Texas A&M.
W3187	6" vase, topaz inside, opal outside, pale pink below with poppies.	Woodall 5/9; Barbe 5/6 SP 40/-	Sold Bonhams, 1999, £16000, now in PC.
W3188	6" red on white on topaz curio vase with spray in stylised container.	Woodall 12/-; Barbe 6/6 SP 55/-	
W3189	6" white on blue vase with iris.	Woodall 6/6 SP 25/-	
W3190	6" opal on eau de nil painted flatsided vase: Flowers, including a parrot.	Woodall 15/6; Barbe 2/6 SP 100/-	
W3191	8" white on raisin brown vase, cherub chasing cherub and 2 butterflies. Signed Geo Woodall & G.C.	Unlisted SP Unlisted	
W3192	6" white on purple vase: Flowers.	Woodall 4/-; Barbe 3/- SP 30/-	
W3194	7½" olive on Burmese vase with unopened flowers.	Woodall 11/-; Cut 1/6 SP 50/-	
W3195	8" white on ruby eau de nil vase: Chrysanthemum with spray on reverse.	Woodall 68/- SP £8.10s	
W3196	8" olive on Burmese vase with figs.	Woodall 34/-; Cut 1/6 SP 90/-	
W3198	4¾" white on blue vase with flowers with spray on reverse.	Woodall estimate 12/6 SP 35/-	
W3199	5" white on blue vase with flowers.	Diaper 2/9 SP 35/-	
W3200	7½" green vase with figs. Neck cut hollow and round. Dated May 1899 in Price Book.	Woodall 15/6; Cut 2/- SP 55/-	Sent to Coldwell in September 1899.
W3200S	Cased green on flint decanter and hollow stopper with plain body.	Unlisted SP Unlisted	Sold to USA in January 1901 for 60/-.
W3201	8" double gourd peach-to-pink on green curio vase with cloud motifs between leafy branches.	Woodall 11/6; Cut 1/6 SP 70/-	
W3202	12" two-handled white on blue vase with stylised fountains, pots and patterns.	Woodall 95/- SP £15	
W3203	8" olive on Burmese vase with intermittent rings of flowers in seven sections.	Woodall 16/6; Cut 1/6 SP 75/-	
W3206	7" brown on flint vase: Blackberry. Painted opaque on the inside by Barbe.	Woodall 10/6; Barbe 2/6 SP 45/-	Sold, Sotheby's 1981, £770.
W3207	4" white on brown bowl: Flowers and Border.	Woodall 12/6; SP 35/-	Due to an error in glassblowing, this vase remained yellow without any Burmese red.
W3209	7" brown on Burmese vase with flowers opening.	Woodall 13/6; Plain Blank 1/3 SP 50/-	
W3210	8" Burmese on lemon vase with gilded neck with swan.	Woodall 14/6; Barbe 6/-; Brushing 1/3 SP 52/6	
W3211	3" white on topaz vase: Sprays.	Woodall 7/- SP 18/-	
W3212	3" white on brown vase: Berries. Dated October 1899 in Price Book.	Woodall 8/6 SP 21/-	
W3214	3" white on topaz vase: Spray.	Woodall 8/- SP 20/-	
W3215	3" white on brown vase: Pattern and diaper.	Woodall 8/6 SP 21/-	
W3216	3¾" white on light blue vase.	Woodall 13/- SP 30/-	
W3217	7½" brownshaded on aqua vase: Passion Flower.	Woodall 9/- SP 25/-	
W3218	8" green, brown and Burmese on flint: Seaweed, Sea Nymph and Fishes.	Woodall 8/-; Barbe 3/-; Brushing 1/6 SP 35/-	Sold USA, 1901, 80/-. Sold, Christie's, 1972, to D Smith on behalf Runyon Coll. Now Texas A&M.
W3219	Burmese on eau de nil vase: Fish, Seaweed and Shells.	Woodall 35/-; Cut 1/6 SP 90/-	
W3220	11" ruby, amber and green vase: Flying Against the Storm with four birds.	Woodall 85/- SP £11	
W3220	12" ivory vase blue inside, and pink outside: Cupid.	Woodall 72/-; Brushing 3/- SP £10	
W3222	6" white on brown vase with stylised flowers.	Woodall 7/6; Barbe 21/- SP £4	
W3222a	6" white on brown vase with stylised chrysanthemums.	Woodall 25/6 SP 65/-	
W3224	6" white on blue vase: 6 Flowers. Sketch book dated February 3rd 1900.	Unlisted SP 65/-	
W3225	7" white on brown vase with seaweed and shells.	Woodall 50/- SP Unlisted	
W3226	10" aqua on white on ruby on flint vase: Birds and Dunes.	Woodall 15/- SP 42/-	
W3236	10" aqua, white and ruby on flint vase with birds and sunset.	Woodall 82/-; Plain blank 2/- SP £12.10s	
W3246	8½" white and ruby on eau de nil vase: Flowers.	Unlisted SP Unlisted	
W3253	8½" pink on lemon vase.	Woodall 17/6 SP 42/-	
W3254	3" white on amber vase: Jasmine.	Woodall 4/-; Barbe 55/- SP £7 approx.	
W3255	8" green on Burmese on green curio vase: Mermaid and Seaweed.	Woodall 11/6; SP 27/6	Formerly Runyon Coll, now Texas A&M.
W3259	7½" olive on Burmese vase with snake, caterpillar and plant. Dated February 1901 in Sketch Book.	Woodall £6.17s SP £15.15s	PC.
W3260	7½" olive on Burmese vase with tree with long grass and treestump. Dated February 1901 in Sketch Book.	Woodall 28/-; Barbe 1/6 SP 70/-	PC.
W3261	7½" olive on Burmese vase with figs. Dated February 1901 in Sketch Book, July 1901 in Price Book.	Woodall 42/-; Barbe 1/6 SP 110/-	
W3265	13" white on dark brown vase.	Woodall 30/-; Barbe 1/6 SP 85/-	
W3270	Bowl with stylised floral patterns.	Woodall 78/- SP 10 guineas	Formerly Runyon Coll, now Texas A&M.
W3271	Vase with six patterns of stylised flowers.	Factory pattern number 26801 SP £3.12s	Formerly Ash Coll, now on loan to V&A Museum.
W3552	Server. 1683	Factory pattern number 26802 SP £1.2s	
W3777	7" green on Burmese with gold enamel vase with yellow birdcage.	Etching 1/-; Painting 1/- SP 5/-	
W3930	17½" white on brown plaque: Cleopatra. Signed T & G Woodall. Dated 11th March 1896 in Price Book.	Unavailable, but work is typical of Jules Barbe SP Unavailable	Woodall £164 SP Unlisted

Index Of Titled Works By The Woodall Team

Selected Bibliography

Beard, Geoffrey *Nineteenth Century Cameo Glass*, The Ceramic Book Company, Monmouthshire, 1956

Corning Museum of Glass, The *English Cameo Glass*, 1994

Grover, Ray and Lee *English Cameo Glass*, Crown Publishers, New York, 1980

Hajdamach, Charles *British Glass 1800-1914*, Antique Collectors' Club Ltd., 1991